Easy Garden Projects
to Make, Build, and Grow

Easy Garden Projects to Make, Build, and Grow

200 Do-It-Yourself Ideas to Help You Grow Your Best Garden Ever

Edited by
Barbara Pleasant
and the Editors of
YANKEE MAGAZINE

Library of Congress Cataloging-in-Publication Data
Easy garden projects to make, build, or grow : 200 do-it-yourself ideas to help you grow your best garden ever / edited by Barbara Pleasant and the editors of Yankee magazine.
     p.   cm.
  ISBN-13 978–0–89909–399–4 hardcover
  ISBN-10 0–89909–399–X hardcover
  ISBN-13 978–0–89909–400–7 paperback
  ISBN-10 0–89909–400–7 paperback
  1. Gardening. 2. Organic gardening. I. Pleasant, Barbara.
  II. Yankee (Dublin, NH).
SB453.E27 2006
635'.0484—dc22   2005037698

2 4 6 8 10 9 7 5 3 1 hardcover
2 4 6 8 10 9 7 5 3 1 paperback

Yankee Publishing Staff

President
Jamie Trowbridge

Book Editor
Barbara Pleasant

Contributing Writers
George DeVault
Melanie DeVault
Erin Hynes
Rose Kennedy
Dougald MacDonald
Deborah Martin
Nancy Ondra
Ilene Sternberg

Book Designer
Jill Shaffer

Illustrator
Michael Gellatly

Copy Editor
Amy Kovalski

Indexer
Lina B. Burton

RODALE

Rodale Inc. Editorial Staff

Editor
Karen Bolesta

Senior Project Editor
Marilyn Hauptly

Designer
Christina Gaugler

Contents

Acknowledgments

By nature, gardeners are generous people who are often eager to share ideas that will help other gardeners enjoy the hours they spend in their gardens. Many of the projects in this book are based on original ideas provided by the editors and contributing writers, while others have been borrowed from public and private gardens throughout North America. As much as we would like to give credit where it is due for every project presented here, the creative roots of some of these ideas are impossible to trace. The editors want to thank the unknown heroes behind each of the projects in this book, as well as people whose expertise served as a basis for specific projects. These include Rose Marie Nichols McGee for her pioneering hands-on experiments with straw bale beds, Dr. Autar K. Mattoo his colleagues at the USDA Vegetable Laboratory in Beltsville, Maryland, for their research on using hairy vetch mulch with tomatoes, and expert gourd grower and crafter Ginger Summit for the excellent information presented in her long list of published books. We are also indebted to Lee Zeike Lee for practical guidance on the growing and crafting of willow branches, and to Dr. Stephen Garton for his tutelage with bamboo and water lotus. Finally, the creative team is deeply indebted to the many hardware department employees from Pennsylvania to Minnesota to Colorado who patiently answered our endless questions about screws, wrenches, and plumbing parts.

Building a Better Garden

On any given day, most gardeners carry a "to-do" list around in their heads. Prune the forsythia, turn the compost pile, order that luscious new mint you read about in a magazine. Each task is a little mission to be accomplished. Afterward comes the special feeling known only to gardeners: the satisfying certainty that we have done a small thing—or perhaps a large one—that will make the world a more beautiful and productive place.

This book is intended to breathe new life into your garden "to-do" list by providing ideas and plans for projects to help you create the most productive, interesting, and satisfying garden you have ever grown. In addition to helping you solve common garden problems—from compost piles that don't quite cook to sneaky slugs that chew holes in your hostas—the projects in this book will actually increase the satisfaction you get from your garden.

Don't believe it? Imagine the pleasure you will feel on a day when you sit down to a dinner that includes freshly dug potatoes seasoned with rosemary, tender steamed snap beans, and juicy tomatoes sprinkled with basil—all grown a few steps from your back door. Now imagine the scene again, and factor in that you grew the potatoes from some spuds that sprouted in your refrigerator before you could eat them (see "Grow New Plants from Produce" on page 58). The snap beans scrambled up a handmade Tie-Together Trellis (see page 98), and the tomatoes spilled out of a Wagon-Ho garden (see page 56) you made from an old red wagon you picked up at a flea market. Your Kitchen Herb Garden (see page 270) provided the herbs, and all of these delights benefited from the compost you made in your Flip-Flop Compost Corral (see page 24). It might be one of the most wonderful meals you have ever eaten!

Nicely accessorized gardens that gain a creative edge from ingenious projects are not only more satisfying to grow—they are also great fun. Even if you don't have trouble with crows in your garden, you might want to give your garden more character with a Flashy Scarecrow (see page 240). Or, build a rock-lined Toad Palace (see page 200) and see who shows up to use it as a summer home. In winter, make a Squirrel Spinner (see page 190) to distract squirrels that are raiding your bird feeder, and enjoy watching their acrobatic antics.

All of the projects in this book have practical value, and many of them can be used for more than one purpose. For example, you might clean out your Slug Jug (see page 226) and use it to gather cut flowers, or make a rowcover tunnel to protect broccoli from cabbage worms, the same way you would use one to grow Undercover Squash (see page 215). Grow spring salad crops in Straw Bale Beds (see page 54), and then use the weathered straw as mulch later in the season.

CRAFTY CROPS

One of the most unique features of this book is Chapter 8, "Special Crops for Handy Gardeners." Craft crops such as ornamental wheat, willow for weaving, or well-behaved bamboo belong in the garden of every resourceful, project-minded gardener. Chapter 8 is a rare source of information on these and other great craft crops, many of which can be used to make projects in this book.

Whether you are setting aside a special area to grow herbs for tea or harvesting grapevines to weave into wreaths, growing your own craft supplies can be a gateway to new gardening adventures that will add a new layer of satisfaction to your garden. Grow your own plant stakes by keeping a clump of bamboo. Store seeds in a small gourd, as people have been doing for thousands of years. Dry flowers for use in potpourri, or bless your kitchen with a hand-woven Wheat Good Luck Charm (see page 264). In addition to showing you how to grow more than a dozen great craft crops, Chapter 8 includes more than 30 creative ideas for projects to make from your garden-grown craft materials.

BASIC TOOLS, SIMPLE HARDWARE

Most of the projects in this book require basic tools most gardeners already have on hand, or tools that are well worth their purchase price that you will use over and over again if you are a project-minded gardener. Don't worry if you don't know a wrench from a screwdriver. These and other basic tools are described in the Glossary of Tools that begins on page 285, which includes buying tips if you are just beginning to build a collection of versatile tools.

Hardware terminology often seems like a foreign language, so care has been taken to make sure the words and phrases used for needed hardware supplies exactly match those you will encounter at any hardware or home supply store. Each project begins with a list of needed tools and supplies, which you can take with you to the store, confident that a salesperson will be able to quickly find exactly what you need. So, even if you don't have the foggiest idea of what a PVC elbow connector looks like, hardware salespeople do! If a hardware item is sometimes known by more than one name, both are included to make shopping for supplies fast and easy.

Just as growing wonderful plants is often habit-forming, expect the same syndrome to emerge as you try your hand with these easy garden projects. Choose projects that interest you, gather together the tools and materials you will need, and delve in when the time is right. The results will amaze you, and you will find yourself looking forward to your next fantastic project.

CHAPTER 1

Digging In: Creating Good Homes for Plants

The importance of soil stewardship extends to even the smallest garden. Growing good soil is as enjoyable and satisfying as growing favorite plants.

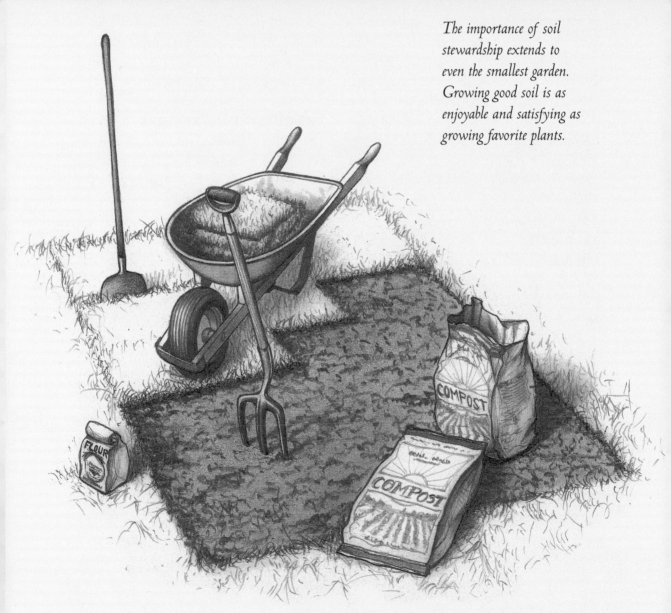

1

Getting to Know Your Soil

The plants in your garden depend on the soil for their survival, because it's where they get the water and nutrients they need. You can keep plants alive in lousy soil, but why spend all your time pumping them with water and fertilizer when healthy soil can take care of a lot of that work for you? Whether you're growing No-Work Tomatoes (see page 18) or stacking a Slope-Taming Terrace (see page 38), the projects in this chapter will make taking care of your soil as much fun as growing a garden. But to nurture your soil, it helps to know what you've got on your hands, as it were.

TAKE A TEST

Whether you are new to gardening or have been at it for years, a soil test from a laboratory gives you priceless insight into your soil. Numerous factors determine a soil's basic characteristics—from the kind of rock from which it was formed, to rainfall and temperature patterns, to how the previous owner cared for it. Bulldozers move soil around when houses are built, so it's possible that your yard includes several different types of soil. If so, you may need more than one soil test.

For a reliable test, obtain a soil test bag or box through your local cooperative extension office, or contact the soil lab of the agricultural college in your state or province. The bag or box comes with instructions for collecting a sample, which is a simple matter of digging

a 4-inch-deep hole and collecting a handful-size sample. When you fill out the information form to mail in with the sample, be sure to specify that you want organic gardening recommendations. The test results will include an analysis of your soil's available nutrients, organic matter content, and pH—all of which will change as you improve your soil.

THE QUESTION OF TEXTURE

One soil characteristic that will change very slowly, and never be radically altered, is your soil's texture. Texture is determined mostly by the size of the soil particles. Sand particles are large, so sandy soil has a light, loose texture, whereas clay particles are very small, so clay soil is comparatively heavy and tight. Intermediate-size particles, such as silt or bits of organic matter, modify extremes in these two soil types. If you are lucky, your soil is either "sandy loam" or "clay loam"—meaning it's basically sand or clay with lots of silt and organic matter. Most gardeners are not so lucky and face the task of improving their soil's texture by adding organic matter. More important, understanding your soil's texture helps you tailor your gardening practices to bring out the best in your soil's hidden talents.

The Scoop on Sand

Very sandy soil drains fast, which is generally good. At the same time, fast drainage means that dissolved nutrients may drain away before plant roots have a chance to absorb them. Sand particles are also slippery, so nutrients don't bind to them. Because sand particles are large, the spaces between them also are quite roomy. For this reason, sandy soil does not need to be cultivated often since its air-holding capacity is already excellent. It does need to be continually enriched with organic matter, which will enhance its ability to hold onto nutrients from fertilizer. If you garden in sand, heavy mulching is so practical and useful that it should become a fundamental method in your soil care practices.

Working with Clay

Tiny clay particles pack so tightly that they trap water and stay wet, so plant roots may find it difficult to push their way through the soil, and then be dissatisfied with constant wetness. On the plus side, clay soils hold nutrients well, so rich forms of organic matter added to clay soil may nurture plants for a long time. Clay soil responds well to cultivation—which introduces much-needed air—as long as you dig or till it only when it is lightly moist to dry. If you add in compost or other soil amendments each time you replant in clay soil, over time you will see a steady lightening of your soil's texture. Avoid walking on clay soil, which compacts it by squeezing out air.

SWEET AND SOUR SOIL

In some regions, the chemical composition of the soil makes the water in the spaces between

Touch Your Texture

To zero in on your soil's texture, you can do the following soil test yourself. All it takes is a clump of soil, a little water, and a willingness to get your hands dirty.

1. Collect a clump of soil about the size of a Ping-Pong ball. Mist or drip a little water onto it and then wait a few moments while the water soaks in. It should be damp, not sopping wet.

2. Try to form it into a ball. If it keeps falling apart and won't form a ball, you have loose sand.

3. If it forms a ball, break off a chunk about the size of a walnut and press it between your thumb and the side of your forefinger with a sliding motion to form a ribbon. Using only one hand, if you can form a flattened ribbon more than 2 inches long, you have tight clay.

4. If it formed a ball but won't form a ribbon more than a half inch long, you have sandy loam—a great soil for gardening.

5. If the ribbon breaks off when it gets to be an inch long, that's good news, too. You have loamy clay, which can be great garden soil when given good care.

the particles acidic—think vinegar or lemon juice. In other regions, the soil is alkaline, also called sweet or basic. The measure of the acidity or alkalinity is called the pH. Distilled water, with a pH of 7, is neutral. Acidic soils have a pH less than 7, while alkaline soils are above 7.

Soil pH is important because it determines what nutrients are available to plants. Some nutrients are tied up in unavailable forms at certain pH levels, while others may be over-abundant to the point of toxicity. Most plants thrive in soil with a pH between 6 and 7.5. A few, such as blueberries and azaleas, require a more acidic soil.

An inexpensive home pH test kit will give you a general idea of your soil's pH, but a soil test is more precise and reliable.

■ If your soil is acidic, you can nudge it toward neutral by mixing in ground-up limestone, simply called lime. Lime is available as a powder, or in easy-to-use pellet form. Adding lime does not give instant results, so it's important to mix it in and allow rain to

The Acid Test

For fun, do this simple litmus test and compare the results to the results from the soil lab—or use it to track changes in your soil's pH from year to year. You'll need distilled water (no fudging—it must be distilled for the results to have meaning) and pH paper, also called litmus paper. Many garden centers and hardware stores carry it, or you can get it at many school supply stores, because taking pH readings is among the most fundamental of chemistry projects. Along with the litmus paper, you will need a color guide. When you buy an inexpensive pH test kit at a garden center, it will include litmus sticks and a color guide.

1. Use a spade to dig up a core of soil 4 to 6 inches deep.

2. Take about a tablespoon of soil from the bottom of the sample, break it apart and pick out bits of root or rock, and place the soil in a small glass cup or jar. Pour in ¼ cup of distilled water, and stir well. Allow the mixture to settle for about 10 minutes.

3. Dip just the edge of a piece of litmus paper into the water.

4. After the paper changes color, compare it to the chart that came with the paper.

5. If you find the color-matching step confusing, try doing multiple pH tests at one time, using soil samples from two or three parts of your yard. The differences may surprise you!

move it through soil crevices before planting seeds or plants.

■ Alkaline soils are harder to modify, and the first step is to add acidic soil amendments such as leaf mold or peat moss. In addition, you can add elemental sulfur as a powder or granules, which will further lower the pH.

Whether your soil is acidic or alkaline, adding organic matter regularly will help bring the pH closer to the neutral mark.

Making Plant-Friendly Soil

Armed with knowledge of your soil's texture and pH, you can choose wisely among the methods and materials available for improving it. When you continue the soil-improvement process season after season, it often gives amazing results. Keep in mind that it took thousands of years to form the soil, and it can take several years to transform dead dirt into dream soil. You'll begin to see some improvement right away, and your plants will reflect their satisfaction by showing steady, sturdy growth.

Regardless of your soil's type, the main way to make it better is to increase its organic matter content. Organic matter is made up of decaying plant and animal materials, such as leaves, roots, dead insects, animal droppings, and just about anything else that was once alive and is now dead. There are four main ways to increase your soil's organic matter content: digging in soil amendments, growing green manures, using organic mulches, and recycling garden and kitchen wastes into soil-building compost. The projects in this chapter provide fun and practical ways to explore each of these options, so you can tailor your choices to suit your personal tastes.

UNDERSTANDING ORGANIC MATTER

Most natural decomposition takes place at the soil's surface, so topsoil contains more organic matter than deeper subsoil. The organic matter content of unimproved topsoil usually hovers around 3 percent, while loamy garden soil contains three times as much. Organic matter feeds a host of soil-dwelling organisms, both large and small—earthworms, insects, fungi, bacteria, and the like. The activities of these organisms enhance the soil both physically and chemically. Earthworms, for example, make tunnels that loosen the soil and improve aeration. Their excretions, called castings, are rich in readily available plant nutrients. Enzymes, acids, and other chemicals result from the biological activities of smaller soil microorganisms. These chemicals become nutrients that are used by plants.

Earthworms and other soil-borne life-forms need oxygen to do their work, so a second function of organic matter is to help hold air in the soil. When you improve soil by adding organic matter, you are creating a better home for plants as well as the organisms that form the foundation of a healthy soil community. .

THE SCOOP ON SOIL AMENDMENTS

A soil amendment is a material that you mix into the soil to instantly raise its organic matter content. You can buy soil amendments in bags at garden centers, or you can buy them by the truckload. Sometimes you can scare up a local supply that's free for the taking, such as decomposed peanut shells, cocoa bean hulls, or ground, composted corncobs. Six of the most widely available soil amendments—and how to use them—are described in the "Six Inexpensive Soil Amendments" chart on the next page.

It's convenient to buy bagged soil amendments, especially if you're in a hurry to create a new garden bed. But what exactly is in those bags of compost, humus, or soil conditioner? You may need to buy a few sample bags to find out, because what one company calls compost may be remarkably similar to what another calls humus. Here is what you are likely to find inside.

- Composted yard waste is made mostly from leaves, which are gathered in the fall and piled into huge heaps, which are turned and watered until they decompose into a soft, fluffy, dark brown to black compost. These products are an excellent choice, because the material still has a little way to go before it is completely decomposed. Purchasing them also supports the recycling of materials that might otherwise end up in landfills.

- Humus can be just about anything, but it often includes blackened chunks of nearly decomposed wood and bark—waste gathered from lumber mills that is mixed with a little soil and then composted. Chunky soil amendments often persist longer in tight clay soil, but they do not give the fast results you are likely to see with finer materials.

- Soil conditioner is a catchall term used on the labels of a range of products. They often are topsoil gathered from floodplains, where the soil is naturally high in organic matter, mixed with other types of compost.

The best advice: Experiment with various products, avoid those that smell rotten or sour, and choose products with light, fluffy textures over those that are heavy and dense.

Once you have a soil amendment, the next step is simple. Spread it over the site you want to improve, and dig it in with a spade

What about Manure?

For thousands of years, gardeners have used animal manure to enrich their soil with organic matter, nitrogen, and other plant nutrients. Yet modern farming methods give gardeners good reason to think twice before using manure, which may contain undesirable chemicals, weed seeds, and potentially dangerous bacteria such as *E coli*. If you can get manure from organically raised animals, and compost it completely, manure can be a valuable soil amendment. A less risky option is to limit your use of manure to organic fertilizer (many of which contain poultry manure) that have been processed to rid them of potential contaminants.

or digging fork, lifting and turning until the amendment and the soil are nicely mixed. If you make a habit of digging in organic soil amendments each time you replant a bed or row, your soil will be well on its way to becoming a fertile, fluffy, well-drained medium that is sure to please your plants.

Keep in mind that soil amendments are not the same as fertilizers. Organic fertilizers do add organic matter to the soil as they decompose, but their primary purpose is to provide nutrients. For more information on organic fertilizers, see "Health Food for Plants" on page 8.

Six Inexpensive Soil Amendments

MATERIAL	WHAT IT DOES	SPECIAL ATTRIBUTES	RISKS
Homemade compost	Increases organic matter and provides some major plant nutrients, along with many minor nutrients and enzymes that support strong growth.	The huge range of beneficial fungi and bacteria in compost made from yard and kitchen wastes can help suppress soil-borne diseases.	Weed seeds and some plant diseases can survive in compost that does not heat up as the materials rot.
Commercial compost	Increases organic matter and provides some major plant nutrients, which vary with the material used to make it.	Usually rich in beneficial fungi and bacteria. Large-volume processing creates high heat that kills most weed seeds.	Compost from community yard waste projects can contain slugs or unwanted debris, so check it carefully.
Mushroom compost	Quickly increases organic matter and overall soil fertility.	Usually made from manure-based compost, further "processed" by fungi (mushrooms), which break down potential contaminants.	Unpleasant odor disappears after several days. Working with heavy mushroom compost is often quite messy.
Spoiled hay	Increases organic matter, provides a few plant nutrients, and lightens soil texture by helping to hold in air.	Improves the way the soil handles both air and water due to the strawlike structure of grass stems, hay's main component.	Often contains dormant weed seeds, as well as fungi that can cause respiratory irritation. Wear a dust mask when handling spoiled hay.
Leaf mold	Increases organic matter, improves drainage, and lightens soil texture while enhancing water retention.	Weed free and easy to make at home. Kept moist, shredded leaves become leaf mold in 1 to 2 years.	Tends to acidify the soil's pH, which can be offset by adding lime. Clumps may need to be pulverized to make leaf mold easier to mix into soil.
Rotted sawdust or wood chips	Increases organic matter, lightens soil texture.	Very slow to decompose, which is useful in clay soils in warm climates, where more fine-textured soil amendments disappear quickly.	If not well rotted, may temporarily decrease available nitrogen in the soil. Additional fertilizer may be needed to offset this effect.

Health Food for Plants

Organic fertilizers contain such a huge range of ingredients that it's difficult to make generalizations as to what you will find in the package. Like synthetic fertilizers, organic fertilizers include three hyphenated numbers on the label, for example 6-4-4, which is called the fertilizer analysis.

- The first number stands for nitrogen, the main nutrient plants need to make new growth.
- The second number stands for phosphorus, an essential nutrient for vigorous root and bloom development.
- The third number stands for potassium, which supports good overall plant functioning.

Animal by-products are a good natural source of nitrogen, so organic fertilizers with a high first number tend to be based on processed manure from poultry, bats, or even crickets. Fish-based fertilizers also are often rich in nitrogen, as are fertilizers that contain ground cotton or alfalfa seeds. To boost their phosphorus and potassium content, dry organic fertilizers often include pulverized rocks, such as rock phosphate or greensand, a sedimentary, gritty silicate that is rich in iron and potassium. Powdered seaweed, or liquid seaweed extract, helps to round things out by providing trace nutrients.

USING ORGANIC FERTILIZERS

There is no single perfect organic fertilizer, and it can be fun to experiment with different products in search of one that is a good fit for your soil, plants, and style of gardening. Always follow the application rates given on the label, because using too much of an organic fertilizer can damage plant roots and cause unnecessary water pollution. If you have very good-quality soil, you may need less fertilizer than the product's label suggests.

When using powdered or granular organic fertilizers, it is also important to thoroughly mix them into the soil. Organic fertilizers do not dissolve rapidly, so inadequate mixing can cause "hot spots" to form around plant roots.

Organic fertilizers break down slowly when soil temperatures are cool, and release more nutrients in warm soil. Sometimes weather conditions cause the sudden release of nutrients, so it's important to watch your plants for signs that they need more or less fertilizer. Underfed plants grow slowly, show pale leaf colors, and may begin blooming while they are still quite small. Overfed plants develop lush stems and leaves, and may produce few flowers and fruits.

SUPPLEMENTAL LIQUIDS

The slow, steady release of nutrients you get with blended organic fertilizers is fine for most plants. If you suspect that a plant is not getting enough nutrients, you can deliver fast relief in the form of a nitrogen-rich, water-soluble organic fertilizer, most of which are made from fish by-products. These nutrients are immediately available to plants, so liquids are good to have on hand—especially if you are growing a "heavy feeder" like spinach or broccoli in cool soil, or when growing anything in soil that's in the early stages of improvement. Plants get 14 nutrients from the soil, but when they are in need of nutrients, they also can take them up through their leaves. For this reason, be sure to drench both the leaves and roots when giving plants a booster feeding with a liquid organic fertilizer.

Fish-based fertilizers provide abundant, ready-to-use nitrogen, but you may want to feed plants nutrients other than nitrogen in a fast-release liquid form. Kelp and seaweed-based products contain plenty of potassium, but their greatest strength lies in their ability to provide micronutrients and other growth-enhancing substances. Seaweed sprays are increasingly popular among tomato growers, and trees and shrubs may root a little faster when soaked briefly in water with a little kelp mixed in. Pepper and rose gardeners often supplement their plants' diets with weak Epsom salt sprays (1 tablespoon per gallon of water); Epsom salt is a good source of ready-to-use magnesium and calcium.

THE WHOLE GARDEN APPROACH

Don't let this discussion of fertilizers make you think you need to regard your garden as a giant chemistry set. Instead, simply approach soil as a living thing that needs care and nurturance. Healthy soil that contains plenty of organic matter does a superior job of retaining both nutrients and water, so the better your soil becomes, the less concerned you will need to be about the details of plant nutrition.

Make a Micronutrient Spray

Not all plant fertilizers come in bags, bottles, or jars. Compost is loaded with micronutrients, so it's the perfect starter material for a nutritious foliar-feed spray. See pages 22 to 29 for four easy compost-making projects. Then use your compost to make this nutrient-rich tonic.

1. Place 1 gallon of finished, crumbly compost in the bottom of a 5-gallon bucket. Fill the bucket to within 3 inches of the brim with lukewarm water. Stir to combine the compost and water, and cover the bucket with a piece of cloth.

2. Let the compost steep for up to a week, stirring occasionally.

3. Strain out the solids through a piece of window screening. Allow the mixture to settle, and strain again through a double thickness of cheesecloth. Add a few drops of dishwashing liquid to help the mixture stick to plant leaves, and apply it using a clean pump spray bottle.

Do a Lawn-to-Garden Turnover

If your yard has too much lawn and not enough garden, turn things around by rolling up the turf like a rug. Then use the right tools to start the soil-improvement process, which is easy if you enlist the help of the special soil-building plants described in the "Eight Great Green Manures" chart on page 15. Or, use the renovated space to build an Easy-Does-It Raised Bed (see page 12) or a space-saving Stepladder Garden (see page 86).

Why not just till in the grass? Many lawn grasses can't be killed by simply turning them under, and the plant parts that do die will tie up soil nutrients as they decompose. Turf also hosts cutworms, grubs, and other insects that coexist peacefully enough with grass but can devastate tender seedlings. Removing the sod, along with a thin layer of soil, reduces these risks.

Sod is heavy, so begin by cutting the turf into smaller squares. It's easiest to peel sod from moist soil, so be sure to water the area lightly the day before you start this project. Also make appropriate plans for the sod you remove. If it's healthy, you can use it to patch thin areas in other parts of your lawn, or put it to work filling in low spots. Sentence weedy patches to your compost pile.

YOU WILL NEED

Tools: Measuring tape, work gloves, garden spade, garden cart or wheelbarrow, digging fork, sturdy bucket, garden rake

One 2-pound bag of all-purpose flour

10 cubic feet of compost (about four 40-pound bags)

1. Use the flour to mark a 4 x 6-foot rectangle on the sod you want to remove. Mark additional lines within the space to divide it into 16-inch-wide squares. Wearing shoes with thick soles, use the spade to cut straight down through the lines of flour.

2. Starting at a short end of the rectangle, push the spade into the soil diagonally around all edges of a square of sod. Firmly grab the two outside corners of the square and flip it over toward the inside of the rectangle. Use the spade to lightly chop into the soil to loosen attached clumps. Lift the square of sod straight up, shake out the loosened soil, and then place the sod in the wheelbarrow. Repeat this procedure with the remaining 15 squares.

3. Use the digging fork to loosen the soil to a depth of 10 to 12 inches. Remove large rocks or roots and place them in the bucket.

4. Spread the compost over the soil, raking it into a 4-inch-deep layer. Use the spade or digging fork to mix the compost into the soil, breaking up clods of soil as you work. You will probably need to turn the soil over twice. Rake the enriched soil smooth with the rake, and get ready to plant.

Smother Your Sod

If you're not in a hurry, you can save yourself several hours of hard work by smothering a patch of lawn instead of digging it up. As long as the grass is actively growing, you can smother it with any material that deprives it of light for at least 6 weeks. Some grass roots will no doubt survive, so be sure to rake them out before using the space to grow vegetables or flowers.

Before you begin, mow the grass as low as possible. Then use one of the materials listed below to turn out the lights on the doomed patch of turf. While you're waiting for the grass to give up its claim on the space, use the site you're smothering for a collection of container-grown plants.

- Sections of dampened newspaper, at least 6 sheets thick, topped with a 3-inch-deep blanket of chopped leaves or grass clippings.
- A sheet of black plastic, held in place with stones, bricks, or heavy pots.
- Scrap carpeting, which can be hidden from view with a thin layer of straw or pine needles.
- Cardboard boxes, flattened into double layers, held in place with pieces of scrap lumber.
- Four to six Straw Bale Beds, described on page 54.

Build an Easy-Does-It Raised Bed

If you're cursed with difficult soil, a raised bed lets you rise above the trouble, with several additional advantages. The soil in raised beds warms up quickly in spring and drains fast in wet weather, and you have unlimited opportunities to alter its texture by digging in the soil amendments of your choice. Raised beds are easy to maintain, too, with less bending required whether you're planting, weeding, or harvesting your crops.

This easy-does-it version is just the right size so you can reach the center of the bed without climbing in, but it still offers 24 square feet of planting space. Once you build one bed, you will soon want more, so locate your first bed with future expansion in mind. Space beds far enough apart so you can work between them, whether that means mowing the paths or trundling between beds with a loaded wheelbarrow.

Don't skip adding this bed's simple yet important accessories—short pieces of PVC pipe attached to the outside of the bed. You can use them as sleeves to hold support hoops for plastic or rowcover tunnels, or they can hold the upright legs of a trellis. If you have two raised beds side by side, you can use the sleeves to attach a wire arch for cucumbers, or perhaps build a rustic arbor that bridges the beds. This is a great way to use the space between beds. It works great as long as you have unrestricted access to the outside edges of the paired beds.

YOU WILL NEED

Tools: Garden spade, rake, measuring tape, wood saw, marker, drill with bits, screwdriver, level, hammer

Two 4-foot-long 2 x 10 boards

Two 6-foot-long 2 x 10 boards

Six 12-inch pieces of 2-inch-diameter PVC pipe

Fifty-six ¾-inch-long wood screws

8 galvanized standard corner brackets

Twelve 2-inch metal pipe strips (also called plumber's brackets)

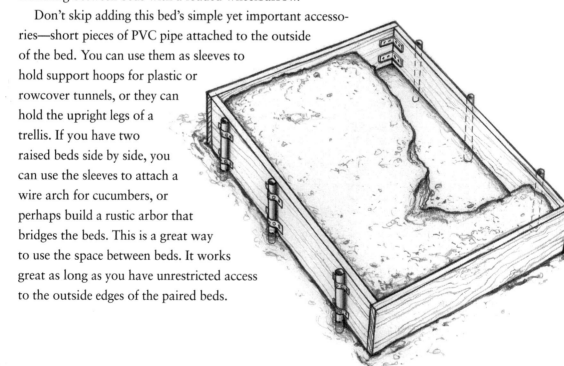

1. Prepare a 4 x 6-foot site for the bed, cultivating the soil at least 10 to 12 inches deep. Work in compost or other soil amendments, and rake the soil into an elongated mound in the center of the site.

2. Use the saw to cut the boards and PVC pipe to the proper lengths.

3. Working on a flat surface, attach 2 corner brackets to the inside edges of the short boards. Hold the brackets in place so that the bends in the brackets are lined up with the end of the board. Mark the positions for the screws, drill guide holes, and then screw the brackets in place.

4. Line up the long side boards to form a butt joint with the short boards. Mark the positions for the screws, drill screw holes, and then screw the brackets in place.

5. Carry the assembled frame to its permanent location (you may need a helper). Use the level to make sure all sides are level. If needed, add or remove soil beneath the corners of the frame to level the top edges.

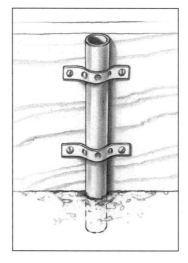

6. Rake out the mound of amended soil to fill the bed. If needed, add additional soil or organic matter to fill the bed to within 1 inch of the top of the frame (it will settle after a drenching rain).

7. Loosely attach the pipe strips, in sets of two, to the outside of the frame, after first checking to make sure they are bent to match the diameter of the pipe. Place one set in the center of each long side, 36 inches from the outside corners, and install the other sets 18 inches from the outside corners.

8. Push the pieces of pipe through the pipe strips until they are in solid contact with the ground. Use the hammer to drive them into the soil 2 inches deep. Firmly tighten the screws to secure the pipe strips.

Good Wood for Beds

Inexpensive pine and rot-resistant cedar are the most readily available woods for framing raised beds. Do not use treated lumber, because the chemicals can leach into the soil. You also can frame a raised bed with lightweight plastic boards, which are available in a range of colors, or you can use composite decking planks made from plastic and recycled wood. Decking planks resist rot and termites, and they are handled just like wood. All lumberyards and home improvement stores sell them, usually in 12-foot lengths.

Grow a Green Manure

Think of green manure as cow manure that never went through the cow. Green manures enrich the soil with organic matter and nutrients, and while they are growing, they suppress weeds and prevent erosion. A green manure is a plant that you grow quickly and then kill by mowing it down, pulling it up, digging it into the soil, or simply letting it die when cold weather comes.

The main difference between a green manure and a cover crop is the age of the plants. Cover crops are usually allowed to grow to maturity, but green manures are harvested or turned under when they are young. Whether you use them as green manures or cover crops, there is a special group of plants that are widely used to improve soil (see the "Eight Great Green Manures" chart at right). These talented plants germinate quickly, grow fast, and do a great job of enriching the soil with nitrogen, organic matter, or both.

USING GREEN MANURES

Farmers use green manures to restore the health of their soil between crops, but in an intensively planted garden, it's more practical to combine them with vegetable plantings. You can grow green manure crops in the pathways between rows, as is done in the Self-Mulching Garden on page 16, or you can grow quick green manure crops between plantings. For example, if you don't plan to use the space vacated by spring peas and lettuce until late summer, you can grow a quick crop of buckwheat. A third option is to sow a winter hardy legume like field peas or hairy vetch as you clean up your garden in fall. This is the method used in the "Grow No-Work Tomatoes" project on page 18.

If you mow, hoe down, or pull up green manure plants, the foliage can be immediately used as mulch, or you can add it to compost. Turning under green manures—foliage and all—is best done with a tiller, and the job goes faster if you cut down the plants with a mower or weed trimmer first. To give the residue time to decompose, wait 2 weeks after tilling to plant your crops. If you rake up the foliage, a spade or digging fork is all you will need to chop and turn the roots of cover crop plants, which will then decompose quickly. The soil should then be ready to plant in 1 to 2 weeks.

THE TRUTH ABOUT LEGUMES

Gardeners often hear that growing peas, beans, and other legumes improves the soil, which is partially true. Legumes do fix nitrogen from the air, which they then store in nodules on their roots. However, they have plans for that stored nitrogen. They use most or all of it to nourish their seeds, leaving little behind in the soil.

The story ends differently when you grow nitrogen-fixing green manures and pull them up or mow them down before they reach maturity. The soil then becomes the beneficiary of the plants' stored nitrogen, which can be used by your vegetables. When grown in soil that's been recently enriched by a strong nitro-gen-fixer, such as hairy vetch, most vegetables need little, if any, supplemental fertilizer. The decomposing green manure plants increase the organic material in the soil as well.

Eight Great Green Manures

PLANT	PROS AND CONS	HOW TO USE
Buckwheat (*Fagopyrum esculentum*)	Adds organic matter, grows fast in warm weather, attracts beneficial insects. Easy to kill by mowing or by tilling under young plants.	Sow from late spring to late summer when soil temperatures are above 50°F. Not frost hardy.
Cereal rye (*Secale cereale*)	Produces abundant organic matter. Difficult to turn under if allowed to grow tall, but good to use in areas managed by mowing.	Sow seed in fall or spring, in combination with a nitrogen-fixing legume. Killed by cold temperatures north of Zone 5.
Cowpea (*Vigna unguiculata*)	Fixes nitrogen, tolerates heat and drought, attracts beneficial insects. Turn under young plants or pull up older ones when planting garden crops.	Sow from early to late summer, when soil temperatures are above 65°F. Not frost hardy.
Crimson clover (*Trifolium incarnatum*)	Adds nitrogen and organic matter, and flowers attract bees. Easily killed by repeated mowing, or by hoeing plants down and cutting them off at the soil line.	Sow seed in fall or spring, in combination with a grain or other legumes. Killed by cold temperatures north of Zone 5.
Field pea (*Pisum sativum* subsp. *arvense*)	Fixes nitrogen, winter hardy, and easy to kill by mowing or tilling. Foliage turned under the soil breaks down quickly.	Sow in fall or spring. Mow or pull plants, and use the stems and foliage as mulch.
Hairy vetch (*Vicia villosa*)	Fixes nitrogen and survives extremely cold weather. Uncut mature plants become large, but they are easy to pull up or cut down.	Plant in late summer or early fall. Hardy to Zone 4. Cut down or pull plants when space is needed for cultivated crops.
Mustard (*Brassica juncea*)	Adds organic matter, and makes a fast crop in cool fall soil. Foliage decomposes quickly when hoed down and then turned under.	Sow in late summer or early fall. Plants survive repeated frosts, but are usually killed by hard freezes.
White clover (*Trifolium repens*)	Fixes nitrogen, persists as a perennial, attracts pollinators. Low-growing plants survive repeated mowing. Can be invasive.	Sow in fall or spring. Hardy to Zone 4. Best used in long-term plantings. Repeated tilling required to kill the plants.

Grow a Self-Mulching Garden

Vegetable gardens have traditionally been laid out in rows so that they could be easily cultivated with a plow or tiller. But why waste the space between the rows where your crops are planted? In this wide-row garden, the row middles, or pathways, are put to work growing soil-building plants. This teeming community of plants doubles as habitat for spiders, ground beetles, and other beneficial insects. Every 3 weeks, one-third of the pathways are mowed, and the clippings are used as mulch for the crop plants. Because only one-third of the pathways are mowed at a time, your core population of beneficials is never deprived of a home—they can simply move to the closest unmowed pathway.

Choose a mixture of plants for the pathways, which should match your mower's cutting width. In addition to the soil-building plants described in "Eight Great Green Manures" on page 15, you can include small nectar-bearing flowers, such as sweet alyssum, or any type of leafy green. The plants suggested here grow well in a wide range of climates and soils and are widely available at farm supply stores.

If your mower has a bagging attachment, use it to gather the clippings and then spread them beneath vegetables to help retain soil moisture and discourage weeds. If you don't have a bagger, you can simply rake the clippings onto adjacent rows. Be sure to set your mower at its maximum cutting height, which is usually 3 to 4 inches. Mowing high makes it easier to mow through the lush vegetation and does less damage to the crowns of the cover crop plants.

This plan is for seven 20-foot rows, with six pathways between them, but you can easily reduce or expand it to fit your garden space. Before getting started, measure the cutting width of your mower. Most walk-behind rotary mowers cut a 20-inch-wide swath, but yours may be slightly different.

YOU WILL NEED

Tools: Tiller or spade and digging fork, hoe, rake, lawn mower

Cover crop seeds to plant 200 square feet:
¼ pound crimson clover seed
¼ pound cereal rye seed
¼ pound white clover seed
3 packets sweet alyssum seed

1. Measure off a 20 x 20-foot square of your vegetable garden, which should be in a sunny, well-drained site. Thoroughly cultivate the soil with a tiller. If you do not have a tiller, hire someone to cultivate it for you in the spring, or dig the site by hand with a spade and digging fork.

2. Use the hoe and rake to form 7 slightly raised parallel rows. Each row, and each pathway, should match your mower's cutting width. Level the tops of the rows with the rake, and then do the same with the pathways.

3. Sow your chosen cover crop seeds in the pathways by scattering the seeds evenly

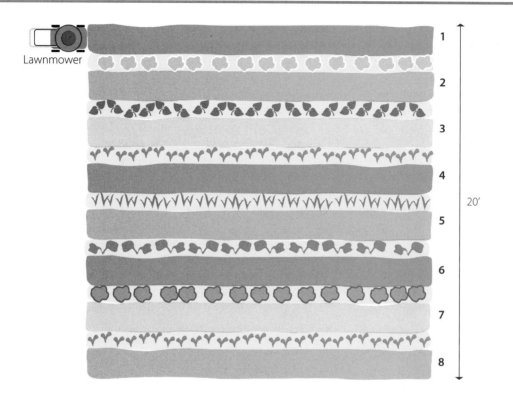

Lawnmower

1
2
3
4
5
6
7
8

20'

over the cultivated soil. As you plant the adjacent crop rows, your footfalls will help firm the seeds into the soil.

4. Assign numbers to the row middles. As soon as the cover crop plants grow 4 to 5 inches tall, mow row middles 1, 4, and 7, and transfer the clippings to adjacent crop rows. The next week, mow row middles 2, 5, and 8. In the third week, mow row middles 3 and 6. Repeat this mowing pattern for the remainder of the season.

Managing Green Middles

In addition to the cover crops you plant in your garden pathways, don't be surprised if you see a number of weeds. This is no problem as long as you mow often enough to keep the weeds from developing mature seeds. When warm temperatures and frequent rain combine to make the middles grow very lush and thick, increase the frequency of mowing to every 4 to 5 days. Should especially nasty weeds like bindweed or Canada thistle threaten to overtake the cover crop plants, dig them out and sow buckwheat, cowpea, or another heat-tolerant green manure in their place.

Grow No-Work Tomatoes

This method, developed by USDA researchers, uses hairy vetch (*Vicia villosa*)—a vigorous, cold-hardy nitrogen-fixing vining legume—as a fall-sown cover crop. Two weeks before tomatoes are set out, the vetch is cut down and allowed to dry into a mulch on the soil's surface. Tomatoes are then planted into holes made in the blanket of mulch. Add stakes or cages, and your tomato plot is on its way—no tilling or weeding required, and the vetch mulch helps keep the soil moist, too. If you need a support plan for your tomatoes, consider building several Windproof Pillars (see page 104). The hairy vetch method is also a great way to prepare soil for a Stepladder Garden (see page 86).

Hairy vetch seed is often available at farm supply stores, or you can order it from one of the mail-order sources listed on page 294. Some varieties are hardier than others. If you live in a cold climate, stick with the straight species, or try the 'Madison' variety developed at the University of Nebraska. Where winters are milder, 'AU EarlyCover,' developed at Auburn University in Alabama, is a good choice.

In addition to saving labor, this system has been found to improve tomatoes' resistance to disease, so it's a great approach to use if you plan to grow heirloom varieties, which rarely have resistance to common tomato diseases. When the system is used with more trouble-tolerant hybrids, many gardeners report improved tomato flavor. The plan includes one small organic refinement—spraying plants every 3 weeks with a seaweed solution—which helps provide trace nutrients, improves plant vigor, and guarantees great flavor.

Try this planting plan with other vegetables, too. It is especially useful with crops that are heavy feeders such as corn, broccoli, and other members of the cabbage family.

YOU WILL NEED

Tools: Rake; string trimmer, scythe, or sharp knife; garden spade; pump spray bottle

1 pound hairy vetch seed per 1,000 square feet

Compost for enriching planting holes

Selection of tomato seedlings

Tomato stakes, cages, or other trellises

1 bottle of liquid seaweed concentrate

1. In late summer, 8 to 10 weeks before your first freeze, decide where you will grow tomatoes the following year. Pull up weeds and spent plants, and rake over the soil to rough up the surface. Plant hairy vetch seeds so that they are about 2 inches apart. Tamp them in with the back of the rake.

2. From late fall through winter, pull any winter weeds that appear, but don't be concerned if the hairy vetch turns purple and flops to the ground. The plants will regrow as the soil warms in early spring.

5. Drench the plants with seaweed solution immediately after planting, and every 3 weeks thereafter for the remainder of the season.

6. Promptly pull out any weeds that appear through the mulch. If needed, add an additional 2-inch-deep layer of organic mulch, such as hay or composted leaves.

3. At about the time of your last spring frost, use a string trimmer, scythe, or sharp knife to cut down the hairy vetch by severing the stems at the soil line. Do not attempt to do this with a mower, because the vetch's stems will clog the blade. Leave the vetch on the soil's surface to dry.

4. Choose planting sites for your tomatoes. Use a spade to open up 12-inch squares in the mulch. Dig a generous spadeful of good compost into each planting hole before setting the tomatoes in place. Install stakes, cages, or other plant supports.

Should You Inoculate?

Like other legumes, hairy vetch depends on the cooperation of certain strains of soil-borne bacteria to efficiently take nitrogen from the air and store it in little nodules on its roots. Hairy vetch utilizes Type C inoculant, which is the same strain used by garden peas. If peas have been grown in the site during the previous three seasons, there should be ample bacteria in the soil to help the vetch work its nitrogen-fixing magic. If you'd rather be sure, purchase a packet of powdered inoculant along with your seeds. Just before planting, place the seeds in a bucket, lightly dampen them with water, and stir in the inoculant. Now you are ready to sow.

Creative Composting

Composting is a way to get organic matter ready for the garden by piling it together and letting it decay, either partially or completely. Besides the obvious advantage of reducing the amount of waste in landfills, composting has several advantages for you and your soil. You get to recycle yard and kitchen wastes into a free, high-quality soil amendment, and your soil isn't challenged to accept undecomposed materials, which often cause a temporary drop in the amount of nitrogen that's available to plants.

Compost is best regarded as a soil amendment rather than a fertilizer, because it often contains only modest amounts of the major plant nutrients. Yet compost is rich in minor nutrients as well as enzymes and beneficial fungi and bacteria. Plants grown in soil enriched with compost tend to do a better job of resisting disease, so you might think of compost as a nutritional supplement, along the lines of your daily vitamin. Making compost is interesting, too, and it's deeply satisfying to nurture plants with dark, crumbly compost that started out as banana peels, coffee grounds, and wilted weeds.

COMPOSTING BASICS

Compost will make itself if you pile materials together, dampen them well, and wait, but you will get better results—and have more fun—if you actively participate in the process. Begin by learning two basic composting concepts.

- Brown and green. Brown materials like leaves and sawdust are high in carbon. Green materials such as grass clippings and vegetable scraps are high in nitrogen. A carbon/nitrogen balance of 25/1 leads to the fastest, highest-quality compost, but you don't need a calculator to make compost. Two parts brown to one part green usually gives good results.
- Cold or hot. Cold composting is done by throwing organic matter into a pile and letting decay organisms do their thing at their own pace. Hot composting involves pampering the organisms by turning the pile often to add oxygen, making a point of balancing brown and green materials, and keeping the pile evenly moist. Cold compost rarely heats up, whereas the middle of a hot compost heap often reaches 130°F. Cold compost is fine for most uses, such as the "Make a Cucurbit in Compost Pile" project on page 28. The main advantage of hot composting is that it gives faster results.

Balancing Moisture and Air

In addition to organic matter, the microorganisms that create compost need moisture and air. Too much moisture favors the growth of foul-smelling bacteria, but it doesn't take much practice to tell if your compost is happy with the amount of water you provide. Moisture is balanced with fresh air that's introduced each time you turn or aerate the mixture.

Exactly how you meet your compost's need for water and air depends in large part on your composting system.

- Open systems, such as those in the next two projects, tend to need more water and less aeration.
- Closed systems, such as the Garbage Can Composter on page 26, usually need frequent turning or aeration more than they need supplemental water.

Before you start, make sure your town has no ordinance banning open compost bins. If it does, the ordinance probably spells out what kind of closed container is acceptable.

When starting any compost heap, it's wise to mix in a little compost from a mature batch, which provides a starter community of beneficial fungi and bacteria. Big batches of compost are often easier to manage than small ones, especially if your goal is to make hot compost. Hot or cold, the most remarkable thing about compost is how much it shrinks as it matures. Six wheelbarrow loads of fresh material usually yield one wheelbarrow load of compost.

What Goes In

Compostable materials that fall into the "green" (high-nitrogen) category include:

- Fruit and vegetable kitchen scraps, coffee grounds (with filters), tea bags, and bread and grain products, including flours and meals
- Green garden plants of any kind, including young weeds that are not bearing seeds, and deadheaded flowers
- Fresh grass clippings

High-carbon, or "brown," materials for your compost include:

- Old mulch materials
- Leaves, preferably coarsely shredded with a mower
- Shredded paper (but not glossy paper with colored ink)
- Sticks, sawdust, or other tree parts

What Stays Out

These materials should not be composted:

- Meat scraps or other animal by-products
- Sugary or fatty foods, such as cake icing
- Waste from dogs, cats, or other meat-eating animals
- Fertilizers, which can be so concentrated that they harm the decay microorganisms
- Household chemicals

Compost Troubleshooting

Gardeners who are new to composting often are mystified by problems in their heaps. Most can be cured by mixing and turning the heap, or adding water if the materials are too dry.

SYMPTOM	CAUSE
Material is slimy and smells rotten or sour	Too much water, or not enough brown materials
Materials do not appear to be breaking down	Not enough water, or materials have not been mixed together well
Ants present in large numbers	Materials too dry; turn heap, adding small amounts of water
Material does not heat up	Normal for most heaps; add green material to increase temperature

Build a Combo Composter

This easily assembled compost bin gives you a place to throw withered plants and food scraps, *and* you can use it to store your digging fork, spade, and other tools you reach for every day. Sturdy enough to resist invasions by the family dog, the Combo Composter is made from wooden pallets—also called skids—which are usually free for the asking at lumberyards or home improvement stores. Open spaces between the pallets' slats allow air to circulate freely, and the front comes off in seconds for easy access. By orienting the pallets so that the outer slats are parallel to the ground, you can slip tool handles through the open spaces at the top edge— or use them to hold one of the Easy Aerators described at right. The finished bin is quite heavy, so it's best to assemble it near its permanent location. To get this bin to perform a fast disappearing act, paint it dark green or brown, and locate it in a shady spot.

YOU WILL NEED

Tools: Work gloves, marker, drill and bits, screwdriver, hammer, measuring tape

4 wooden shipping pallets

6 galvanized corner brackets

Twenty-four 1-inch wood screws

Four 4-inch-long pieces of scrap wood or furring strips

Eight 2-inch nails

Two 12-inch bungee cords (utility tie-downs)

1. Place the pallets that will be the sides of the bin on the ground, with the outer slats horizontal.

2. Attach a corner bracket to the edge of the top cross-board, another to the middle cross-board, and another to the second board from the bottom. To attach each bracket, hold the bracket in place with the bend in the bracket aligned with the outside edge of the pallet. Mark the screw holes, drill guide holes, and then screw the brackets in place. Repeat this procedure as you attach 3 brackets to the other side.

3. To attach the sides, rest the back pallet against a wall or tree, or have a helper hold it for you. Beginning with the center bracket, attach the side pallets to the back pallet the same way you did in Step 2.

4. To make compartments for tools, nail short pieces of scrap wood across the top of the back pallet at 6-inch intervals.

5. Position the bin in its permanent location. If necessary, dig out or add soil beneath the base to make the bin sit solidly on the ground.

6. Fill the bin with kitchen scraps, yard waste, and refuse from your garden. When you are not working the heap, close up the bin by securing the fourth pallet to the front with the bungee cords.

PLAY IT AGAIN

Easy Aerators

You can use a pitchfork or digging fork to mix materials and fluff air into a compost pile, which is the best way to give fungi and bacteria the oxygen they need to work quickly. In between turning sessions, try some of these easy aerators to keep your compost cooking.

- Each time the size of the pile grows 6 inches, lay a short pole over the top before adding more material. You can use a piece of PVC pipe, an old broom handle, or even stout sticks, provided they are a few inches longer than the width of your heap. Every week or so, grab the end of each pole and jiggle it back and forth and up and down. It might not move much—especially if it's near the bottom of a heavy pile—but air will still find its way in.

- When you build a new pile, bury the head of an old garden rake or cultivator in the middle, with its handle standing straight up. To aerate the pile, simply rock the handle from side to side.

- Attach a coat hook to a broom handle, stick, or piece of PVC pipe. Wriggle it into the pile as far as you can, and then pull it back out again. Repeat in different areas of the pile.

Make a Flip-Flop Compost Corral

This circular compost corral is incredibly easy to put together, yet it still gives you the versatility of a two-compartment bin. Gradually fill one wire-enclosed side with compostables, and when you're ready to dig in and begin some intensive turning to finish off the composting process, simply flip the bin to the other side of the central post, and start all over again.

The most challenging part of this project is installing the post. As long as the soil is moist, you should be able to pound a metal fence post into the ground by placing a piece of scrap lumber over the top and pounding away. If you prefer, install a wood post in a narrow posthole dug 18 inches deep. When installing either type of post, make sure there is 2 feet of free space on both sides. You can use the leftover lawn fencing for other projects, such as the Movable Melon Trellis on page 96.

YOU WILL NEED

Tools: Wire snips, staple gun, hammer, pliers

1 roll of 3-foot-wide vinyl-coated 2 x 3-inch mesh lawn fencing

Two 48-inch-long 1 x 2 furring strips

One 6-foot-long metal fence post

1 small piece of scrap lumber

8 to 10 plastic cable ties

Two 6-inch lengths of 2-inch-diameter PVC pipe

1 thick rubber band

1. Use the wire snips to cut one 6-foot-long piece of fencing. To keep the fencing from rolling up as you try to cut it, it helps to have a helper hold the roll. Snip off protruding pieces of wire to create clean edges.

2. Use the staple gun to attach the furring strips to the cut ends of the fencing. Center the fencing so that about 6 inches of wood extends beyond the top and bottom of the fencing.

3. Cover the top of the fence post with the piece of scrap lumber, and pound it into the ground until the protruding metal wings near the base of the post are just below the soil's surface. To land sound blows, you may want to stand on a sturdy stool.

4. Using the plastic cable ties, attach the midpoint of the fencing to the fencepost at several points, with the bottom of the fencing flush with the ground.

5. On one side of the post, form a circle with the two sides of the fencing and mark the ground where the furring strips meet. Pound one of the pieces of pipe 5 inches into the ground, and then use pliers to pull it back out. Push a stick through the plug of soil to clear the center of the pipe, and then pound it back into the hole again, leaving the top ½ inch above the soil line. Install a second pipe sleeve the same way on the other side of the post.

6. On the first side you want to fill with compost, bring the two furring strips together and insert the bottom ends into the PVC pipe sleeve. Secure the top ends of the furring strips together with a thick rubber band.

Fire Up a Slow Heap

The materials that go into a compost pile are often pretty random, so it's not uncommon for a heap to decompose very slowly—unless you give it a little help. First try chopping and mixing the materials, stopping every few minutes to add water to get all of the pieces evenly moist. If the heap still feels cold 2 days later, you can heat up the heap fast by adding any of these compost fire-starters.

- A wheelbarrow load of fresh green grass clippings, evenly fluffed into the heap
- A 5-pound bag of cheap dry dog food (corn meal should be the main ingredient)
- One gallon of alfalfa pellets (sold as animal feed)
- Two cups of powdered or pelleted organic fertilizer
- More of everything! Small compost piles lose heat fast, especially in winter. A pile less than 2 feet high and wide can be bulked up with shredded paper, grass clippings, spoiled hay, or the leftovers from your last compost heap.

Construct a Garbage Can Compost System

Contained compost systems are more challenging to manage compared to open piles. They are harder to aerate; they tend to be smaller (and thus slower to decompose); and it's easy to overwater the materials, so they become slimy. But if your town requires closed compost containers—or your dog likes to dig in an open pile—an enclosed system may be your best choice.

This easy system consists of two modified garbage cans with snap-on lids—an upright can for collecting materials, and a second can that sits on rolling casters for easy turning. To facilitate drainage, the bottom is removed from the collecting can. The rolling can includes interior baffles that help to mix the materials each time the can is turned. Having two containers that serve differing purposes helps to avoid the most common pitfalls of closed compost systems, and it makes the composting process more enjoyable, too. A bag of packaged compost is used to help get the compost off to a good start, or you can use compost you have made yourself.

1. To enhance aeration and drainage in the collection can, drill approximately 30 holes all over the sides of the can. Turn the can upside-down, and use the utility knife to cut out the bottom, leaving the curved bottom edge and 1 inch of the can's bottom intact.

2. Set the can in place and fill the bottom 6 inches of the can with loose material such as straw, pruned branches, or spent plants pulled from your garden. Cover with a 2-inch layer of damp, finished compost. Close the can and

YOU WILL NEED

Tools: Drill with bits, utility knife, hammer, measuring tape, screwdriver, adjustable wrench, garden hoe

Two 32-gallon plastic garbage cans with locking lids

One 20-quart bag of finished compost

Sixteen 2-inch nails

Two 36-inch-long pieces of 2 x 4 lumber

Two 15-inch-long pieces of 2 x 4 lumber

Two 18-inch-long pieces of 2 x 4 lumber

4 heavy-duty casters with wood screws

Four 30-inch-long pieces of 1 x 2 furring strips

Twelve 3-inch-long bolts with washers and nuts

One 18-inch bungee cord (utility tie-down)

lock on the lid. You can now begin using the can to collect kitchen trimmings and yard waste, alternating with 1-inch layers of finished compost.

3. To make the base for the rolling bin, build a frame by nailing the 36-inch-long 2 x 4s and the 15-inch-long 2 x 4s together into a rectangular frame. Place the frame on a level surface, and nail the two 18-inch-long 2 x 4s over the top, with their outer edges 12 inches in from the edge of the assembled frame. Mark the centers of each crosspiece, and make four more marks 6 inches from the center marks. Use wood screws to attach the casters to the cross-pieces at each mark.

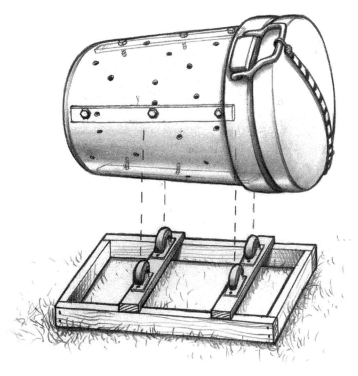

4. Turn the second can on its side. Hold one of the 1 x 2 furring strips against the outside of the can, and use the drill to make 3 guide holes for the bolts that go through the furring strip and the can. Switch the furring strip to the inside of the can, and install the bolts by threading on washers, inserting the bolts from the outside so they go through the can and the furring strip and extend into the interior

of the can. Then screw on and tighten the nuts. Repeat with the 3 remaining furring strips.

5. Use the drill to make approximately 30 aeration holes in the sides and bottom of the second can. Snap on the lid, and place the can on the casters.

6. Whenever the collection can is halfway full, transfer its contents to the rolling can. The easiest way to do this is to lay the collection can on

its side, and pull batches of material into the lid with a hoe. Then dump them into the rolling can.

7. Secure the lid of the rolling can with a bungee cord. Roll the can several times to mix the materials, and add water if needed to lightly dampen the contents. Roll the can every few days. In 3 to 5 weeks, the compost should be ready to use in your garden.

Make a Cucurbit Compost Pile

If you've ever thrown your jack-o'-lantern into your compost pile in November, you have probably been surprised to find young pumpkin vines sprouting there in the spring. All plants of the cucurbit family have a long history of thriving in compost piles, which is how gourds, winter squash, and pumpkins became staple crops for many native North American tribes. But you need not rely on chance. Create a strategically located compost pile in the fall, when leaves and withered plants are in abundant supply, and plant cucurbits in it the following spring. In addition to nurturing winter squash or pumpkins, a custom-built compost heap makes a great summer home for gorgeous gourds (see page 280).

A compost pile destined to be a home for cucurbits can be created from yard waste without the addition of kitchen scraps, so it will be of little interest to dogs or other animals. Where should you put it? Long-vined cucurbits don't mind having their roots in the shade as long as most of their leaves get plenty of sun. This is an ideal project for the outer edge of your vegetable garden, or you can station your cucurbit compost near the edge of your lawn and let the vines tumble into the grass. If you're short on space, consider providing the vines with a trellis such as the Movable Melon Trellis on page 96.

Don't skip making little pockets of soil for your seedlings. Good contact between soil and seeds enhances germination and helps to keep the pile moist.

When the vines wither in fall, gather them up and compost them, and spread the remaining compost over your garden. Then get busy creating another Cucurbit Compost Pile!

YOU WILL NEED

Tools: Lawn mower (preferably with bagging attachment), wheelbarrow, watering can, digging fork, spade

Grass clippings

Shredded leaves

2 cubic feet of garden soil

1 cup of garden lime

4 to 6 cups of organic fertilizer

1 packet of winter squash, pumpkin, or gourd seeds

1. In fall, build a layered compost pile to form a heap about 2 feet high, 6 feet long, and 3 feet wide. Tailor the heap to the needs of growing plants by including the last green grass clippings of the season (for nitrogen), leaves that have been finely chopped by two passes with your mower (for bulk), and several thin layers of soil (to add weight and retain moisture). Thoroughly water the pile between layers. As you build the pile, also scatter in lime (to offset the acidity of the leaves) and organic fertilizer. The fertilizer is needed to enrich the pile with nutrients, and it will help to keep the

decomposition process active during the winter months.

2. As soon as the heap thaws in early spring, use a digging fork to thoroughly turn and mix the pile. Stop often to add water, so that the pile is thoroughly moist. Don't be concerned if many of the chopped leaf pieces are still intact. As soon as temperatures warm, they will rapidly decompose. If you encounter many dry pockets when turning the heap, you may need to turn it a second time after one to two weeks to make sure all the material is uniformly moist.

3. Soon after your last spring frost passes, dig three 8-inch square holes in the top of the heap. Fill them with garden soil. Plant 4 seeds in each pocket of soil. After the seeds germinate, thin them if necessary to one plant per pocket.

Provide water as needed to keep the heap moist, and your cucurbits will soon be off and running.

JUST FOR FUN

Grow a Sunflower Patch Compost

You can accomplish four things at once by installing a pole-mounted bird feeder in a plantable compost pile like the one described here: make compost, feed birds, grow self-sown sunflowers, and prepare a site for a new bed. Choose a place where you would like to create a new bed, and install a bird feeder before building a cold compost pile around its base from fall yard waste and soil. Sunflower seeds dropped into the pile in winter will sprout and grow in spring. After their bloom time passes, you can dig the leftover compost into the soil, and be well on your way to having a fertile new spot for veggies, herbs, or flowers.

Make an Indoor Worm Farm

Remember the ant farm you had as a kid? You can have just as much fun growing worms, which will reward you with rich fertilizer for your garden. Specifically, the worms create worm castings—excretions high in nitrogen, phosphorus, and potassium, as well as micronutrients and enzymes. Castings are slightly more acidic than garden compost and are a more concentrated source of plant nutrients. You can add them directly to the garden, sprinkle them over the soil's surface of your potted plants, or mix them into potting soil.

Vermicomposting can be done indoors year-round, and it is not stinky when you have the right balance of bedding, water, worms, and food scraps. Bad odors are a sign that you're overfeeding or the bedding is too wet. Fortunately, vermicomposting is easy to do correctly, and it gives you an alternative use for kitchen scraps in winter, when outdoor compost often freezes. It also makes a great science project for kids.

For best results, use red worms (*Eisenia foetida*), which are also known as red wrigglers. They are raised commercially for fishing bait, so you often can buy them by the pint at fishing supply stores. For this project, you will need 1 pound of worms, which is roughly equal to 3 pints of fishing worms. The worms can process about 3 pounds of kitchen waste per week.

This project uses a plastic storage bin, modified to meet the needs of the worms. Keep the bin in a dimly lit place where the temperature stays between 55°F and 77°F. Place it on bricks above a sheet of plastic, and use newspapers to catch any liquids that drain from the bottom. Newspapers enriched with "worm juice" make great garden mulch.

YOU WILL NEED

Tools: Drill and ¼-inch drill bit, bucket, pump spray bottle, hand trowel

One 12-inch-deep 50-quart plastic storage bin with lid

Shredded paper for bedding; enough to fill the bin ¾ full

1 quart peat moss

1 cup cornmeal

1 pound of red worms (*Eisenia foetida*)

1. Drill 30 evenly spaced ventilation holes in the bottom and sides of the bin.

2. Place the bedding material and peat moss in the bucket and moisten it uniformly until it is as damp as a wrung-out sponge. Mix in the cornmeal. You may need to prepare the bedding in bucket-size batches.

3. Dump the prepared worm bedding into the plastic bin. Fluff the bedding gently to create air pockets. Mist bits of paper that remain dry.

4. Add the worms to the top of the bedding. Begin adding small amounts of food scraps

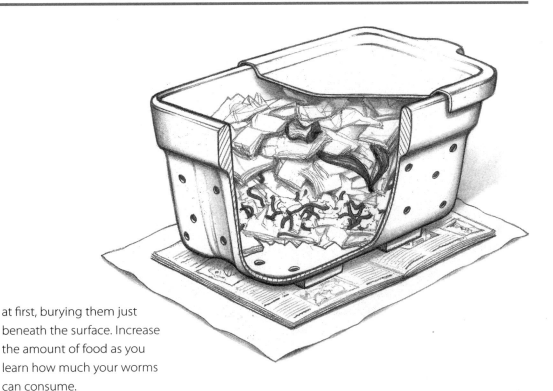

at first, burying them just beneath the surface. Increase the amount of food as you learn how much your worms can consume.

5. Mist the bedding as needed to keep it slightly damp. Soggy bedding causes odors.

6. After 2 to 3 months, when the worms have converted most of the bedding to castings, use a hand trowel to move the compost and worms to one side of the bin. Add fresh bedding and food scraps to the empty side of the bin. Give the worms a few days to move to the fresh side and then remove the compost. Fill the empty side with fresh bedding.

Feeding Your Worms

Keep your wriggly livestock on a vegetarian diet to avoid odors and bacterial complications. Red worms also tend to reject spicy foods, such as garlic or onions. Banana skins, apple peels, and wilted lettuce are earthworm favorites, and they also love eggshells that have been rinsed well and crushed. Cut vegetable and fruit scraps into small pieces before putting them in the bin. Include paper filters and tea bags when feeding your worms coffee grounds or tea. In summer, add a few handfuls of fresh grass clippings to the bedding material. Anytime you want to energize your worms, a light sprinkling of cornmeal will do the trick.

Improving Soil with Mulch

Nature's favorite way to improve soil is to cover it with mulch. This happens naturally in the fall, when deciduous plants shed their foliage and grasses and other plants die back to the ground. Rain then leaches out soluble substances, and by the time the weather warms in spring, the material is well on its way to becoming soil-enriching organic matter.

By mimicking this natural plan—with a few refinements—mulch can become a labor-saving way to cultivate healthy soil. Any organic material that's left on the soil's surface is a mulch. Mulches form physical barriers that bring additional benefits that include retaining soil moisture, suppressing weeds, and moderating soil temperatures. As long as you use mulches thoughtfully, they will enhance the growth of your plants and your soil.

HOW MUCH MULCH?

Some gardeners have good luck keeping their soil mulched year-round—a method often called perpetual mulching, which became popular in the 1960s and continues to have many advocates. However, sites that are constantly mulched also are constantly moist, so they become a prime habitat for leaf-eating slugs and snails, and perhaps mice as well. Perpetually mulched soil also is slow to warm up and dry out in spring, which may delay planting. Shrubs that have shallow roots benefit from perpetual mulch, but in vegetable and herb gardens, intermittent mulching generally works better. "Grow a Triple-Mulched Garden" on page 34 presents an ideal model for smart seasonal use of mulches.

Popular mulches such as those described in the "Seven Super Mulch Materials" chart have special quirks that influence the best ways to handle them in a garden. When deciding how to use any mulch, think about the plant that produced it. Mulches that started out as grasses, such as grass clippings, hay, or straw, will decompose much faster than mulches that originated from trees. Materials that take a long time to decompose may temporarily borrow nutrients from the soil, but you can intervene by working with mulches in layers. Place fast-rotting mulch materials on the soil's surface, and then cover them with another mulch material that benefits from being weathered by sun and rain.

FEEDING MULCH TO YOUR SOIL

As the growing season ends, you have several choices as to what will become of your garden's mulch. For maximum gain in organic matter, turn under weathered mulch in the fall, and then top the cultivated soil with a fresh mulch of shredded leaves. Another option is to leave the mulch in place until late winter, at which time you can either turn it under or rake it up and compost it. Either way, it is best to rake up mulch in spring to help the soil dry out and warm up.

Seven Super Mulch Materials

MATERIAL	PROS	CONS	HOW TO USE
Grass clippings	Free, easy to obtain, and rich in nitrogen.	Clippings from other people's yards may contain chemical residues or weed seeds. When piled more than 2 inches thick, the clippings can dry into a mat that repels water.	Spread over bare soil in thin layers, no more than 2 inches thick. Can be used under or over a paper mulch.
Hay	Inexpensive or free, breaks down quickly when exposed to rain.	Often contains weed seeds, molds, and mites. Wear a dust mask when handling spoiled hay to avoid breathing mold spores.	Spread over bare soil, or over a paper mulch. Turn under in fall, or rake up residue first thing in spring and compost it.
Leaves	Free, easy to obtain, and provide long-lasting organic matter.	Whole leaves must leach for several months before they begin to decompose. Shredding is necessary to speed decomposition and make leaves easier to handle.	Spread shredded leaves over bare soil, or over a paper mulch. Ideal for lowering soil temperatures for cool-season plants.
Paper	Free, suppresses weeds, and decomposes quickly when kept moist. Sheets make useful barrier between soil and mulches that decompose slowly.	Colored inks, glossy papers, and other substances may introduce unwanted chemicals to soil.	Layer with other mulches to suppress weeds. When using shredded paper, cover with another organic mulch.
Sawdust	Inexpensive or free, attractive, provides long-lasting organic matter, easy to store for future use.	Slow to decompose. Fresh sawdust may tie up soil nitrogen as it rots. Sawdust from building projects may include residues from treated wood.	Layer over newspapers or grass clippings. Sawdust that has weathered for more than 1 year can be spread over bare soil.
Straw	Attractive, easy to apply, and often free of weeds, and you can grow your own if you grow grains (see page 260).	Fresh oat and wheat straw may leach natural chemicals that inhibit growth of sensitive seedlings.	Spread weathered straw over bare soil, or use to cover a paper or grass clipping mulch.
Wood chips	Free and widely available, usually free of weeds, provide long-lasting organic matter.	Slow to decompose, and may tie up soil nitrogen as they decompose.	Spread over a paper mulch no more than 2 inches deep. Wood chips that have weathered for 2 years may be spread over bare soil.

Grow a Triple-Mulched Garden

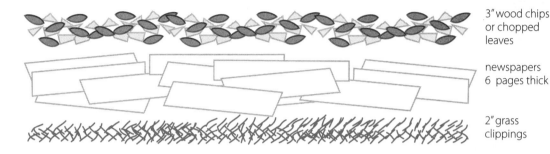

3" wood chips or chopped leaves

newspapers 6 pages thick

2" grass clippings

If rampant weeds and worn-out soil turn your summer garden into a disaster area, you need more than one layer of mulch. Why not go for three that work together? By using a method sometimes called sheet composting, you can improve the soil, frustrate weeds, and drought-proof your garden at the same time.

You will need to spend some time gathering mulch materials, but once they are in place, your garden will require much less weeding and watering, so you can even enjoy a vacation without worrying that you will return to a parched patch of weeds. In the fall, either turn under the weathered mulches or rake them up and combine them with pulled-up plants to create a king-size compost pile.

The exact materials you use are not as important as the order in which you layer them onto your garden. By using grass clippings or well-dampened hay as the base layer, you are setting the scene for robust activity by beneficial soil-borne fungi, which will begin working on the next layer when they've finished the first. Dampened newspapers are ideal for the second layer, or you can use large pieces of unwaxed cardboard; both block out light to sneaky weeds and form a barrier that allows the woody top layer to leach and weather with minimal impact on the soil's nutrient balance. The measurements given are for an area of approximately 400 square feet—a 10 x 40-foot rectangle, or a 20 x 20-foot square.

YOU WILL NEED

Tools: Rake, sprinkler, wheelbarrow

5 bushels of fresh green grass clippings or 3 bales of spoiled hay

Three 12-inch-high bundles of folded newspaper

4 cubic yards of wood chips, sawdust, or shredded leaves

1. In spring, cultivate the soil, rake out weeds, and plant your favorite garden crops. About 2 weeks after your last frost passes, thoroughly weed and water the garden.

2. Spread a 2-inch blanket of fresh green grass clippings or spoiled hay over the garden. Wait 1 to 2 weeks for the material to dry and settle into crevices.

3. Station the wheelbarrow at the garden's edge, and fill it halfway with water. Dip sections of folded-out newspaper, about 6 pages thick, into the water and spread them over the garden. Stop when you have covered about 50 square feet.

4. Before the newspapers can dry, cover them with a 2- to 3-inch layer of wood chips, sawdust, or shredded leaves.

5. Repeat Steps 3 and 4 until your entire garden is secured beneath three layers of mulch. Use a sprinkler to water the garden until all of the layers are thoroughly damp.

Mushrooms in Mulch

Damp straw, wood chips, or sawdust often are colonized by fruit-bearing fungi, which we call mushrooms. Almost all are inedible, and some are poisonous, so do not eat mushrooms that appear in your mulch. It is not necessary to pick them, either, because they are there for a reason. Mushrooms use special enzymes to penetrate woody plant materials, which promotes faster decomposition. Wild mushrooms are definitely beneficial life forms.

There is one type of edible mushroom that can easily be grown in a bed of wood chips or sawdust mulch, and it also thrives in damp, shady soil that is rich with organic matter. Commonly called winecap stropharias or king stropharias (*Stropharia rugoso-annulata*), these mushrooms typically grow 3 to 4 inches across, and fruit soon after the soil warms in spring. To grow them, you will need to order spawn (immature mycelium) from a specialty supplier, and then simply provide a suitable site. Fruiting usually begins in the second year, and continues for several seasons as far north as Zone 5.

How can you tell a winecap stropharia from a "weed" mushroom? Winecaps are an extremely vigorous species, which colonize mulch and soil with thick patches of white, threadlike mycelium. The large mushrooms appear in small clusters and have wine-red caps that lighten to tan within a few days. If you pick one and set the cap on a white piece of paper, it will make a dark purple spore print. Cooked winecaps have a mild flavor, similar to that of portobellos.

Solarize Sick Soil

Healthy soil is teeming with a diverse community of microorganisms, but sometimes soil becomes "sick" with fungi that invade plant roots and cause disease. This may be a problem if you want to grow heirloom tomatoes, which lack resistance to two common soil-borne diseases—fusarium and verticillium wilt. Soil solarization uses heat from the sun to kill these problem fungi, as well as insect eggs, destructive nematodes, and many types of weed seeds. Because solarization affects beneficial as well as harmful organisms, it's best used only when the soil is so badly infested that more moderate restorative measures—such as adding compost—have not been successful. Earthworms manage to escape danger by moving into surrounding soil.

The solarization process is simple: You install a tight plastic bubble over damp soil, and then let the summer sun cook it for several weeks. Soil that is solarized in August and left undisturbed until the following spring should still be free of unwanted weeds and fungi, but the effects of soil solarization decline after 12 to 18 months.

For solarization to work, the area must get several hours of direct sunlight each day—the more, the better. It's also important to time solarization to make the most of summer heat and solar intensity. If you solarize soil when the daily high temperature reaches 85°F, temperatures beneath the plastic may rise to 130°F or even higher.

YOU WILL NEED

Tools: Spade or digging fork, rake, garden hose, scissors

Clear plastic sheeting, 3 to 6 mil thick, wide enough to cover the area

Clear shipping tape

1. Prepare a square or rectangular area by digging the soil 12 inches deep and raking out all weeds, rocks, and debris (see "Make These Nifty Soil Sifters" on page 40). Dig a trench about 12 inches wide and 8 inches deep around the area, setting the excavated soil along the outside edge of the trench.

2. Water the soil until it is thoroughly soaked. Soil organisms are more active in moist soil, and moist soil is more likely to develop plenty of steam during the solarization process.

3. Cover the area with the plastic sheeting, and cut the plastic to fit so that the edges rest in the deepest part of the trenches. Bury one long edge with the excavated soil, and stretch the plastic tight before burying the opposite edges. Do the same with the other two edges.

4. Leave the plastic in place for 4 to 6 weeks. Check regularly for holes by looking for clear areas without condensation. Use clear shipping tape to patch any that appear. Walk on the plastic only to repair holes, either barefooted or wearing socks.

5. Remove the plastic and allow the soil to cool for 2 days before planting.

6. In the first season after the solarization process, avoid digging deeper than 6 inches, where weed seeds are likely to have survived.

Solarizing in Containers

You can apply the principles of solarization on a small scale by using the sun's heat to sterilize used potting soil, potting soil that has been kept in open bags, or garden soil you want to mix with potting soil and then use to grow tomatoes or other plants that are susceptible to soil-borne diseases. You just need the soil, a number of black plastic containers, and a place that bakes in hot summer sun.

To begin, cover a sunny spot of asphalt or concrete with a black plastic garbage bag. Place black plastic containers filled with soil on the black plastic, and soak them well. Cover the setup with a sheet of clear plastic, and secure the edges tightly with bricks, stones, or milk jugs filled with water.

Aboveground containers heat up faster than in-ground beds, so the container method usually works in only 2 weeks, provided the weather is hot and sunny. Store solarized soil in tightly closed containers until you are ready to use it for container gardening projects.

Stack a Slope-Taming Terrace

Sometimes the biggest problem with a site is not the soil itself, but the fact that the place you want to garden is a sloping hillside. The best way to turn a slope into a good place for plants is to build a terrace stabilized by a low wall, which creates a flat bed at the slope's base. In addition to its beautiful appearance, a stone wall controls erosion and creates an ideal place to grow plants that demand excellent drainage. Plus, you can tend the plants with less worry of tumbling down the hill.

This terrace-building project uses the cut-and-fill method, in which soil removed to form the foundation for the wall is temporarily set aside, amended with compost, and then used to backfill the area behind the wall. Very long, steep slopes may benefit from more than one terrace, but it's best to begin with one, located near the base of the slope, and then work your way upward if additional terraces are needed.

As long as you limit the height of a stone wall to about 15 inches, you can use dry-stacked stone, which requires no mortar. The measurements here are for a single stone wall, 20 feet long and 15 inches high.

YOU WILL NEED

Tools: Measuring tape, heavy work gloves, spade, wheelbarrow

1 cubic yard of fine gravel or crushed stone (two 1.5 cubic foot bags)

1 ton of faced stacking stone

1 cubic yard of compost (three 40-pound bags)

1. Measure the location of the wall to make sure you purchase enough stone. It's better to have too much than not enough. After you get your stone, sort it into sizes. Use the largest stones for the base of the wall, and make a pile of flat, uniform stones for the wall's top edge.

2. Use the spade to dig a 12-inch-deep horizontal shelf that will form the base of the wall. Place the excavated soil in the wheelbarrow, and dump it in a place where it will be convenient to get to when you're ready to fill in the space behind the wall. Go back and sculpt the shelf so that it slants backward, with the front edge about 1 inch higher than the back edge.

3. Spread a 1-inch-deep layer of gravel or crushed stone over the base of the prepared foundation.

4. Use your largest stones to lay the first course over the gravel or crushed stone. Then lay two or three additional courses, setting stones so that vertical crevices do not run continuously from one tier to the next. Also set each new course ¼ inch behind the one below it, so the front of the wall tilts slightly backward toward the slope.

5. When the wall is 8 inches high, stop to backfill behind it with some of the excavated soil, and pack it firmly in place. Reposition any stones that seem wobbly, using small stones or pieces of gravel as shims. Lay the remainder of the stones in place, stopping just before you lay the top tier in place.

6. As you backfill behind the wall, amend the soil with compost to help it do a good job of supporting plants. Place flat stones on the top of the finished wall, with their back edges pushed into the soil.

7. Fill the new bed behind the wall with your favorite plants.

Good Stone for Walls

When you shop for stone—or collect it from ruined structures—choose a type that is in good supply. Later, if you build additional walls or other stone features, you will want to match the stone you used for your first wall. "Faced" stone has at least two flat sides, so it's easy to stack. You can use the same steps used to make a natural stone wall to build one using preformed concrete landscaping blocks, which are heavy but otherwise not difficult to handle. Before buying either stone or landscaping blocks, make sure you have a place to put them while you work. Building even a small stone wall is a big project that will require several work sessions.

Make These Nifty Sifters

Soil sifters separate the big stuff from the little stuff, whether that stuff is the rocks from your garden soil or undecomposed broccoli stalks from your compost. Use different sifters for different jobs; the Rock-Removing Roll is great for sifting out rocks, while the Cheap Seat Sifter will make quick work of turning chunks of compost into fine crumbles.

Rock-Removing Roll

YOU WILL NEED

Tools: Heavy-duty gloves, wire snips, pliers, wheelbarrow

One 6-foot-long piece of 36-inch-wide chicken wire (poultry netting)

6 feet of insulated wire

1. Cut the chicken wire to length, and roll it into a cylinder. Crimp and fold the side edges to close it.

2. Close one end of the cylinder by bending in

12 inches of the chicken wire on all sides. Thread the insulated wire through the side edge seam and through the closed end to keep them closed. Use pliers to wrap the ends of the insulated wire through the mesh to keep them from coming loose.

3. Fill the wire roll with rocky soil, and shake it vigorously to remove soil while retaining rocks. Dump the rocks in the wheelbarrow, and use them for another garden project.

Cheap Seat Sifter

YOU WILL NEED

Tools: Utility scissors, staple gun, bucket

One 14-inch-wide cardboard box

One 16-inch square of aluminum window screening

1 old wood chair without seat

Duct tape

1. Remove the flaps from one end of the box, and cut two of them into 1-inch-wide strips.

2. Place the screening over the seat area of the chair, and trim the edges if needed to make them the proper size. Staple the edges in place, sandwiching the cardboard strips between the staples and the screening.

3. Open out the flaps on the other end of the cardboard box, and place it over the screening. Tape the opened flaps to the chair.

4. Place a bucket of compost in the cardboard hopper, and then place the bucket under the Cheap Seat Sifter. Use a hand trowel or gloved hand to stir and scrape the compost across the screen.

CHAPTER 2

Raising Them Right

Whether you're sowing seeds, rooting cuttings, or dividing and replanting beloved perennials, plant propagation will bring out your nurturing side.

How Great Gardens Are Born

Every plant has the ability to produce offspring, and participating in that process is what plant propagation is all about. Annual plants, which include most vegetables and some flowers, reproduce by shedding seeds, so knowing how to help seeds germinate and grow is a fundamental gardening skill. Some seeds seem to germinate as soon as they are tucked into moist soil, while others require special handling. The first part of this chapter includes several projects to help you refine your seed-starting skills, whether your heart is set on growing heirloom tomatoes or a rainbow of summer flowers.

Propagating plants is not only about seeds though. In less than an hour, you can triple your supply of many clump-forming perennials by digging and dividing them. A bit more patience is required to grow new plants from rooted cuttings, or you can try the low-risk propagation method known as layering. The best way to learn these easy techniques is to take them on one project at a time. Expect success when you set stem cuttings to root in a Double Pot Propagator (see page 70), or raise skimpy divisions to transplanting size in a Propagation Bed (see page 68).

SECRETS OF SEEDS

Unlike most animals, plants are not able to see to it that their offspring receive nurturing care. Instead, they use a miraculous plan in which they package up everything their babies need to start a new life in a tiny seed. The outer seed coats may include hooks or prickles, which help the seeds hitchhike to new homes on the feet of unsuspecting animals. Or, seeds may be covered with a substance that turns sticky when it gets wet—a great way for a seed to slide into a wet soil crevice. The coats of parsley seeds even contain a natural herbicide that leaches into the soil and inhibits the germination of nearby weeds.

Seeds come in all shapes and sizes, and even the tiniest seed contains enough food to support the seedling until it grows roots and is able to begin feeding itself. Changes in temperature and moisture are the most common factors that trigger a seed to make the transition from seed to seedling, so managing these factors becomes your job when you start plants from seed. From the moment the first leaves break through to the surface, seedlings use light as their primary energy source. So you will need to provide light, moisture, and warm temperatures to keep your seedlings growing strong.

THE BENEFITS OF STARTING SEEDS

Why should you take on the responsibilities of growing plants from seeds? Beyond the fun of this project, there are several important advantages.

■ You can grow unusual varieties that are seldom available as seedlings, such as purple-skinned carrots or gourds that are the exact shape and size of goose eggs.

- You can experiment with flowers in unique colors, or grow numerous plants of a single color.
- You know your plants are free of growth regulators, pesticides, and other unwanted chemicals.
- You can have healthy seedlings for planting in fall, when bedding plants often are not available.
- You can save money, because a packet of 50 seeds is much less expensive than two flats of the same plant.

CHOOSING GOOD SEEDS

It is a tradition among gardeners to spend the second half of winter drooling over the beautiful pictures in seed catalogs, most of which are now available online and in printed form. Seed racks in retail stores often offer great treasures, too, or you can swap seeds with fellow gardeners. If you hope to save and replant seeds produced by the plants you grow, start with good open-pollinated varieties rather than hybrids. However, if a hybrid variety provides a form of disease resistance that's important in your area, the hybrid is probably a better choice. Whether the seeds you choose are hybrid or open-pollinated, look for ones that have been organically grown, or at least have not been treated with fungicides. Store your purchased seeds in an airtight container, and keep it in a cool, dry place.

SOWING ON SCHEDULE

Some seeds can wait in the soil for years until they sense just the right combination of temperature, moisture, and light. These factors are under your control when you raise seedlings indoors, but nature is in charge when you sow seeds or set out seedlings in your garden. Getting the timing right is not difficult if you carefully read the suggestions given on seed packets or in catalogs, which usually describe ideal planting times in relation to first and last frost dates.

Sowing Seeds in Spring

As a general rule, most vegetable seeds can be started indoors 4 to 8 weeks before the last spring frost, and slower-growing annual flowers should be started 6 to 8 weeks before the last frost. You can use season-stretching tricks such as Tube Hoop Cloches (see page 160) or a Sliding Window Bed Topper (see page 154) to get an earlier start in spring, but only with seedlings that are started indoors and set out under protection. With direct-sown seeds, it's best to wait to plant until the soil is warm enough to promote fast germination.

Planting Seeds for Fall

Several rewarding vegetables grow better in fall than in spring—broccoli, bulb fennel, and leafy greens are good examples. But the same factors that encourage fall crops to prosper—days that are getting shorter, and temperatures that are becoming cooler—slow the rate at which they grow. When planting seeds in late summer or early fall, add 3 to 4 weeks to a variety's "expected days to maturity" rating when planning your sowing schedule. For example, a cauliflower variety rated at 60 days to maturity when grown in spring may need 90 days when grown in fall. Many fall garden vegetables have no trouble surviving light frosts; use the average date of your first hard freeze as an end date when choosing planting dates for most fall vegetables.

START WITH EASY SEEDS

If you're new to seed starting, begin with seeds that are easy to please before trying more challenging subjects. Most plants that develop branched, fibrous roots can be started indoors and set out as seedlings, while those that send taproots straight down into the soil perform better when seeds are sown directly in the garden. The "15 Easy Plants to Grow from Seed" chart below describes the germination requirements of 15 popular vegetables and flowers, along with how long the seeds will keep when stored under cool, dry conditions. More details on how to grow seeds indoors begin on page 46.

15 Easy Plants to Grow from Seed

10 EASY VEGETABLES

NAME	BEST GERMINATION TEMPERATURES	WHEN TO PLANT	SPECIAL NEEDS	SEED LONGEVITY
Beans	70°F–80°F	Direct sow beginning 1 week after last spring frost; make last planting 10 weeks before first fall frost.	High germination rate, so seedlings often need to be thinned.	3 years
Broccoli	60°F–80°F	Start indoors 6 weeks before last spring frost; plant fall crop 8 to 10 weeks before first fall freeze.	Often grows better in fall than in spring	5 years
Carrots	55°F–85°F	Direct sow 1 week before last spring frost; make last planting 10 weeks before first fall freeze.	Cover with a cloth or shade cover if needed to maintain constant moisture.	3 years
Cucumbers	65°F–85°F	Direct sow beginning 1 to 2 weeks after last spring frost; make last planting 10 weeks before first fall frost.	Bears all at once, so several small plantings are better than one large one.	5 years
Lettuce	50°F–70°F	Direct sow beginning 3 weeks before last spring frost; make last sowing 6 weeks before first fall frost.	Must be eaten fresh, so make several small sowings rather than one large planting.	3 years
Peas	45°F–70°F	Direct sow beginning 3 weeks before last spring frost.	Inoculate with beneficial rhizobium when planting peas in new garden soil.	3 years

NAME	BEST GERMINATION TEMPERATURES	WHEN TO PLANT	SPECIAL NEEDS	SEED LONGEVITY
Peppers	70°F–85°F	Start indoors 4 to 6 weeks before last spring frost.	Warm temperatures and light moisture promote fast germination.	4 years
Spinach	45°F–75°F	Direct sow 4 weeks before last spring frost; make last sowing 6 to 8 weeks before first fall frost.	Spring spinach bolts as days become long; fall crops often survive winter.	5 years
Squash	65°F–90°F	Direct sow beginning 1 to 2 weeks after last spring frost; make last sowing 10 weeks before first fall frost.	High germination rate, so fast-growing seedlings often need to be thinned.	5 years
Tomatoes	65°F–85°F	Start indoors 6 to 8 weeks before last spring frost; plant rooted stem cuttings after midsummer.	Bright light required to support fast growth.	4 years

5 EASY FLOWERS

NAME	BEST GERMINATION TEMPERATURES	WHEN TO PLANT	SPECIAL NEEDS	SEED LONGEVITY
Celosia	70°F–85°F	Start indoors 4 weeks before last spring frost; direct-seed outdoors 3 weeks after last spring frost.	Seeds must be covered, as darkness promotes germination.	4 years
Marigolds	60°F–85°F	Start indoors 4 weeks before last spring frost; direct-seed outdoors beginning 2 weeks after last spring frost.	Sow shallow, so seeds are barely covered.	2 to 3 years
Nasturtiums	60°F–75°F	Direct sow beginning 1 week before last spring frost; continue planting through the spring season.	Nicking and soaking seeds overnight before planting speeds germination.	5 years
Sunflowers	60°F–75°F	Direct sow beginning 1 to 2 weeks after last spring frost; make additional plantings until 10 weeks before first fall frost.	High germination rate, so plants often need to be thinned.	2 to 3 years
Zinnias	65°F–85°F	Start indoors 3 weeks before last spring frost; direct sow outdoors beginning 2 weeks after last spring frost.	Barely cover seeds with fine soil; deep planting delays germination.	5 to 6 years

Starting Seeds Indoors

There are five basic factors to keep in mind when starting seeds indoors. Remember these few points, and you're on your way.

- The seeding medium, or soil, needs to be light in texture and free of soil-borne fungi. The best way to meet this need is to use seed-starting mix, which is typically a blend of peat moss and vermiculite, with a few minerals added. In addition to using it to start seeds, seed-starting mix makes a great medium for rooting stem cuttings (see "Make a Double Pot Propagator" on page 70). Buy a small bag, and keep it closed between uses. If the bag does not have a zip-top closure, fold down the top and secure it with clothespins.

- Containers should be large enough to hold 2 to 4 square inches of seed-starting mix. Smaller containers (such as egg cartons) dry out quickly, and larger containers increase the risk of damping off (fungal diseases that cause seedling stems to shrivel and collapse at soil level).

- Good drainage is important. If you use drinking cups, yogurt containers, or other recycled items, use an ice pick or nail to poke several holes in the bottom before filling them with damp seed-starting mix.

- Most seeds need warmth to germinate. You can buy heating cables or mats made for providing gentle bottom heat, or simply keep planted containers in a warm place, such as atop your refrigerator or near your hot water heater. You could also use a heating pad set on low, with planted containers set on a metal cookie sheet held above the heating pad with empty food cans.

- The seeding medium needs to be kept moist until the seeds germinate. You can replenish moisture with light sprays of water from a pump spray bottle, or enclose the containers in a roomy plastic bag.

KEEPING SEEDLINGS HEALTHY

As soon as seeds sprout, the leaves need plenty of light, which they photosynthesize into the energy needed to grow new stems and leaves. A very sunny windowsill may suffice, though you will need to turn the seedlings daily to make sure that all sides of the plants get plenty of direct light. It is often easier to use a fluorescent light, kept on for 12 to 14 hours a day. It's best if you can adjust the height of the lights so they are about 2 inches above the tops of the seedlings. Inexpensive shop lights, hung from chains attached to the ceiling, are a good investment, or you can try the project on page 50, "Make a Light Box from a Drawer."

Seedlings also need fresh air, so remove plastic coverings as soon as seeds germinate. The most common problem with indoor-grown seedlings, called damping off, occurs when various fungi attack the tender stems and roots, causing the seedlings to fall over and die. Plenty of light and fresh air and the right amount of water are the best ways to protect seedlings from damping off; overwatering can cause many problems.

Damping off also can be caused by using containers that are not clean. Before planting seedlings in cell packs or flats saved from the previous season, wash them with warm, soapy water, and then swish them through a mixture of 1 part bleach to 10 parts water. If you rinse containers well and allow them to dry, they should be free of any residual fungi.

SUPPORTING STRONG GROWTH

Seeds contain enough food to sustain seedlings until the germination process is complete. But seed-starting mix seldom includes plant nutrients, so you should begin feeding seedlings with an organic liquid fertilizer like fish emulsion or kelp about a week after they sprout. Start by mixing the fertilizer at half the recommended rate given on the package, and then gradually increase the strength of the solution as the seedlings grow.

Seedlings also need more light as they gain size, which is best provided by gradually exposing them to real sunlight. If you don't have a cold frame, find a protected spot outdoors where you can place your seedlings for a few hours on mild, sunny days. Seedlings that are able to gradually adapt to outdoor light—as well as moving air from gentle breezes—are less likely to suffer setbacks when they are transplanted to the garden.

Are They Still Good?

Seed packets bear a date that tells you the year for which they were packaged. Seeds in partial leftover packets often are fine for planting. Most seeds remain viable for at least 2 years when stored in a cool, dry place, but if you're not sure that your seeds are still good, use this simple test.

1. Moisten a paper towel, fold it in half, and arrange 10 seeds near the center, so they are not touching.

2. Fold the paper towel into thirds, letter-style, and tuck it into a plastic sandwich bag. Place the bag in a warm place, such as the top of your refrigerator.

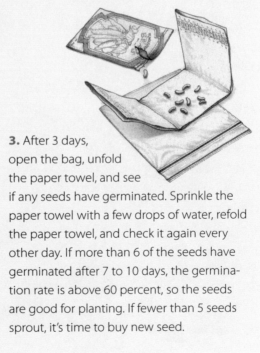

3. After 3 days, open the bag, unfold the paper towel, and see if any seeds have germinated. Sprinkle the paper towel with a few drops of water, refold the paper towel, and check it again every other day. If more than 6 of the seeds have germinated after 7 to 10 days, the germination rate is above 60 percent, so the seeds are good for planting. If fewer than 5 seeds sprout, it's time to buy new seed.

Plant a Homegrown Six-Pack

Learning to start seeds indoors opens the door to unlimited possibilities for exploring unique vegetable varieties and unusual herbs, and you can grow flowers in exactly the colors you want. If you've never grown your own seedlings before, this easy procedure is guaranteed to give great results. Except for a bag of seed-starting mix and a packet of seeds, you probably already have everything you need to get growing.

YOU WILL NEED

Tools: Plastic or paper cup, bucket, pencil, plate, pump spray bottle, plastic dishwashing detergent bottle

1 small bag of seed-starting mix

1 plastic 6-cell seedling container, cleaned and dried

1 packet of seeds

1 clear or opaque plastic produce bag

Package of organic water-soluble plant food

1. Scoop 2 cups of dry mix and place it in the bucket. Stir in 1 cup of warm water, and allow the mixture to sit for at least 2 minutes.

2. Fill the container cells to the rim with the moistened mix. Lightly pat the surface, adding more mix if needed to make the cells almost full.

3. Use your fingertip or a pencil to make 2 shallow holes in the surface of each cell. Plant 1 seed in each hole at the planting depth recommended on the package. Cover the

seeds with dampened mix. Add labels (see page 61) if you are planting more than one type of seed.

4. Place the planted cell pack on a plate, and spray the surface lightly with lukewarm water from a pump spray bottle. Slip the plate and cell pack inside the plastic bag, tuck under the edges, and set it in a warm place, such as on top of your refrigerator.

5. After 3 days, begin checking daily to see if seeds have sprouted. When you see the first sprouts breaking the surface, move the cell pack to a brightly lit place (see page 50 for lighting suggestions).

6. Spritz the surface with room-temperature water twice daily until all the seedlings are up. If more than 2 seedlings appear in a cell, pull out the ones closest to the edges with tweezers, or cut them off at the soil line with a small pair of scissors.

7. Two weeks after the seeds germinate, begin feeding your seedlings with an organic, water-soluble plant food, mixed at half the strength

recommended on the package. Place the mixture in a clean dishwashing detergent bottle, and dribble a small amount into each cell every 3 days, or as often as needed to keep the seed-starting mix constantly moist.

8. When the seedlings are 4 to 6 weeks old, begin preparing them for their move to your garden. If you do not have a cold frame, harden them off by placing them in a protected spot outdoors for a few hours each day for 1 week.

PLAY IT AGAIN

Containers for Starting Seeds

Beyond plastic cell packs saved from last year's purchased pansies or petunias, you can use any small containers that hold at least 2 square inches of seed-starting mix for starting seeds. To promote good drainage, use an ice pick or nail to punch several holes in the bottom of yogurt cups, small Styrofoam cups, or other small containers. Do you sometimes buy salad to go? Add drainage holes to a plastic salad bowl, pop on the clear lid, and you have an instant mini-greenhouse!

Paper towel or bathroom tissue rolls make great containers for starting seeds. Cut them into 2-inch lengths, slit them down the side, and then use a small piece of tape to tape the sides back together. Line the bottom of a plate or dish with a ¼-inch layer of damp seed-starting mix, place the prepared rounds on top, and use string to bundle them into groups of 4. Fill with damp seed-starting mix, and start planting. As you set out the seedlings or transplant them to larger containers, gently remove the rolls (remove the tape and spread open the roll from around the plant) so the roots can quickly grow out into surrounding soil.

Make a Light Box from a Drawer

Providing ample light is often the most challenging aspect of growing your own seedlings. An inexpensive fluorescent light can do the job—provided you keep the bulb 2 to 3 inches from the seedlings' topmost leaves, and paint all nearby surfaces bright white to reflect every last light ray. This light box, made from an old drawer, can accommodate about a dozen seedlings at a time, and you can raise or lower the lights in keeping with the size of your plants. Between seed-starting seasons, simply take it apart for easy storage.

To make sure seedlings get as much light as they need, leave the lights on for about 14 hours a day (fluorescent lights give off very little heat, so don't worry about "cooking" your plants). If you like, add a timer to turn the lights on and off automatically. If the seed-starting mix dries out quickly (indoor air in late winter can often be quite dry), cover the box and lights with a sheet of clear plastic at night, after the lights are turned off. Be sure to remove it before turning the light back on, because it could pose a fire hazard.

Making More Light

The more seedlings you grow indoors, the more light you will need. Ordinary fluorescent shop lights work well and are widely available in 24- and 48-inch lengths. Look for a model that includes a reflective hood, and suspend it from the ceiling with hooks and chains. In addition to providing the light your plants need to grow, an illuminated group of seedlings brings a cheery note to any room.

YOU WILL NEED

Tools: Measuring tape, handsaw, drill, marking pencil, screwdriver

1 wood dresser drawer at least 19 inches wide

One 24-inch-long piece of poplar, ¼-inch thick and 4 inches wide

One 24-inch-long piece of poplar, ¼-inch thick and 3 inches wide

1 can of bright white spray enamel paint

Four 32 x 1 bolts with matching wing nuts

One 18-inch-long under-counter fluorescent light fixture

8 small ½-inch screw eyes

1. To make the frame for the lights, measure the exact width of the drawer between the outside edges. Cut the 4-inch-wide piece of poplar to this length to form the top piece. For the sides, cut the 3-inch-wide piece of poplar into two 12-inch-long pieces.

2. In a well-ventilated place or outdoors, paint the cut pieces and the inside of the drawer with white enamel paint.

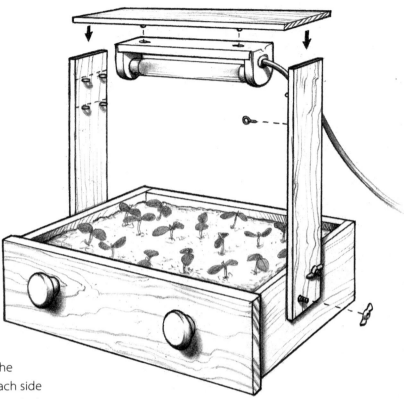

3. Drill 2 holes in the lower section of each side piece for the bolts, with the holes about 2 inches apart and diagonal rather than straight across. Check to make sure the bolts will barely pass through the holes. Center one of the side pieces upright against the outside of the drawer, and use the pencil to mark where you should make matching holes in the side of the drawer. Drill holes through the pencil marks, and loosely attach the side piece to the drawer with bolts and wing nuts. Repeat on the other side.

4. Check to make sure the top piece fits correctly between the two side pieces. Follow the manufacturer's directions to attach the light fixture to the top of the light frame.

5. Unscrew the wing nuts to disassemble the sides. Use a small drill bit to make guide holes for the screw eyes in matching sets of two, which will support the lights at two different heights. Install one set of screw eyes 2 inches from the tops of the side pieces, and another set 2 inches below the first set.

6. Reassemble the side pieces, and firmly tighten the wing nuts. Slide the top into place at either of the two heights, so the ends rest on the screw eyes. Plant your seedlings in the drawer, and turn on the lights. Or, place seedlings started in small containers inside the drawer.

Direct Seeding

Digging in the soil and tucking seeds into the ground feels wonderfully invigorating—especially after a long, dreary winter. In addition to its sheer pleasure, one of the benefits of direct-seeding is that it saves time. Plants that grow right where they sprout mature quickly, in part because they are never set back by the transplanting process. And many plants have such fragile roots that they always grow best when planted directly in the garden.

Good timing is important, especially in spring when the soil is cool and wet. You can avoid planting delays due to wet soil by preparing spots for cool-season plants in the fall, but seeds sown too early often rot when forced to wait for warmer temperatures. A few vegetables—notably peas, radishes, and many leafy greens—will germinate in cool soil, but most others need soil temperatures above 60°F to sprout quickly.

SEED DEPTH AND SPACING

Pay attention to the seed packet directions for seeding depth, as well as the space needed between plants and rows. Most seeds should be planted at four times their size, which usually means planting large bean and squash seeds 1 inch deep, and covering tinier seeds with less than ¼ inch of soil.

If you are new to growing plants from seed, it's a good idea to space seeds slightly closer than the packet suggests. If all the seeds germinate, you will need to thin them by pulling out excess seedlings about 2 weeks later. On a positive note, having plenty of seedlings popping up makes it much easier to tell the difference between desirable seedlings and weeds. The same factors that help seeds germinate promote the sprouting of weed seeds, so direct-sown vegetables and flowers often have plenty of wild company.

IMPROVING GERMINATION

The first stage in the germination process is taking up water, and large seeds like peas and beans may spend several days plumping up before they can sprout. Soaking the seeds in room-temperature water overnight is an easy way to speed germination of large seeds, or seeds with very hard seed coats, such as okra.

If you have clay soil, another possible problem is the formation of a hard crust over germinating seeds. The simplest way to avoid this problem is to sow seeds in furrows, and cover them with used potting soil or compost instead of garden soil. In hot weather, placing a board over the furrows for a couple of days will help keep the soil moist.

Keeping a seeded bed or row constantly moist can be a challenge when you are planting in dry weather. Using a sprinkler is a good way to keep large areas moist, or you can simply cover a small bed with a damp blanket for the first few days after seeding. To provide temporary shade for a newly seeded row, make a Movable Sun Shade (see page 170).

SEEDS WITH SPECIAL NEEDS

Some seeds are covered with such thick, hard seed coats that they take forever to germinate—if they germinate at all. Solving this problem requires that you make an opening in the seed coat, which enables the seeds to take up water. This process is called scarification. Seeds that benefit from scarification include sweet peas, morning glories, moonflowers, New Zealand spinach, and gourds. Nasturtiums will germinate without being scarified, but they will sprout faster with a little help.

The easiest way to scarify seeds is to use a nail clipper to make a shallow nick in the side of the seed. Another method consists of placing seeds inside a piece of coarse sandpaper, folded in half, and rubbing the seeds until they are thoroughly scratched. You also can scarify seeds by rubbing them against a metal file, such as the one you use to sharpen your hoe and other garden tools.

To further speed germination, soak scarified seeds in water overnight before planting them. Any seeds that were not adequately scarified will not take up water and will remain small and hard. Give them another little nick with nail clippers before planting them in prepared soil.

Make Your Own Seed Tape

Many seed companies sell seeds of their most popular varieties as seed tapes—biodegradable ribbons to which seeds have been attached at the proper spacing. It's easy to make your own, which insures exact spacing, saves time-consuming thinning, and doesn't waste seed. Plus, making seed tape is a great project for a cold winter night, and it's easy enough for kids to do with ease.

1. In a small saucepan over medium heat, mix 1 tablespoon of cornstarch and 1 cup of cold water. Stir until the mixture boils. Remove from heat and cool to room temperature.

2. Cut newspapers into strips 1 inch wide. Use a ruler and pencil to mark the proper spacing for seeds.

3. Place the cornstarch mixture in a zip-top sandwich bag. Cut off a tiny corner of the bag, and squeeze a dot of the mixture onto each mark on the paper. Place a seed on each dot, and allow the seed tapes to dry (about 2 hours).

4. Write the name of the seeds on the end of each seed tape, roll them up, and store in a cool, dry place.

5. At the proper planting time, unroll the seed tape and place it in a furrow. Cover with soil and water well.

Make Straw Bale Beds

Raise your garden to new heights and get an up-close experience with direct-sown seeds by planting lettuce, bush beans, and trailing flowers in a straw bale bed. You won't have to bend far to tend your plants or contend with weeds, and at the end of the season you can use the decomposing straw as mulch. Get extra mileage from this project by positioning three beds in a semicircle, which creates a protected pocket for hardening off tender seedlings started indoors. If you have a new bed planned for the next season, the bale beds will smother weeds and grasses, so the spot will be ready to dig by fall.

The decomposing straw creates gentle bottom heat, so straw bale beds also are a good way to get a head start on spring. On cold nights, simply cover them with plastic or old blankets, held aloft with sticks stuck into the bales. Bale beds need frequent watering, so keep a hose or watering can handy. In rainy weather, don't be surprised to see mushrooms sprouting from the bottoms of the bales. These "weed" mushrooms are not edible, but their appearance is evidence that naturally occurring fungi are busy promoting decomposition within the bales.

YOU WILL NEED

Tools: Scissors, garden hose, handheld digging fork

3 bales of wheat straw

20 yards jute or hemp string

Water-soluble organic all-purpose plant food

Three 20-pound bags of compost

1 packet each bush bean, lettuce, and nasturtium seeds

1. Place the straw bales in a sunny spot, with the cut ends of the straw facing up. The baling twine or wire should be parallel to the ground. To reinforce the baling twine, tie string around the sides of

Bale Bed Banquets and Bouquets

You can grow any plants that are not heavy feeders in a straw bale bed. If there is still time left in the growing season, follow lettuce and bush beans with quick crops of fall radishes, turnips, or baby bok choy. If you'd rather grow flowers, stud the middle of the bale beds with upright zinnias, and flank them with cascading petunias. For fall, fill bale beds with bright chrysanthe-

mums, and add a few pumpkins, gourds, or winter squash to complete the display. Keep in mind that wet bales of straw are heavy, so it's best to put them in their permanent places before you plant them. They also become fragile as the straw begins to decompose, so the bales should not be moved until you're ready to tear them apart to use the straw as mulch.

each bale to help hold them together as the straw begins to decompose.

2. Thoroughly dampen the bales, which may require you to water them 3 days in a row. On the third day, drench the moistened bales with plant food, mixed according to label directions.

3. Wait 1 week. Wet down the bales again, wait a few hours for the straw to soften, and then use the small digging fork to chop into the top of the bales. Leave a 2-inch margin of intact straw around the edges. Pry out enough straw to create 6-inch-deep bowls inside each bale.

4. Place half of the compost in the hollowed-out bales, and lightly chop it in with the digging fork to sift it down into the straw. Spread the rest of the compost over the top.

5. Nick the nasturtium seeds with a nail clipper. Soak the nasturtium and bean seeds overnight. Plant the beans 1 inch deep down the center of each bale, and water well. Scatter lettuce seeds down either side of the bean row, and firm them in by patting lightly with the palm of your hand. Poke the nasturtium seeds into the compost 2 inches inside each corner.

6. Keep the compost moist until the seeds germinate, and then thin the seedlings if they are too crowded. Every 2 weeks, give your straw bale beds a thorough drench with liquid plant food.

Grow a Wagon-Ho Garden

That little red wagon that's a little too unsteady for the children or grandchildren is great for moving seedlings indoors and outdoors, so it makes hardening off a breeze. When most of your seedlings are in the ground, use the wagon as a novel container for a compact patio tomato, grown in the company of robust nasturtiums. In the fall, simply clean out the wagon and put it back to work moving plants or other gardening supplies. You can use an old wheelbarrow for this project, too.

YOU WILL NEED

Tools: Hammer and nails, tape measure, wood saw, watering can, garden trowel, strips of stretchy cloth

An old child's wagon

One 48-inch-long wood tomato stake

Newspapers

One 20-pound bag of potting mix (more for a large wagon)

1 patio tomato plant

1 packet of nasturtium seeds

All-purpose water-soluble organic plant food

1 stout stick, 2 inches longer than the width of the wagon (optional)

1. Wash and dry the wagon, and use the hammer and a nail to make 10 drainage holes in the bottom of the wagon.

2. To prepare a stake to support the tomato, measure the width of the wagon between the inside edges. Use the saw to cut off the bottom of the tomato stake at exactly this length. Place the long piece of the tomato stake on a flat, solid surface, and center the short piece across the bottom

edge to form a T. Nail the two pieces together.

3. Cover the bottom and sides of the wagon with 4 thicknesses of newspaper. Twelve inches from the front of the wagon, install the stake by pushing the base inside the wagon. If it fits very tightly, use the hammer to tap it into place. If the fit is so loose that the stake falls over, shim the ends of the base with squares of folded newspaper.

4. Thoroughly dampen the newspapers before filling the wagon with potting soil. Plant the tomato near the base of the stake, laying its roots and lowest section of the stem at a diagonal angle. Nick the nasturtium seeds with nail clippers before planting them 4 inches apart in the rest of the wagon. Water well, and move the wagon to a place that gets at least 6 hours of full sun each day.

5. To keep the soil from drying out, cover the soil's surface with damp newspapers until the nasturtium seeds germinate. After the nasturtium seeds sprout and begin to grow, thin them to 4 plants.

If desired, lift the extra seedlings and transplant them to your garden.

6. Water your Wagon-Ho Garden as often as needed to keep the soil lightly moist. Topping the soil with mulch will help retain moisture. Every 2 weeks, give the soil a deep drench with a water-soluble organic plant food, mixed according to label directions.

7. As the tomato grows, tie it loosely to the stake with strips of stretchy cloth. When the tomato vine becomes heavy with fruit, reinforce the upright stake by placing a stout stick across the top edges of the wagon, if necessary. Tie it snugly to the stake.

PLAY IT AGAIN

Creative Containers

From old work boots to discarded Easter baskets, perhaps your storage room is a treasure trove of whimsical containers for just the right plants. When using boots or shoes as planters, use a hammer and nail to make a few drainage holes in the soles, and stick with plants that don't mind dry conditions, such as sedums or other succulents. To turn porous baskets into containers, simply line them with a piece of cloth before filling them with soil.

Look for ways to use old pieces of furniture, too. The phrase "garden bed" takes on a whole new meaning when an old bed frame is sunk into the garden and filled with colorful pansies or petunias. And few planters are more charming than an old seatless wooden chair that's been retrofitted to hold a large container of small-fruited cucumbers, or a frothy pot of verbena. Making a sturdy platform for the container is usually a simple matter of cutting two wood slats that can be laid over the chair's rungs.

Grow New Plants from Produce

The best way to grow a perfect potato patch is to start with organically grown, certified disease-free seed potatoes, but it's not the only way. Next time you have small potatoes that start sprouting before you can eat them, plant them instead. Small potatoes—including egg-size new potatoes and elongated fingerling types—grow faster than big baking potatoes, so they always make a crop. The best time to plant potatoes is early to mid spring, which is prime planting time for onions, too. "Grow a Potato Salad Patch" on page 60 puts this coincidence into action, but there are other types of produce you can plant in addition to potatoes and onions.

MINT AND OREGANO

If you really like the flavor of fresh mint in a special recipe and usually have to buy sprigs, try treating a few sprigs like rooted cuttings and grow them into new plants yourself. Mint is such a willing rooter that stems will often strike roots in plain water (see page 74), or you can use a Double Pot Propagator (see page 70). Other culinary herbs that often can be grown from produce department packages include oregano and marjoram. You may have luck with sage, rosemary, and tarragon, too. To increase your chances of success, promptly remove the herbs from their packaging, snip off the ends of the stems, and treat them like any other rootable stem cuttings, as described on page 66. Mint can be invasive, so it's best

to grow it in an aboveground or sunken container rather than a garden bed.

SWEET POTATOES

Sweet potatoes often begin sprouting when kept at room temperature, but unlike regular potatoes, they should not be planted outdoors until late spring when the soil is thoroughly warm. Meanwhile, you can grow a sweet potato in plain water by using toothpicks to suspend the tuber's root end in a jar of water. Better yet, plant the tuber on its side in a broad flowerpot, and place it near a sunny window. When the weather warms, either set the entire plant in your garden, or break off individual stems with a few roots attached, and plant them in a sunny, well-drained spot.

HORSERADISH

Hard horseradish roots may not appear to hold much promise, but a 4-inch piece planted a few inches deep will usually produce a big plant in only a few months. Horseradish is quite cold tolerant, so it makes a great edible perennial. Harvest roots in the fall by digging up the plant and cutting off several inches of root. Discard old, woody sections, and replant a 4-inch piece where you want the next season's crop to grow.

GARLIC

The type of garlic sold in supermarkets is called artichoke garlic, and it grows quite well in Zones 6 to 9. The best time to plant garlic is mid-autumn, after the soil has become cool. Break apart a bulb into cloves, and plant the largest outer cloves 8 inches apart in rich, well-drained soil. The following summer, dig up the plants when the tops begin to die back—but before they turn totally brown.

At other times of year, grow sprouting garlic cloves into "gallions"—slender scallion-type plants with a strong hint of garlic flavor.

As long as the green tops are young and tender, they can be eaten either raw or cooked. The white shanks are delicious when sautéed with other vegetables.

Make a Planting Bar

When you're planting lots of garlic or onions, or dropping large seeds into the ground, a planting bar can save time and help you get spacing perfect. When you're not using the planting bar for planting, hang it from a wall and use it to hold bunches of herbs or flowers as they dry.

YOU WILL NEED

Tools: Measuring tape, handsaw, pencil, drill with ½-inch bit, hammer
One ½-inch-diameter wooden dowel
One 36-inch-long piece of 2 x 4 lumber
Five 2-inch-long finishing nails

1. Use the saw to cut five 3-inch pieces from the dowel.

2. Mark 6-inch increments down the middle of the broad side of the 2 x 4.

3. Drill holes through the board at each mark. Insert a piece of dowel into each hole.

4. Place the assembled planting bar on a solid surface, narrow edge down. Nail

through the edge of the bar and into each dowel piece to secure them in place.

5. To use the bar, place it on prepared soil and jiggle it back and forth to make 5 perfectly spaced planting holes. When planting a broad bed, pick up the planting bar and, with the end dowel still in the first planting hole, pivot the bar to make a perpendicular set of holes. Then make a row at each end hole, and so on down the row.

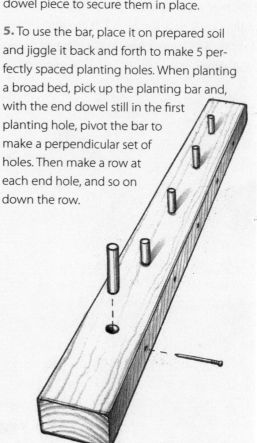

Grow a Potato Salad Patch

Want to teach a child where fresh food comes from and have some fun in the process? This easy garden plot is mapped out for you, and the veggies are all easy to grow. Of course, you don't have to be a kid to enjoy the thrill of growing armloads of produce from three packets of seeds and a few items from the supermarket. If you've never grown vegetables before, this project will get you hooked.

Depending on your soil, additional fertilizer may be needed to make sure your vegetables grow as well as they should. However, all of these crops are "light feeders," so they do not require extremely fertile soil. If growth is slow despite warm weather and regular water, providing water-soluble plant food—such as fish emulsion fertilizer—will solve the problem.

YOU WILL NEED

Tools: Spade, rake, knife, scissors, watering can

Two 40-pound bags of compost

4 small red-skinned potatoes

2 bunches of slender green onions, with roots attached

1 packet each of zucchini, leaf lettuce, bush bean, and radish seeds

1 bale of hay

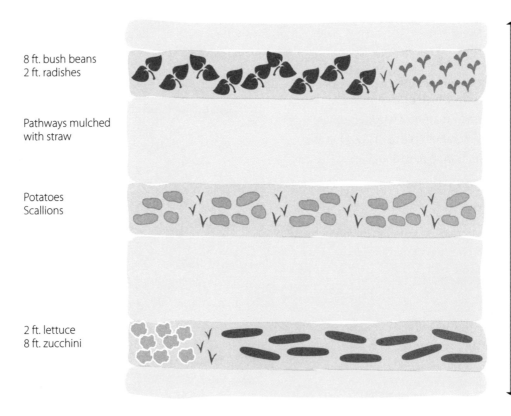

8 ft. bush beans
2 ft. radishes

Pathways mulched with straw

Potatoes
Scallions

10'

2 ft. lettuce
8 ft. zucchini

1. Use the spade to dig and turn a 10 x 10-foot square of soil in a sunny spot. Rake out weeds, spread the compost over the soil, and turn it again, breaking up large clods of dirt.

2. Starting in the middle of the plot, use the rake to create 3 slightly raised parallel rows. Rake the tops of the rows to give them flat tops. They should be about 14 inches wide.

3. Cut the potatoes in half, so that each half has at least one wrinkled "eye." Plant the potatoes, 2 inches deep and 12 inches apart in the middle row, with their cut sides down. Poke 3 green onion into the ground in between the places where the potato halves were planted.

4. Plant 20 zucchini seeds, 1 inch deep and 6 inches apart, in all but 2 feet of one of the outside rows. Fill the unplanted space with lettuce seeds, scattered over the top of the soil and patted into place. Plant bean seeds, 1 inch deep and 3 inches apart, in all but 2 feet of the other outside row. Fill the unplanted end with radish seeds, pressed into the soil 2 inches apart all over the top of the row. Use onions to mark the divisions between the zucchini and lettuce, and between the beans and radishes.

5. Cut the twine from the hay, and scatter the hay evenly down the pathways between the rows. Don't worry if some gets on the row planted with potatoes, but brush away hay from the tops of the other rows.

6. Fill the watering can, and water all three rows. Water as often as needed to keep the soil moist until the seedlings and potatoes are up and growing—usually about 2 weeks. Pull out any weeds that pop up, and harvest green onions anytime you need them in the kitchen.

7. The lettuce and radishes will be ready to start picking in a month, followed by beans and zucchini about 2 weeks later. When the potato stems begin to turn yellow, pull up the plants. You should find six or more tender potatoes beneath each plant.

Make Merry Markers

While you're waiting for your garden to grow, mark your plantings so they'll be easy to find. Slip the empty seed packet into a plastic sandwich bag, stick it between the tines of a plastic picnic fork, and push the handle into the ground. Or, use a laundry marking pen to write the name of your crops on old mini-blind slats, along with decorative doodlings. Feeling creative? Get a few paint-stirring sticks, paint them white, and paint or stencil the name of your crop in a darker shade of paint. Everyone will notice the neat signs and want to know where to get them—and they'll last several seasons, too.

Potting Up Purchased Plants

When growing your own seedlings indoors, the most difficult thinning is the last one, when you must decide which of two seedlings will be allowed to remain. Many greenhouse growers skip the last thinning, intentionally leaving two or three seedlings in a container so the consumer will see a fuller, healthier-looking specimen. When shopping for plants, it is not unusual to see pots containing several basil, parsley, or impatiens plants. Multiples also are common with cutting-grown flowers, such as hibiscus or geranium, in which three cuttings have been rooted and left to grow in one small pot. If you provide such crowded plants with roomier quarters and appropriate after-care, you can save money and end up with many more plants.

Look for pots in which the main stems of multiple plants are spaced at least 1 inch apart—a good sign that each plant will emerge from repotting with an ample supply of roots. Thoroughly water the plants, and then get ready to repot or plant them. Work in a shady place. Have clean pots and potting soil ready, or ready-to-plant space in your garden. You also will need three necessary pieces of equipment.

- A plastic fork from which the two outside prongs are broken off, leaving two prongs. This is the perfect tool for separating intertwined roots from adjoining plants.
- A sharp knife, which you can use to cut apart the roots of plants with thin, fibrous roots, such as impatiens and begonias.
- One large cardboard box with its top flaps removed, which you can set on its side and use as a temporary shade chamber for newly divided seedlings or cuttings that are moved into pots. If you are planting divided seedlings directly in the garden, be ready to cover them with small boxes or flowerpots for 3 to 5 days.

SEPARATING CROWDED SEEDLINGS

Before you begin, pinch off any flowers or leggy stems. Pinching back the growing tips will encourage the plants to develop new branches, and reduce demands made upon injured or traumatized roots.

Remove crowded seedlings from their containers by pushing them out from the bottom, or use scissors to slice through the sides of thin plastic pots. Don't touch the main stems any more than necessary, and lay the mass of plants on its side. Use a fork or knife to separate the plants, and immediately pot them up or set them in the garden. Water thoroughly, and then provide the divided plants with some type of shade. Don't worry that they will suffer because they are deprived of light. Instead, they will be free to concentrate on growing new roots, the plant part most needed in the days immediately following division.

Make a Handy Sink Screen

On busy gardening days when you're constantly washing out pots or grooming plants, you will spend less time cleaning up after yourself with the help of a sink screen. Keep your sink screen in a cabinet between uses, or let it do double duty as a drying rack for kitchen herbs (see page 266). This 12 x 12-inch version fits perfectly into a standard-size kitchen sink.

YOU WILL NEED

Tools: Tape measure, handsaw, hammer, scissors, staple gun

One 6-foot-long 1 x 2 furring strip

Sixteen 1½-inch nails

1 small roll of polyester window screening

1. Cut the furring strip into six 12-inch-long pieces. Place two of the cut pieces on a flat surface, broad side down, and partially drive 2 nails into each end, ½ inch from the outer edge. Position two pieces at right angles to the first two, overlapping the corners, and nail them together to form a box.

2. Cut a piece of screening 12 inches wide and 12 inches long. Staple it to the frame.

3. Place the remaining two pieces of 1 x 2 along the high sides of the frame, flat side down, so they cover the edge of the screening. Nail them in place.

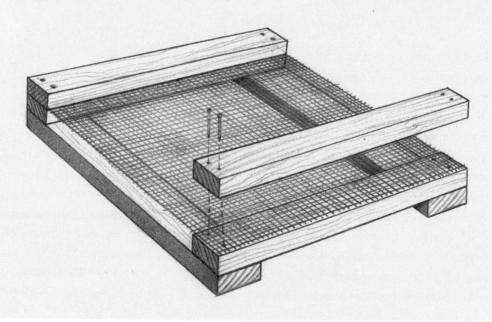

Build a Potting Table

Potting up seedlings or newly propagated plants is most enjoyable when you can stand and move about freely, which is why you need a potting table. Unlike regular tables, which are usually about 30 inches high, a potting table stands several inches taller, making it easier to work while standing up. If you prefer to work sitting down, a tall kitchen stool will be the perfect size.

This model requires minimal carpentry skills and only a few simple tools, and it includes a hole in the top so you can quickly sweep spilled soil into a bin or bucket stationed below. Use space beneath the table for storing pots and other supplies, or as a place to keep freshly repotted plants, which often benefit from a few days of shade.

Accessorize Your Potting Table

Whether you are potting up seedlings or houseplants, it's best to work in a shady spot, which is more comfortable for you and less stressful to your plants. You will need a water supply close by, too. In addition to a hose, a tub or wheelbarrow that can be filled with warm, soapy water is handy for cleaning pots, or for rinsing dirt from your hands.

Necessary accessories to hang from the hooks on the side of your table include a small whisk broom, a hand trowel, a rag for wiping down pots, and a small pail for carrying trimmings to the compost heap. With a well-equipped potting table always ready for action, you may find yourself looking for excuses to repot your plants.

YOU WILL NEED

Tools: Measuring tape, wood saw, hammer, drill with ⅛-inch bit, screwdriver

Three 8-foot-long pine 2 x 4s

Four 3-inch nails

One 8-foot-long 1 x 8 piece of pine lumber

Thirty-two 2½-inch galvanized wood screws

4 cup hooks

1 plastic storage bin

1. Use the saw to cut each 2 x 4 into 3 pieces: two 36-inch-long pieces and one 24-inch-long piece.

2. On a level surface, build the frame for the table by placing two 36-inch-long pieces and two 24-inch-long pieces into a rectangle, with the long pieces butted against the edges of the shorter ones. Nail together with the 3-inch nails. Turn the frame up on its side.

3. Place one of the 36-inch-long legs inside a corner of the assembled frame so it is parallel with the ground. Place the remaining 24-inch piece of 2 x 4 beneath the leg to support it, and position the top of the leg so it is flush with the top edge of the frame. Holding it firmly in place, drill 2 guide holes through the outside edge of the frame and into the leg. Insert screws through the guide holes, and tighten them firmly.

4. Gently turn the frame top side down, and drill guide holes for two more screws in the other side of the leg. Insert screws through the guide holes, and tighten them firmly.

5. Repeat Steps 3 and 4 to install the other 3 legs. Set the table right side up.

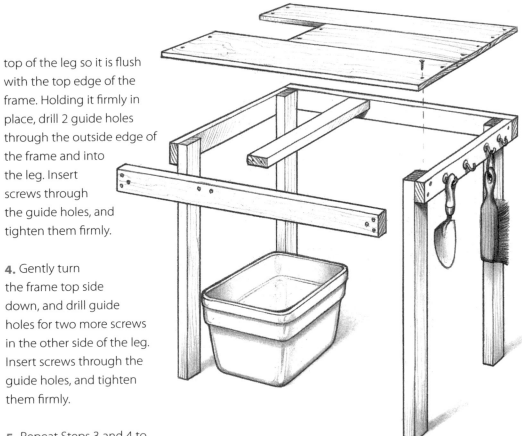

6. Measure across the center of the inside of the frame. Trim the remaining piece of 2 x 4 to this length, which should be about 21 inches. Position it inside the frame, 13 inches from one of the inside edges, with its broad side up and flush with the top of the frame. Drill guide holes through the outside of the

frame, and screw both ends of the brace in place.

7. Use the saw to cut the 1 x 8 into 3 pieces: two 36-inch-long pieces and one 24-inch-long piece. Place them across the top of the frame, with the short one in the middle. Drill 2 guide holes in the ends of each board before screwing them in place. Screw the

end of the short board to the brace.

8. Screw cup hooks into the outside of one side of the frame. Use them for hanging hand tools or gloves. Place the plastic bin under the hole in the top of the bench. Between potting sessions, put the top on the bin to keep potting soil clean and dry.

Multiplying Your Plants

Most vegetables can be grown from seed, but some herbs and many flowers must be multiplied using vegetative propagation methods. The three propagation methods every gardener should know are division (often called digging and dividing), rooting stem cuttings, and layering. Once you learn these simple techniques, you can rejuvenate old plants you love, accept "starts" from generous gardening friends, and grow plenty of plants to share with others.

PROPAGATING BY DIVISION

A tendency to grow into clumps makes a plant a prime candidate for propagating by division, which involves lifting part or all of the clump, and then pulling or cutting the clump into smaller pieces. Division is much faster than growing new plants from seed, and each division will be an exact duplicate of the parent plant. Many of the most popular garden perennials—and all bulbs—are best propagated by division.

Divide plants when they are just beginning to emerge from dormancy, which is early spring for most perennial flowers. You can replant the divisions right away, put them in pots, or buy some time by sinking them into a Propagation Bed (see page 68). Thrifty gardeners often look for multiple crowns, or growing points, when buying new perennials, and divide them before adding them to their gar-

dens. Whether you dig them from your garden or buy them in pots, the following perennials are prime candidates for honing your skills at propagating by division.

Aster	Monarda
Chrysanthemum	Ornamental grasses
Coneflower	Phlox
Daylily	Sedum
Hosta	Shasta daisy

ROOTING STEM CUTTINGS

Although it's not as fast and foolproof as propagating plants by division, rooting stem cuttings is the most commonly used method of vegetative propagation. It's the best way to grow new coleus, geraniums, hydrangeas, impatiens, sedums, and roses. Most perennial herbs are propagated from rooted stem cuttings, too.

The same plant parts that grow new leaves and stems, called nodes, can be coaxed into growing new roots. To prepare a cutting, select a 4-inch-long section of stem that has no flowers, and use a sharp knife or a pair of clean scissors to sever it from the stem. Some cuttings root best if you take a little "heel" with the stem, which is a bit of tissue taken from where the stem joins a larger stem. Trim back the tips of heel cuttings until they are less than 4 inches long. With both stem tip and heel cuttings, pinch off all the lower leaves until only a few remain at the top of the cutting.

It is not necessary to use rooting powder with soft-stemmed plants that root readily, such as tomatoes. Harder stem cuttings, such as those taken from roses, will root faster if you dip the cut ends in water, then in rooting powder, before you set them to root. Do use a special rooting medium, such as damp seed-starting mix, vermiculite, or a half and half mixture of peat moss and sand. In addition to keeping the rooting medium moist, you'll want to place the rooted cuttings where there is high humidity, which keeps the leaves from drying out while new roots are forming. The Double Pot Propagator on page 70 makes it easy to maintain moisture in the rooting medium and the air.

LAYERING GARDEN PLANTS

Many houseplant growers are familiar with air layering, in which schefflera or other large houseplants are tricked into growing roots into a packet of damp moss attached to a stem. A much simpler technique can be used to multiply numerous garden plants. The "Layer a Lovely Clematis" project on page 72 shows how to layer the most popular flowering vine, and once you learn this method, you will find yourself using it all over the garden. Is a gaura or rose stem bending over a little too far? Why not layer it by cutting a little nick in the stem, and then covering it with soil held in place with a stone? Buttercup types of winter squash are self-layering—they often develop roots from parts of the vines that touch bare ground. You can encourage this talent by mounding a little soil over the new roots.

Every time you use a vegetative propagation method, it quickly becomes an absorbing project. As you become more proficient with these easy methods, you may find yourself enjoying propagating plants so much that part of your yard becomes a home nursery! When you run out of room for plants in you yard consider donating your extras to plant sales held by non-profit garden groups.

Wows for Willow Water

Many commercial rooting preparations offer enough warnings to make you want to wash your hands after you've simply looked at the label. But willow twigs contain natural plant hormones that can offer an added boost for cuttings—or divisions—you are trying to coax to develop new roots. Snip a few willow twigs and cut them into pieces a few inches long. Add 3 to 4 inches of water to a bucket and soak the twigs for a day or two. Then use the willow water as an overnight soak for cuttings you plan to root, or use it to water newly divided plants. When rooting cuttings in plain water, a willow stem added to the jar often will help roots form a little faster. See "Grow Great Wood for Weaving" on page 252 for versatile willows to grow in your garden.

Build a Propagation Bed

The more you garden, the more you need a holding bed for plants you're not quite ready to plant, as well as those that need some growing time before they are set out in the garden. As temporary quarters for perennials you've divided, or plants given to you by a generous friend, a quickly constructed propagation bed is hard to beat. Locate it in a spot that gets afternoon shade, so plants with skimpy roots won't have to struggle against the demands of hot sun. Reinforced by a sturdy plywood bottom, this bed can be moved if needed to give plants exactly the exposure they prefer. When left situated in one place, the bottom serves as a barrier to tree roots and soil-dwelling insects, and keeps the propagated plants from settling in too deeply as well.

This bed measures 2 x 4 feet, which is the same size as a quarter sheet of plywood. Most home supply stores carry precut pieces, so the only sawing required is cutting the frame pieces, which can be done with a handsaw. The light, loose texture of the sand–peat moss mixture promotes fast root development, discourages soil-borne diseases, and makes it easy to lift plants when their new homes are ready. You also can sink container-grown plants into the propagation bed to help keep their roots cool and moist.

YOU WILL NEED

Tools: Tape measure, pencil, handsaw, hammer, drill with ¼-inch bit, garden spade, wheelbarrow, garden hose

12 feet of 1 x 8 pine or cedar lumber

Thirty-four 2-inch nails

One 2 x 4-foot piece of ¼-inch plywood

One 6-foot-long 1 x 2 furring strip

One 50-pound bag of play sand (1 cubic foot)

One small bale of peat moss (1 cubic foot)

1. To make the frame, measure and cut the 1 x 8 boards into two 4-foot-long pieces and two 2-foot-long pieces. Nail them together at the corners to form a box.

2. Place the plywood over the assembled frame, and nail it in place. Use at least two nails for each short side, three nails for each long side, and one nail at each corner.

3. Cut the furring strip into three 2-foot-long pieces. Nail one to each end of the frame, broad sides down, sandwiching the plywood between the furring strip and the frame. Nail the remaining piece across the center of the frame.

4. Use the drill to make 12 evenly spaced drainage holes in the plywood. Move the bed to its permanent location.

5. Use the spade to thoroughly mix the sand and peat moss together in a wheelbarrow. Dump the mixture into the assembled bed, and drench with water. Wait a few

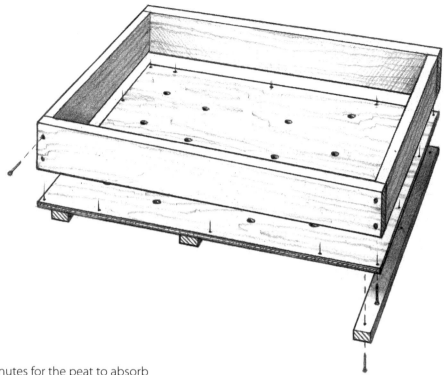

minutes for the peat to absorb the water, stir the mixture, and water it again. Repeat if necessary until the peat particles appear dark with moisture.

6. To use the bed, simply sink plants into the sand–peat moss mixture and keep them moist until you are ready to lift them out and plant them in your garden.

7. To move your bed, remove some of the sand–peat moss mixture, and allow the rest to dry out. Get a helper to help you move the dry, partially filled bed.

Adding Shade

Plants with skimpy roots cannot withstand strong sun, so it's important to provide your propagation bed with some type of shade. If you cannot locate the bed in a spot that gets dappled sun, install a shade cover. One of the simplest ways to shade the bed is to bend three 4-foot-long slender saplings or pieces of 12-gauge wire into hoops, and stick the ends inside the long edges of the bed. Then cover the hoops with lightweight cloth, such as an old sheet. Remove the shade cover on cloudy days, and begin leaving it off on sunny days when you see evidence of new growth. Plants that gradually become accustomed to sun will experience little trauma when they are moved to the garden.

Make a Double Pot Propagator

This easy system, which makes use of the porous nature of inexpensive terra-cotta clay pots, sets up in a snap and always gives good results. Water poured into a sealed small pot is slowly absorbed by the rooting medium, and a plastic tent provides the humidity needed by rootless cuttings. A half-and-half mixture of sand and peat moss makes a good medium for rooting cuttings, or you can use damp seed-starting mix or perlite. Regardless of which medium you choose, start over with a fresh batch for each new crop of cuttings. Develop your propagation skills with fast-rooting cuttings such as chrysanthemums, coleus, or some of the other plants listed on page 66 before moving on to woody plants, which need more time to develop new roots.

YOU WILL NEED

Tools: Bucket, hand trowel, measuring cup, pump spray bottle

One 8-inch-wide clay flowerpot

One 4-inch-wide clay flowerpot

One 6-inch clay pot saucer

1 quart clean sand (such as play sand)

1 quart pulverized peat moss

Two 1-inch-square pieces of duct tape

1 cup small, clean pebbles

4 chopsticks or wood skewers

8 to 10 prepared stem tip cuttings (see page 66)

1 opaque plastic produce bag

1. Thoroughly clean the pots and pot saucer. If you are using new ones, place them in a tub of clean water to soak for 10 minutes, and then allow them to drip dry.

2. Place the sand and peat moss in a bucket, and use a hand trowel to mix them together. Add 2 cups of lukewarm water, mix, and then add another 2 cups of water. Mix again, and allow the mixture to sit for 10 minutes. If pieces of the peat moss still appear dry, add more water until the mixture is the consistency of raw cookie dough.

3. Cover the drainage hole in the bottom of the 4-inch pot with the pieces of duct tape. Place one on the inside of the pot, and the other on the outside.

4. Place the pebbles in the bottom of the 8-inch pot. Add a 2-inch layer of the sand/peat moss mixture. Set the 4-inch pot in the center, and press lightly. Add more of the sand/peat moss mixture if needed to raise the top rim of the smaller pot ½-inch above the top rim of the larger pot.

5. Fill the space between the two pots with the sand/peat moss mixture. Spray lightly with water, and add more sand/peat moss mixture if needed until the space is filled to within ½-inch of the top of the 8-inch pot. Gently lift and rinse out the smaller pot, and then put it back into place.

6. Use one of the chopsticks or skewers to make 8 to 10 evenly spaced holes in the sand/peat moss mixture for cuttings. Stick the prepared cuttings into the holes, and use your fingers to make sure they are in firm contact with the rooting medium.

7. Insert the chopsticks or skewers along the outside of the 4-inch pot. Place the Double Pot Propagator on the saucer, and position it in a warm place out of direct sunlight. Pour 1 cup of lukewarm water into the small pot, and then cover the Propagator with the plastic bag, arranging the folds so the plastic is held above the cuttings by the chopsticks or skewers.

8. After 2 days, remove the plastic bag and use your finger to see if the sand/peat moss mixture is still moist. If it feels dry, add ½ cup water to the small pot. Replace the plastic cover.

9. Check the moisture level again every other day, and add ½ cup water to the small pot whenever it becomes empty. Remove any cuttings that have wilted. Leave the plastic cover off at night, but put it on during the day.

10. Three weeks after setting the cuttings to root, pull gently on cuttings that show evidence of new growth. If you feel slight resistance, use a fork to lift them and transplant them to small individual pots. Keep the transplanted cuttings in a shady place outdoors, or indirect light indoors, and keep moist. Increase light as new growth appears.

Layer a Lovely Clematis

When you have a beautiful large-flowered clematis, it's only natural to want another to plant in at the base of a new trellis, or perhaps to share with a friend. Clematis are nearly impossible to propagate by division, and stem cuttings often refuse to root. Yet there is a propagation method called layering that is guaranteed to work with any clematis. How does it work? A section of stem is tricked into sensing that it is broken, and then it's tucked into moist soil. There it slowly grows roots, and the next spring you have a robust new plant.

For best results, wait until the second half of summer, or even early fall, to begin this project. Stems that are so mature that they are nearly woody are much less likely to rot than tender new green growth. The layered section of stem will grow a few roots in the weeks after it is set in the ground, followed by much more vigorous root development the following spring, just before it is cut from the parent plant.

YOU WILL NEED

Tools: Garden spade, wheelbarrow, sharp knife, pliers

1 mature clematis vine

2 gallons of good compost

Two 8-inch-long pieces of 12-gauge wire

1. On the plant you want to propagate, select a sound stem that can be detached from the trellis and placed on the ground in a place that is shaded from hot midday sun. After identifying the spot where 12 inches of the stem can be buried, set the selected stem aside so it won't be damaged as you prepare the site.

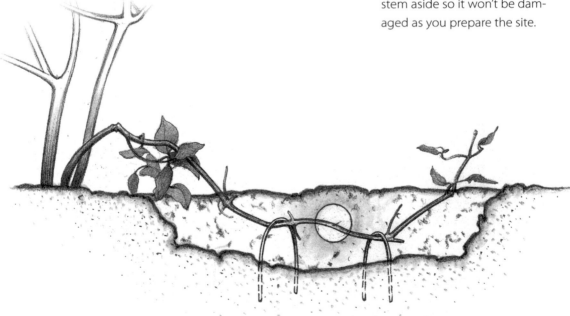

2. Dig an 8-inch-deep trench for the stem, 6 inches wide and 18 inches long, and place the excavated soil in a wheelbarrow. Mix it well with the compost, and refill the trench halfway.

3. Lay the stem in the trench, and pinch off any leaves that would be buried. Leave at least two sets of leaves intact at the stem's tip end. Use the knife to make a shallow diagonal cut into the stem 1 inch from a node (the place on the stem where leaves are attached). The cut should go no more than halfway through the stem.

4. Use the pliers to bend the pieces of wire into U-shaped hoops. Position the prepared section of stem in the trench, and use the wire hoops to pin it in place. Cover with the remaining amended soil. Keep the soil moist.

5. The following spring, as soon as the parent vine begins to leaf out, cut the layered stem just above the soil line on the side closest to the parent vine.

6. Wait 4 weeks before digging the rooted section of vine and transplanting it to its permanent location.

7. Water the new vine as needed to keep its roots constantly moist through its first growing season.

More Good Plants for Layering

You may learn the art of layering to propagate a clematis, but it also can be used to propagate other popular plants. Any climbing vine, such as climbing hydrangea or noninvasive native or hybrid honeysuckles, is a good candidate for layering, and it's the easiest way to propagate lanky roses that grow on their own roots. Forsythias are so willing to develop roots near the tips of their branches that they often layer themselves, as do many raspberries. Lanky tomato stems layer easily too. If you get into growing "Great Wood for Weaving" (see page 252), you can use layering to propagate redstem dogwoods and other woody plants that are grown for their pliable branches.

Many herb gardeners use the layering method to propagate rosemary, lavender, tarragon, and other herbs that tend to become lanky and woody as they age (see "Grow a Kitchen Herb Garden" on page 266 for more information on growing and using these plants). When layering herbs or other plants that have very thin stems, it is usually easier to distress the section of stem you want to grow roots by scraping it with your fingernail than to try to nick it with a knife. And, while you can layer a stem from a plant growing in a container by pinning it into a second container set nearby, oblong planter boxes are easier to use than pairs of pots.

Make More Tomatoes

The most popular crop in home vegetable gardens, tomatoes are typically started from seeds sown indoors 6 to 8 weeks before the last spring frost, or you can begin with plants purchased from a garden center. Either approach will get your tomato patch off to a strong start, but there are four more ways to make more tomatoes.

RECRUIT VOLUNTEERS

If you keep a compost heap, chances are good that some tomato seeds will survive the composting process. Seedlings will spring up in a resting heap, or in rows or beds where you have spread your black gold. There is no way to know their genetic background; they could be offspring from last year's crop, or they might be seeds from purchased tomatoes. Either way, digging and moving a plant or two to a sunny spot will diversify your collection, and may yield some pleasant surprises.

SOW MORE SEEDS

The main reason to start tomato seeds indoors is to get a head start on spring. Once the soil has warmed, you can sow tomato seeds directly into fertile garden soil. This is an easy way to make sure you have vigorous plants that will bear their fruits in late summer, when your earlier planting may be showing signs of exhaustion. Use small-fruited varieties, which do a better job of setting fruit in hot weather than tomatoes that bear very large fruits.

ROOT SOME CUTTINGS

Five- to six-inch-long tomato stems quickly develop new roots, and they will even root in a jar of plain water. Cuttings taken from the lowest sections of the plants, which already show little bumps (root buds) along the stems, will root in a matter of days, but even suckers pinched from the tops of plants willingly develop roots. Pinch off any flowers before setting the cuttings to root.

It's interesting to watch roots form on cuttings kept in water on a sunny windowsill, but the types of roots that grow in water are not as sturdy as those that grow from cuttings set in soil. Tomatoes (and other plants) rooted in water will eventually suffer from lack of oxygen and minerals. To keep this from happening, transplant the cuttings to containers filled with damp potting soil as soon as the roots are ½ inch long. Two weeks later, they will be ready to move to the garden.

GROW WINTER TOMATOES

If you have a large, sunny window that faces south or west, you can grow tomatoes through the winter months indoors. Plant rooted cuttings of small-fruited varieties in 5-gallon containers, and bring them indoors in fall, when nighttime temperatures drop below the mid-50s. Provide a trellis, because the stems will become quite lanky due to limited indoor light. When flowers appear, jiggle the blossom clusters twice a day to move pollen from one blossom to another.

CHAPTER 3

Teepees, Trellises, and Other Smart Plant Supports

Plants that grow upward make great use of space and raise fruits and flowers to eye level. This chapter includes more than a dozen trellises you can make and use for many seasons, together with information on more than 30 great plants to grow in your garden.

The Benefits of Vertical Gardening

Good soil and healthy plants form the foundation for a successful garden, but where do you go from there? Most vegetables and flowers stay close to the ground, so trellised vines are unique in their ability to add a vertical dimension to any outdoor scene. In the vegetable garden, growing plants up rather than out pays off by increasing yields and improving plant health. Trellised pole beans, for example, typically produce 40 percent more beans per square foot than bush beans, and tomatoes must be trellised to prevent problems with diseases. With cucumbers and other small-fruited cucurbits, a trellis often coaxes plants to produce more leaves, which in turn gather more energy from the sun, resulting in larger, higher-quality crops.

As landscaping devices, trellises offer an easy way to block out unwanted views, create beautiful focal points, and enhance privacy. You can use trellised vines to create living walls for a lush, private retreat, or locate them so they will throw a curtain of shade over a hot spot on your patio, or give your deck plants much-needed relief from intense summer sun. But the best part of working with trellised flowers is the plants. From fragrant sweet peas to long-limbed miniature roses, flowers that reach for the sky always get plenty of attention.

Taking care of plants at eye level rather than in a bed is a bit easier for most gardeners, but you'll probably see fewer problems in the first place. Trellised plants dry off quickly after rain, which reduces their risk of leaf-spot diseases. Controlling insect pests is simple because you can see unwanted visitors as soon as they appear, and early intervention is the second best way to limit insect damage—right after prevention. Even your body benefits from vertical gardening, since you can tend, pick, and enjoy your plants with much less bending over.

GETTING STARTED

Once you decide you want to grow a plant that is willing to scramble up a trellis, there are several types of structures to consider, from lightweight string trellises to wood or wire panels to triangular teepees. But before you start building, look around and see what you already have.

- An ordinary chain-link fence makes a fantastic trellis for most vining vegetables and flowering vines.
- You can easily add a wire trellis to the back side of a wood fence that will provide easy moorings for curling tendrils or twisting stems.
- Deck railings can be put to work as a ready-made trellis for container-grown vines, and you can transform entryways by using porch posts—or your front-step handrail—to support a well-behaved vine.
- Get double duty from wood posts that are already serving another purpose, whether

they are holding up a mailbox or birdhouse or are part of an existing fence. Add a few nails and screws, attach some strings or wire, and create an instant pillar for edible or ornamental vines.

CHOOSING THE RIGHT SITE

Before you decide where to place a new trellis—or how you will make use of a structure you already have—consider the site from the vine's point of view. Of course you want to pick a spot where a trellis will look good or block your view of an eyesore next door, but you should make sure your plants will grow well in their new home, too. Begin by digging an exploratory hole. You can amend poor soil to improve its fertility, but make sure the soil can be dug deeply enough to accommodate new posts that may need to be set in place. If you encounter a buried boulder, you will need to look for an alternate site. Underground utilities also may restrict where you can dig deep holes for posts.

Tracking Sun and Shade

Sun exposure will affect your choice of sites, too. The sun rises in the east and sets in the west, and in the Northern Hemisphere, it always arcs a little to the south as it moves across the sky. The sun's angle matters little to low-growing plants, but it causes tall plants and trellises to cast shadows. To minimize the shade created by trellised plants, try to locate trellises on a north-south axis when growing plants that need abundant sun. This means that one side will face east while the other faces west. The west (afternoon) side will get more intense sun than the east (morning) side, but the difference will be less than it would be if the trellis faced north-south.

If you want to use a trellised vine to create shade, this will happen naturally if you locate a trellis on the south or west side of a hot spot in your landscape, or if you build an overhead arbor. For example, if your goal is to be able to sip tea on your deck on a summer afternoon while hummingbirds dart in and out of a lush screen of scarlet runner beans, locate the trellis on the west side of your favorite sitting spot, because intense afternoon sun always comes from the west.

You can take the confusion out of studying a site's exposure by pounding a wood stake into the ground and watching it for a few days, making mental note of where its shadows fall. Don't worry about the shade that is created at the base of a trellis, because most vines thrive when they have their roots shaded and their heads in the sun.

Plan for Easy Reach

Whether you are planning to support cucumbers or a clematis, you'll also need to position the trellis so you can get to the plant for watering, pruning, and harvesting. It is usually best to allow vines to run no higher than you can reach. Choose vines that fit the space you have to offer and your notions of reasonable maintenance, and keep in mind that a vine capable of growing 10 feet tall does not necessarily require a 10-foot trellis. Once vines reach the top of their support structure, they usually turn back toward the ground, creating a cascade of foliage, flowers, and fruit.

SIZING UP STRUCTURES

The projects in this chapter provide an array of trellising options, including tied-together teepees, versatile wire panels, wood pillars and trellises, and simple techniques for using plants to support other plants. Most are quite easy and inexpensive to build or make and require little or no carpentry experience. If you can hammer a nail or install a screw, you can make these projects. However, very heavy plants do require super-sturdy support such as the T-trellis described on page 108, which requires the joint effort of two people to construct. On the other hand, you can make trellises for container-grown plants in only a few minutes using the projects that begin on page 112.

Regardless of size, the sturdiness of any trellis depends on how well it is anchored. In some situations, you may want to set a post as securely as possible, which will require anchoring it in concrete. Concrete is messy but not especially difficult to handle. Still, before you decide that concrete is needed, consider simpler solutions. If you do want to set a post in concrete, follow the directions on page 80.

Some trellises need no posts at all. The pyramid shape of teepee trellises often makes them self-anchoring. With trellises that do depend on buried posts to hold them upright, keeping posts as close to each other as possible can enhance the structure's sturdiness. Post size affects sturdiness, too. Stout posts can bear more weight than narrow ones, but they are heavier to handle and more troublesome to move. Posts only 2 inches square, installed 18 inches deep and 4 feet apart, do a good job

of supporting tomatoes, peas, and beans in the vegetable garden, and they are easily moved by wiggling them a bit before pulling them up. Moderately heavy, long-lived plants such as climbing roses and clematis will be better served with a trellis that's attached to sturdier 2 x 4-inch posts. Permanent landscape structures call for 4 x 4 or larger posts.

Safe and Sturdy Posts

When selecting posts for your garden trellises, do not use pressure-treated lumber or wood treated with creosote if edible plants or herbs will be grown nearby. Whenever possible, use weather-resistant wood such as cedar, redwood, or locust as your first choice. Chemicals leaching from pressure-treated or creosote-coated wood can contaminate the soil. Several of the hundreds of chemicals in creosote are known carcinogens that can leach into the soil and be taken up by plants. Similar problems exist with the chemicals that have been used for the last 20 years to make treated wood posts more resistant to rot and termites, so grow only ornamental plants on posts made of treated wood.

Once you've taken stock of the trellising potential of structures that you already have, you can start having fun with vines and add to your collection of supportive plant structures. The "22 Garden-Worthy Vines" chart on page 82 lists excellent options to consider for your garden. You should have no trouble finding just the right vine for any spot in your yard. Study what various sites have to offer because vines differ in their needs for sun, moisture, and the sturdiness of their support.

Guy Wires

If a trellis is not as sturdy as you think it should be, you often can fix the problem by installing guy wires attached to nearby stakes, in much the same way that camping tents are secured in place. Two guy wires that pull on a trellis post from opposite directions work better than one, especially when the stakes are installed at angles that are diagonal from the trellis itself. Install the stakes at an angle, with their tops tilted away from the trellis. You also can use guy wires to attach a trellis to a nearby structure such as a building or fence.

Guy wires need not be actual wires at all. You can use whatever you have on hand to tie the trellis to stakes, including string, twine, or hemp cord. The main disadvantage of using stakes and guy wires is that they are easy to trip over, but this is less likely to happen if you paint them a noticeable color. Tying a few colorful ribbons to guy wires also makes them easy to see.

TAKE IT EASY

The Dead Man

If you have little confidence in the ability of a post to hold a trellis as firmly as it should, but you don't want to resort to concrete, outfit the base of the post with what is called a dead man. Create a dead man by attaching a piece of scrap wood to the side of the post crosswise, nailing it near the bottom (but not on the bottom). Buried securely in the soil, the dead man increases the post's resistance to movement. You can make a dead man from scraps of PVC pipe, too, by using screws to attach the pipe to the side of a wood post.

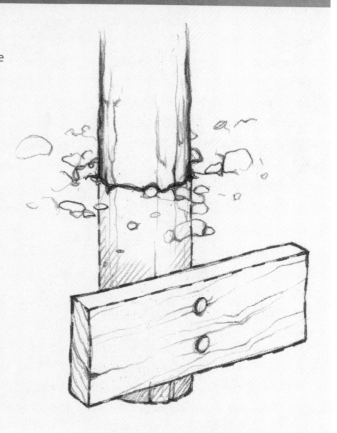

Setting Posts in Concrete

Working with concrete is not hard, but posts set in concrete are so difficult to remove that you should think carefully before you decide a trellis needs concrete feet. Ask yourself: How big are the posts? What are they made of? How much weight and wind must the trellis bear? How deep will the posts be set? Will the soil do a good job of holding the post firm, or does it have a loose, sandy texture? Will you be satisfied if the trellis lasts a few years, or do you want it to support very long-lived plants, such as grapes?

If all of your answers to these questions steer you to concrete, here are the steps you should follow. When the goal is to attach trellises or fences to posts set in concrete, it is best to set the posts first, let the concrete harden, and then build the trellis. If the tops of matching posts are not quite even, trim them after the concrete has cured.

1. Dig a 2-foot-deep hole for each post with a posthole auger or digger. Place 2 inches of gravel in the bottom to enhance drainage.

2. Set the post in the hole and secure it in place by nailing a piece of scrap 2 x 4 to the post, angled down to the ground. Use a level to make sure the post is perfectly straight.

3. Use a spade to mix water and dry, pre-mixed concrete in a wheelbarrow. Add only enough water to make the mixture as thick as wet cookie dough.

4. Fill the hole with concrete, poking with the spade to force out any air bubbles. As the concrete begins to set, mound 1 inch of concrete around the base of the post to discourage water from pooling. Check the post again to make sure it is plumb. Install a second scrap piece of 2 x 4 to hold it perfectly straight.

5. Let the concrete cure for at least 48 hours before removing the 2 x 4s and continuing with your project.

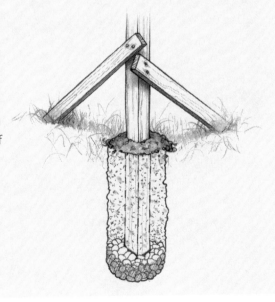

MATCHING PLANTS WITH TRELLISES

Posts serve as a trellis's legs, but most trellises also have a body made of wood, string, wire, or some type of fencing. The projects in this chapter show how you can use several versatile, inexpensive trellising materials, but there are loads of other ingenious possibilities. Creative gardeners often fashion unique trellises from flexible copper tubing or bent twigs and even tie together plastic six-pack holders to support their peas.

You can use whatever suits your taste and the needs of the plants you decide to grow. Vines are never snobbish about the support they receive as long as it matches the "growing equipment" they use to twine from point A to point B. These ingenious plant structures may be curling tendrils, curving stems, or sticky rootlets.

Curling tendrils reach out and wrap around whatever is available: Wire, string, branches, and woven-wire fencing all are fair game. Tendril-producing plants, such as peas and cucumbers, also wrap tendrils around their own leaves and stems. Young plants may need a little guidance to find their trellis, but once they get growing, they know what to do. Plants that produce curling tendrils often do best with a wire or mesh trellis.

Twining stems spiral around their support, and twining species vary in whether they twine clockwise or counterclockwise. Twining vines like pole beans and morning glory grow best when supported by poles, taut cords, or other trellising materials that resemble tree limbs or upright plants. Teepee trellises are ideal, and with a little encouragement, twining plants will cover a chain-link, wire-mesh, or lattice fence. When they run out of trellis, twining plants will twist around themselves.

Tethered vines, such as tomatoes and climbing roses, have no way to attach themselves to a support structure, so they must be fastened to their trellis. String or wire can damage the stems, so it is best to use strips of soft, stretchy cloth or discarded panty hose to tie them in place. You also can use green, plastic-coated wire twist ties. In addition, you often can train some stems manually by weaving them between the slats of a sturdy wooden trellis. Choose a solid, stationary trellis that does not move when pushed by strong wind.

Clinging vines, such as Virginia creeper, Boston ivy, and English ivy, have special holdfast roots that grow from the stems and attach themselves to surfaces (including tree trunks and wood, siding, or brick walls). The holdfast roots and the vines' foliage retain moisture, which can damage buildings. These vines should be watched closely and pruned as needed to control their spread. Although popular and beautiful, English ivy becomes aggressive when it is abandoned by the gardener who planted it. It is easiest to control when grown in containers.

22 Garden-Worthy Vines

SEVEN VINES FOR THE VEGETABLE GARDEN

PLANT NAME	HOW IT CLIMBS	DESCRIPTION	IDEAL TRELLIS
Cucumber (*Cucumis sativus*)	Curling tendrils	Fast and productive, cucumbers often need to be tied to their trellis because cucumber tendrils are sparse and weak.	Try a 3-foot-tall teepee or a diagonal trellis made with wire mesh or plastic hardware cloth.
Lima Bean (*Phaseolus lunatus*)	Twining stems	Heat tolerant and pest resistant, heirloom varieties often run 10 feet and produce beans with maroon markings. Limas grow best where summers are long and warm.	Provide a teepee-type trellis 8 feet tall or grow on a wire-mesh fence.
Malabar Spinach (*Basella rubra*)	Twining stems	A vigorous grower in hot weather, this plant's glossy young leaves taste like Swiss chard when cooked. Unpruned vines grow to 15 feet and often reseed in warm climates.	Grow three plants on a single sturdy teepee or pillar.
Pea (*Pisum sativum*)	Curling tendrils	Short varieties of snow, shell, or snap peas grow to only 18 inches, but taller ones reach 5 to 6 feet. Plant first thing in spring because peas love cool weather.	A light net or string trellis is sufficient for peas.
Pole Bean (*Phaseolus vulgaris*)	Twining stems	Easy to grow, with a huge selection of varieties. Some have purple or yellow pods, and vine length varies with variety, from 4 to 10 feet.	Provide a teepee-type trellis 4 to 8 feet tall, or grow pole beans on a wire-mesh fence.
Scarlet Runner Bean (*Phaseolus coccineus*)	Twining stems	Young pods are edible and so are the flowers. Vines run 6 to 8 feet and grow best where summers are not extremely hot.	Adapts to many types of trellises, from teepees to rustic twig fences to old stumps.
Yard-Long Bean (*Vigna unguiculata*)	Twining stems	Vigorous plants grow fast in hot weather, often growing to 10 feet. Harvest the beans when they are less than 18 inches long for best flavor.	A pair of tall, sturdy teepees connected at the top.

NINE ANNUAL FLOWERING VINES

PLANT NAME	HOW IT CLIMBS	DESCRIPTION	IDEAL TRELLIS
Asarina (*Asarina scandens*)	Twining stems	Dainty, well-behaved vine usually grows to 6 feet, laden with jewel-toned snapdragon-like flowers. Grows best where summers are not extremely hot.	Choose an attractive wood, wire, or string trellis. Can be grown in containers.
Black-Eyed Susan Vine (*Thunbergia alata*)	Twining stems	In addition to the common yellow varieties, there are others that bloom white and coral pink. Vines run to 8 feet and can be grown in containers.	Use wire or sturdy string to train up a mailbox post or other pillar; excellent cover for chain-link fence.
Cup and Saucer Vine (*Cobaea scandens*)	Curling tendrils	A robust grower with stems to 20 feet long, this vine makes a good shade screen where summers are quite warm. Flowers emerge greenish white and ripen to purple.	A sturdy wood or wire trellis is required because vines become lush and heavy by late summer.
Gourd (*Lagenaria* or *Cucurbita* species)	Twining stems and tendrils	Small-fruited egg or spoon gourds mature fast enough to be grown in any climate, and the vines grow to only 10 feet. Large-fruited varieties grow to twice that size.	Grow small-fruited varieties on a pillar, diagonal, or teepee trellis. Large-fruited varieties become very heavy and need a sturdy support made of wood or wire.
Hyacinth Bean (*Dolichos lablab*)	Twining stems	Sometimes called ornamental butter bean, this plant's 10- to 20-foot-long violet stems produce lavender flowers, followed by glossy purple seedpods.	One or two plants can be supported by a string trellis, but a larger planting needs sturdy wood or wire support.
Morning Glory (*Ipomoea* species and hybrids)	Twining stems	Easy to grow and widely adaptable, morning glories come in numerous colors. Vines run 10 feet or more. *Often invasive in warm climates.*	Grow on a sturdy wire trellis, pillar, teepee, sunflower stalks, or a chain-link fence.
Purple Bells (*Rhodochiton atrosanguineum*)	Twining stems	Tender perennial grown as an annual, this vine likes rich soil in partial shade. Grows to 10 feet and produces exotic two-toned purple flowers.	Choose an attractive wood trellis. Can be grown in containers.
Spanish Flag (*Mina lobata*)	Twining stems	Sprays of tubular blossoms open red and ripen to yellow. Vines run to 15 feet, and seeds germinate best when soaked for a day or two before planting.	Grow on a sturdy wire trellis, teepee, or wood pillar.
Sweet Pea (*Lathyrus odoratus*)	Curling tendrils	Beautiful and often fragrant, most sweet peas climb to about 5 feet. Grow in cool weather, and nick the seeds to help them germinate faster.	A string or net trellis is sufficient for sweet peas. Can be grown in containers.

SIX LONG-LIVED PERENNIAL VINES

PLANT NAME	HOW IT CLIMBS	DESCRIPTION	IDEAL TRELLIS
Clematis (*Clematis hybrids*)	Twining stems and tendrils	Gorgeous flowers in a wide range of colors with attractive green foliage on 10-foot vines. Adapted in Zones 4 to 9, pruning times vary with variety.	Can be trained to grow into small shrubs or trees or on a wood or wire support.
Climbing Rose (*Rosa hybrids*)	Curved thorns, requires tying	Stiff arching canes bloom heavily in late spring, and often repeat bloom. Adapted in Zones 4 to 9, canes must be tied or wired to a stiff trellis.	Choose an attractive wood trellis to accompany the classic beauty of a climbing rose.
Cross Vine (*Bignonia capreolata*)	Curling tendrils	Improved varieties of this native evergreen vine bear orange or red flowers that attract hummingbirds. Vines grow to 20 feet in Zones 5 to 9.	Choose a sturdy wood or wire trellis that needs little maintenance since the plants are never fully dormant.
Grape (*Vitis* species)	Curling tendrils	Woody plants may live for decades. Adapted in Zones 4 to 9, grapes bear sweet fruit, and you can use the pruned branches for other projects.	Provide a very sturdy wood and wire trellis, or grow grapes over an arbor.
Hardy Kiwi (*Actinidia arguta*)	Twining stems	Large, woody plants become quite massive; mature female plants produce flavorful fruits. Adapted in Zones 4 to 9, hardy kiwis need periodic pruning.	Provide a very sturdy trellis constructed of wood and wire.
Passionflower (*Passiflora* hybrids)	Twining stems	Exotic blossoms followed by green egg-shaped fruits on 10-foot vines. Hardy in Zones 7 to 9, but can be grown as an annual farther north.	Best grown on a post, pillar, or stump or combined with annual vines on a larger trellis.

Beware of Invasive Vines

When vines are perfectly suited to their site and soil, some reseed so successfully that they become weedy pests. A prime example is morning glory, which seldom causes problems in the North, but can become so weedy in warmer climates that it is listed as a noxious weed in Arkansas and Arizona. And, even though it is a native plant, love-in-a-puff (*Cardiospermum*) is on the noxious weed lists of six southern states.

If you want to grow a vine with a questionable reputation, start with a small planting, and locate the trellis near a walkway, driveway, or other paved surface. Or, place it where you can mow around it on all sides. Unwanted seeds can't sprout in concrete, and those that sprout in mowed grass can quickly be clipped into submission.

Avoid These Unsocial Climbers

Nicknamed "unsocial climbers" by botanists, a number of once-popular perennial vines have proven so invasive that they should not be planted at all. Even though you may be able to control the behavior of one of these vines in your yard, you cannot guess where a bird may drop a seed or what will become of the vine if you move away. Fortunately, there are plenty of safe native plants to take the place of these exotic invaders. Vines to avoid planting include:

- Climbing euonymus (*Euonymus fortunei*)
- English ivy (*Hedera helix*)
- Japanese honeysuckle (*Lonicera japonica*)
- Oriental bittersweet (*Celastrus orbiculatus*)
- Porcelain berry (*Ampelopsis brevipedunculata*)

JUST FOR FUN

Garden Tool Vine Post

Got a bunch of old hand tools that no longer work? Or can you pick up some rusty relics for pocket change at a flea market? Either way, add them to an existing wood fence post for a quick and easy "vining post" with character. Use glue, wire, nails, or screws to fasten the tools to the post at 6-inch intervals, with the handles protruding from the sides. They don't need to look uniform, but each cross arm should protrude at least 4 inches from one side of the post to give the vine something to cling. If you want to add height to the top, try a perpendicular rake or grass rake (be sure to allow for clearance if it's near a foot traffic area). Then let morning glories, hyacinth beans, or passionflowers (to name a few) elaborate on your handiwork.

Grow a Stepladder Garden

Here's a novel way to get your veggie vines to climb the ladder of success. Train them up an old wooden stepladder! A single ladder and a few square feet of soil will support a small garden—complete with tomatoes, beans, savory herbs, and edible flowers. At the end of the season, you can take it apart in minutes and store it until next year. This is a fantastic trellis for a small garden plot. You can even tuck a tiny compost heap beneath the ladder, where it will be hidden from view by your robust vegetables. Be sure to keep a hose or watering can handy for this garden because the containers will dry out quickly in hot weather. The plants in pots will also need to be fed with a balanced, water-soluble plant food every 2 weeks, but any extra plant food that drips down to the tomatoes will be put to good use.

YOU WILL NEED

Tools: Scissors, drill, screwdriver, garden spade

6-foot wooden stepladder with pail shelf

1 heavy-duty plastic garbage bag

8 large rubber bands

Four to eight 2-inch screws

2 to 3 bushels of organic mulch

Hemp or jute cord

One 12-inch-diameter pot each of pepper, nasturtium, basil, and parsley

2 tomato plants

1 packet of pole bean seeds

1. To slow the decay of the ladder's wood, cut four 8-inch squares from the garbage bag, fasten them around the ends of the ladder's legs with rubber bands.

2. To make pegs that will stick through the drainage holes of containers set on the ladder's rungs and hold them steady in the wind, install 2-inch screws in the center of the second and fourth rungs from the bottom, as well as the top platform of the ladder and the pail shelf. If the containers have drainage holes near the edges rather than in the center, adjust the position of the screws accordingly. Work from the undersides of the rungs, so that the screws protrude at least an inch from the tops of the rungs, platform, and pail shelf.

3. Pick a sunny 4 x 6-foot site for your stepladder garden. At one end of the 6-foot width, prepare two planting holes for tomato plants. At the other end, prepare a 3-foot-long planting row for pole beans. Open the ladder and set it in place, spanning the 6-foot width and having the step

side next to the tomato holes. Bury the plastic-wrapped legs about 3 inches deep. Blanket the space beneath the ladder with 3 inches of mulch.

4. Weave the hemp or jute cord between the horizontal rails, as well as between the open legs of the ladder. Follow any pattern you like to create a support grid for both the pole beans and the tomatoes.

5. Place the peppers on the pail shelf, the nasturtiums on the top platform, and the basil and parsley on the second and fourth rungs.

6. Plant the beans alongside the back ladder rails, and the tomatoes by the ladder steps. The beans will know where to go, but you will need to tie the tomatoes to the side slats of the ladder as they grow.

Change the Ladder Garden Crop Mix

There is no end to the possible mixes and matches for this versatile little garden. Substitute peas for beans and eggplant for tomatoes, or let cucumbers, cantaloupes, or small-fruited winter squash sprawl up, under, and around the base of the ladder. If you love cooking greens, heat-tolerant Malabar spinach makes a great stepladder garden plant. Fill pots with lettuce or other salad greens. Of course, you can plant your stepladder garden entirely with rambunctious gourds, or turn it over to flowers, such as sweet peas, hyacinth beans, or scarlet runner beans. For great special effects on a flowering ladder, choose a light-colored cascading petunia for the highest containers, and echo it with a darker shade of petunia planted around the base. In sites that get afternoon shade, try the same trick with different shades of impatiens.

Make a Primo Portable Trellis

As handy as a pocketknife, a portable trellis made with chicken wire attached to 1 x 2s can work as a freestanding support in an open vegetable or flower garden, or you can place it next to a wall or wood privacy fence. You can change its shape, too, so the same trellis that supports a straight row of peas in spring can be changed into a circular cage for summer tomatoes. When winter arrives, simply pick off the dead vines and roll up the trellis like a scroll for storage, or use it as a collection bin for leaves. Best of all, this trellis comes together so quickly that you can make several in one afternoon.

Farm supply stores often stock chicken wire (also called poultry netting) in 36-inch or wider widths, but most home supply stores sell the 24-inch-wide version. Plain galvanized wire is fine, but many gardeners prefer chicken wire that has been covered with a vinyl coating because it looks better and is easier to clean at the end of the season. Both types are inexpensive to buy, and you will find plenty of uses for small leftover pieces. A 12-inch square piece, crumpled into a ball and placed in a teapot, is a flower arranger's best friend. See page 236 for ways to use chicken wire to deter four-legged garden pests, and check out the Flip-Flop Compost Corral on page 24. You may decide to buy a bigger roll!

YOU WILL NEED

Tools: Thick gloves, tin snips, staple gun, hammer, spade, scissors, carpenter's level

10-foot roll of 24-inch-wide 20-gauge chicken wire (poultry netting)

Four 5-foot-long pieces of 1 x 2 cedar lumber

Eight 1½-inch galvanized finishing nails

Cord, twine, or wire for use as guy wires

Four 18-inch-long wood stakes

1. Wearing gloves, use the tin snips to cut two pieces of chicken wire 4 feet long.

2. Set two of the 1 x 2s on a flat surface, 4 feet apart, with their broad sides down. Use the staple gun to attach the chicken wire to both 1 x 2s, beginning at the top edge and allowing a ½-inch margin between the outer edge of each 1 x 2 and the chicken wire. Attach a second piece of chicken wire below the first one.

3. Top each 1 x 2 with another, sandwiching the edges of the chicken wire between them. Nail them together with the finishing nails.

4. Dig two 12-inch-deep holes for the trellis legs. Set the trellis in place, and refill the holes. Firm in the soil around one leg, and stabilize it with two guy wires attached to two stakes. Use the level to make sure the trellis stands up perfectly straight.

5. Adjust the position of the second leg, stretching the trellis tight as you work, before installing the last two stakes and guy wires. Check to make sure the trellis is straight before firming the soil around both legs.

How Much Can You Grow in a 4-Foot Row?

Perhaps more than you think! First thing in spring, prepare a planting row 18 inches wide and install a chicken-wire trellis down the middle. Plant snap peas (the most productive kind) on both sides, 2 inches apart in rows 4 inches from the trellis. Move out 3 more inches, and plant a row of onions down one side, using sets, seedlings, or scallions from the grocery store. On the other side, flank the peas with a 2-foot-long planting of radishes, and 2 feet of leaf lettuce. Total yield? Expect 4 pounds of peas, 3 pounds of onions (some pulled green), 2 pounds of radishes, and 2 pounds of lettuce.

But you're not done yet. In midsummer, replace the peas with cucumbers, with companion crops of weed-smothering turnips and mustard. You'll need to tie the cucumbers to the trellis as they grow, but by season's end, your trellised row should produce 20 pounds of delicious, garden-fresh vegetables. Not bad for only 6 square feet of growing space! To reward and replenish your hard-working soil, dig in a generous helping of compost before bedding it down for winter beneath a thick organic mulch.

Grow a Three Sisters Circle Garden

Planting one crop that can support another is not a new idea, but it's still a wise one. Native Americans have long valued the practice of planting The Three Sisters—squash, corn, and pole beans—as a congenial plant community. The corn supports the beans, the beans add nitrogen to the soil for the corn, and the squash forms a groundcover that smothers weeds and helps the soil retain moisture.

Growing The Three Sisters also presents a fitting opportunity to grow beans with very long vines, such as the 'Genuine Cornfield' snap bean—one of the oldest beans cultivated by the Iroquois. And you can maximize the flavor of the mix by using tall sweet corn such as 'Silver Queen' and naturally pest-resistant squash such as butternut. Let most of the squash grow to maturity, but harvest a few and eat them as summer squash. Do the same with the beans, which can be picked young and used as snap beans, or allowed to mature into shell beans.

YOU WILL NEED

Tools: Garden spade, rake, watering can or garden hose, hoe

Two bushels or two 40-pound bags of compost

1 packet of 'Silver Queen' sweet corn seed

1 packet of pole bean seeds

1 packet of butternut squash seeds

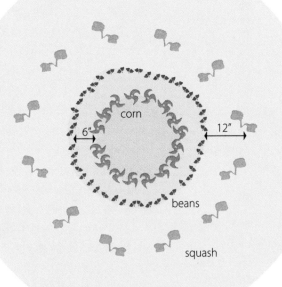

corn

6"

12"

beans

squash

8'

1. As soon as the soil can be worked in the spring, cultivate a circle of soil 8 feet across, and mix the compost into the center. Use the rake to create a flat-topped mound in the center, 10 inches high and 4 feet across.

2. Two weeks after the last spring frost passes, sow 15 corn seeds in a ring in the center of the growing circle, spacing them 4 inches apart and planting them 1 inch deep. Water the planted circle.

3. When the corn is 10 inches tall, thin the plants to 12 inches apart. Hoe out any weeds, and mound 2 inches of loose soil around the base of the corn plants.

4. Plant about 20 pole bean seeds in a ring 6 inches outside the ring of corn, spacing the seeds about 6 inches apart and planting them 1 inch deep. Water the planted beans.

5. A week after the beans sprout, sow 10 squash seeds in a ring 12 inches outside the beans. Space seeds 12 inches apart and plant them 1 inch deep.

6. As the beans begin to climb, guide them toward the corn stalks, and they'll carry on from there. Occasionally turn some of the squash vines toward the center of the mound to help the plants cover the entire circle, but do not move them after they begin to set fruit.

7. When the silks emerge from the ears of corn, hand pollinate the corn by shaking some pollen from the tassels into your palm, and sprinkle pinches onto the silks. Repeat 3 days in a row. It's essential to hand-pollinate small plantings of corn if you want big ears packed with kernels.

JUST FOR FUN

Grow a Sunflower Teepee Playhouse

You can grow a single-season garden structure that doubles as a hideout for kids, and harvest homegrown bird feed, by growing a living teepee from sunflowers. After the soil warms in spring, plant seeds of a tall, single-stemmed sunflower in a 6-foot diameter circle, leaving a 2-foot space open for the playhouse door. Two to 3 weeks later, when the sunflowers are 6 inches tall, plant scarlet runner beans just outside the base of the sunflowers. When the sunflowers reach their almost-full height of 6 feet and have formed flower heads, gently draw the tops together and loosely tie them into a teepee with the legs from panty hose or strips of soft, stretchy cloth, tying just below the flower heads. Leave some slack at the tops and don't worry if the flowers don't touch in all spots—the vines will eventually fill in the playhouse's roof and walls. Pave the floor of the playhouse with mulch to create a cozy play space

Working with Living Trellises

Any plant that grows lean and tall can be used to support twining vines. In spring, short peas are often happy to cling to clumps of ornamental wheat, and in the summer garden, you can use amaranth, corn, Jerusalem artichokes, or okra to support pole beans or long-vined limas. Single-stemmed sunflowers make great support plants in either a vegetable or a flower garden, where they can be used as living trellises for dainty asarina or more muscular purple-podded hyacinth beans.

There are a few things to keep in mind when using plants as trellises. Drenching rain combined with wind can cause tall plants to fall over, which becomes even more likely if the plant is top-heavy with the added weight of a vine. Giving the support plant a 2-week head start on the vine is important, too, because once vines get growing, they seldom slow down. Should a plant being used as a living trellis start to look like a leaning tower, tying it to a tall, slender stake may provide a temporary remedy.

USING AN UNEMPLOYED STUMP

When a treasured old tree must be removed, leaving a stump about 3 feet high instantly creates a great trellis for perennial vines such as passionflower or trumpet creeper. Tree roots often dominate the soil around a stump, so you may need to use a short rebar stake to probe about in search of a suitable planting pocket

for a vine. If the stump is too short to provide vertical growing space for a vigorous vine, perhaps you can drill holes into the top that will support upright stakes. A single sturdy stake topped with a small weather vane or piece of metal sculpture can transform a vine-covered stump into a beautiful garden focal point.

Another option is to hollow out the top of the stump to create a planting space for cascading flowers or annual vines. If this seems like too much work, grow your vines in a large, heavy container placed on the stump. As the vines sprawl, they will cover both the container and the stump.

PLANT PARTNERS FOR CLEMATIS

One of the most beautiful vines you can grow, clematis also makes a great team player when trained to wind its way through a small tree or shrub. The host plant provides support for the clematis, which in turn furnishes a bit of shade for its living trellis. In most cases, the clematis will bloom after its support plant has leafed out, so each blossom floats on a sea of lush foliage.

Clematis vary in color, bloom season, and ideal pruning times, but because there are hundreds of varieties to choose from, it is not difficult to coordinate them with exactly the right host plants. Don't worry that the host plant will shade out the clematis, because the vine will seek out sunny pockets in the tree or

Six Sure-Fire Clematis Combos

HOST PLANT	CLEMATIS	COMMENTS
Star Magnolia (*Magnolia stellata*), grows 15 feet tall	White 'Henryi,' blooms early summer and fall, prune in late winter	These two white bloomers look great when given a dark evergreen backdrop. The tree blooms in late winter on bare branches. Both plants grow well in Zones 4–9.
Japanese Maple (*Acer palmatum atropurpureum*), grows 15 feet tall	Pale pink 'Belle of Woking,' blooms early summer, prune in late winter	Pairing any pink clematis with a burgundy-leafed Japanese maple creates breathtaking special effects. This pairing is adapted in Zones 5–8.
Smoke Tree (*Cotinus coggygria*), grows 10 to 15 feet tall	White petals with plum centers *C. florida* 'Sieboldii,' prune in late winter	While the airy panicles of the smoke tree are filling in, this shade-tolerant, fine-textured clematis will steal the show. Combo adapted in Zones 4–8.
Azalea (hardy, deciduous *Rhododendron* species), grows 10 feet tall	Purple *C. x jackmanii*, prune in late winter	This vigorous clematis forms a river of purple weeks after the azalea's spring blossoms fade away. Try this plant combination in Zones 4–8.
Variegated Dogwood (*Cornus alba*, 'Argenteo-marginata'), grows 10 feet tall	Burgundy-red 'Niobe', prune in late winter	Partnering a bold red clematis with any shrub with variegated or gray-green foliage is always a winning combination. This one works best in Zones 5–7.
Redbud (*Cercis canadensis*), grows 20 to 30 feet tall	Creamy-white Sweet Autumn Clematis (*C. terniflora*), prune in early spring	A muscular little redbud will look like it's wearing a fragrant white cloak in late summer or fall, and this clematis attracts beneficial insects, too. Adapted in Zones 5–9.

shrub's canopy and eagerly fill them in. The "Six Sure-Fire Clematis Combos" chart lists several proven partnerships between clematis varieties and widely adapted host plants.

To begin one of these lovely liaisons, plant a clematis 2 feet from the base of the host plant. Clematis need rich, fertile soil with a near-neutral pH, so be sure to mix in some lime if your soil is naturally acidic. As the clematis grows, secure a slender stake between the vine and a low branch of the tree or shrub to help the clematis find its way. When pruning clematis trained this way, you can avoid future training sessions by pruning it back only to where it threads into the lowest branches of its host plant.

Make a Tied Teepee Trellis

Pretty, practical, and resistant to wind, a trellis made from tripods of bamboo connected with a net of hand-tied strings can be assembled in less than an hour. In the fall, when your crops are ready for the compost heap, snip the strings and compost them along with the spent plants. Then tie the poles into a bundle, and store in a dry place until spring.

Despite its light weight, this trellis is very sturdy because the plants pull it downward as they grow. This bean–size version is 5 feet tall and 10 feet long, but you can change its height, depending on what you plan to grow. Cucumbers are happy with a 3-feet-tall trellis, while many heirloom beans prefer longer, 8-foot poles. To increase the length of the trellis, simply add more tripods. If you do not have access to bamboo poles, you can make poles from 1 x 2-inch furring strips, quarter-round molding, or long saplings cut from the woods.

New Teepee Twists

Strong enough to form the framework for animal hide–covered houses, teepee architecture has plenty of uses in the garden. The minimum number of posts for any teepee is three, and three posts are usually adequate when the teepees are attached to one another at the top. Increase the number of poles when making single teepees. Tall, broad teepees with five legs are ideal for vigorous yard-long beans, or you can add a lovely vertical accent to your flower garden by growing asarina vines on a 4-foot-tall teepee with four legs. Get more creative by attaching a finial, or top piece, to teepees used to support flowering vines. Good possibilities include rustic round grapevine globes, or spirals made from flexible copper tubing.

YOU WILL NEED

Tools: Stepladder, scissors

Nine 6-foot-long bamboo poles, 1 inch in diameter

Large ball of jute or hemp string (about 75 yards)

Two 5-foot-long bamboo poles, ½ inch in diameter

1 packet of pole or runner bean seeds

1. Prepare a 10-foot-long planting row 18 inches wide. Position 3 of the 6-foot-long bamboo poles at one end of the row, so that one leg of the tripod is placed just outside the center of the row. Standing on a stepladder, bind the tripod together at the top with string. Assemble a second matching tripod at the other end of the row.

2. Make a third tripod in the middle of the row by first placing one of the poles in the center of the row. The base of the middle tripod will be a more acute triangle than the ones at the ends. Connect the tops of the three tripods by tying the two 5-foot-long bamboo poles in place.

3. Tie six horizontal strings between the end poles, spacing them about 8 inches apart and looping them twice around the center pole. The lowest horizontal string should be about 3 inches above the ground.

4. Cut twelve 8-foot-long pieces of string. Starting at the top, tie them to the cross pieces at the top of the trellis, spacing them about 8 inches apart. Loop each one around the horizontal strings to form a grid, and tie them off at the bottom string.

5. Plant pole bean seeds 1 inch deep and 6 inches apart in two parallel rows beneath the trellis.

6. After the beans grow 6 inches tall, mulch with hay or grass clippings to retain soil moisture and discourage weeds. If needed, use small sticks to guide the seedlings to the string trellis.

Try Restrained Runners

Most beans are classified as bush or pole types, but several varieties fall in between. Often called half-runners, varieties such as 'Mountaineer,' 'White Half Runner,' and 'Royalty Purple Pod' produce a first crop as compact bushes, and then develop vining stems that often grow 3 to 4 feet long. When given modest support from a 4-foot-tall trellis, half-runners produce beans longer than bush beans, and they are easier to pick than long-vined varieties that reach for the sky.

Make a Movable Melon Trellis

Lightweight and versatile, you can set a pair of these wire-mesh panels in the garden diagonally to form an inverted V. Set diagonally, they make a great trellis for sprawling plants such as melons, cucumbers, bush-type winter squash, or even tomatoes. There is no need to provide slings for the melons, because they receive ample support from the fencing. At season's end, snip the cord holding the panels together, gather the panels, and store them until next year. The directions here are for 2 panels, but they are so handy that you will probably want to make more.

YOU WILL NEED

Tools: Handsaw, wire snips, staple gun, hammer, scissors

Two 8-foot-long 1 x 2s

Two 6-foot-long 2 x 2s

Roll of 3-foot-wide vinyl-coated 2 x 3-inch mesh lawn fencing

Sixteen 1½-inch nails

Four 18-inch-long wood stakes

Jute or hemp cord

Packet of cantaloupe seeds, or 6 seedlings

TAKE IT EASY

Multipurpose Panels

To keep dogs, birds, or other critters from ruining newly seeded beds, set one of these panels over beds on bricks or upturned flowerpots. In the fall, tie four panels into a square to make a quick collection bin for leaves.

1. Use the saw to cut the 1 x 2s into four 4-foot-long pieces. Cut the 2 x 2s into four 3-foot-long pieces.

2. Unroll 5 feet or so of fencing, using bricks or other heavy objects to weight the free edge. Measure a 4-foot section and cut with wire snips. Then cut another 4-foot-long section.

3. Lay two 2 x 2s on a level surface, parallel with their outer edges 3 feet apart. Use the staple gun to attach panels of wire, stapling 1 inch inside the outer edges about every 4 inches. Repeat with the remaining 2 x 2s.

4. Still working on a flat surface, position the 1 x 2s across the top and bottom edges of the panel, with the edge of the wire sandwiched between the 1 x 2s and 2 x 2s at the corners. Nail in place, placing 2 nails in each corner. Repeat with the other panel.

5. Flip the panels over, and staple the edge of the wire to the back side of the 1 x 2s.

6. Prepare two parallel 3-foot-long planting rows, 12 inches wide and 8 feet apart. To keep weeds from growing under the trellis, mulch over the 5 x 3 rectangle in the center with several thicknesses of newspaper, held in place with grass clippings or another organic mulch.

7. On the inside of the planting rows, pound stakes into the ground at the corners, 3 feet apart. Set panels in place to form an A-frame, with the bottom corners of the panels pushing against the stakes. Use the jute or hemp cord to tie the panels together at the top, and to tie the panels to the stakes.

8. Plant seeds or seedlings in the prepared rows. Set seedlings 14 inches apart. If you direct-seed, plant seeds 6 inches apart, and thin them to 14 inches apart 2 weeks later.

Grow Your Greatest Melons Ever

Melons grown on the ground often develop problems with spots and rots, but they will stay clean and dry held aloft by a diagonal trellis. All you will need to do is choose a sunny site and a luscious variety, and then generously enrich the soil with good compost. These varieties bear small fruits that are so delicious that you may eat a whole one at a single sitting.

- 'Amy' canary melon bears sweet, 2- to 3-pound fruits with white, honeydew-type flesh. The vines run only 6 feet, and the fruits turn bright yellow when ripe.
- 'Savor' is a juicy French melon that produces 2-pound gray-green fruits with bright orange flesh. These melons smell as good as they taste.
- 'Jenny Lind' has a flattened shape and is not as uniform as modern hybrid melons, but fans of heirloom varieties love the sweet flavor and rich muskmelon perfume of the small, 1- to 2-pound fruits.

Make a Tie-Together Trellis

Looking for a way to expand your garden space without doing much digging? This tied-together fence panel stands high, leaving plenty of room near the ground for layering on compost, leaf mold, and other soil amendments, lasagna-style. It's strong enough to hold additional strings for vines that cling with curling tendrils, or you can tie on taller vertical pieces for long-vined pole beans. Because it's tied together, you can take this trellis down at the end of the season by snipping the knots. When you're ready to use it again, setting it in place and tying it back together takes less than half an hour.

YOU WILL NEED

Tools: Tape measure, pencil or marker, fine-toothed wood saw, drill with 1-inch expansion bit, keyhole saw, scissors, garden spade

Three 5-foot-long 1 x 4 cedar boards

2 bamboo crossbars, 8 feet long and 1 to 1½ inches in diameter

2 bamboo vertical bars, 45 inches long and about 1 inch in diameter

4 bamboo vertical bars, 36 inches long and about ¾ inch in diameter

Ball of jute or hemp 80-pound weight cord for tying

1. Mark diagonal lines on the tops of the boards and cut them using the saw. Also use the saw to cut the bamboo pieces to length, and to remove any sharp stubs present at the joints. See page 248 for more details on working with bamboo.

2. Measure and mark 12 inches and 24 inches down from the top of each of the cedar boards. Drill 1-inch holes in the center of the board at each mark. Check to see if the bamboo crossbars will fit through the holes. If needed, use the keyhole saw to enlarge or refine the shapes of the holes.

3. Lay the boards on their back edges on a flat surface. Push the bamboo crossbars through the holes. Measure and adjust the boards and crossbars to make sure the center board is exactly the same distance from each end board. Mark the correct positions where each crossbar passes through the holes. Using the jute or cord, tie the crossbars tightly in place.

4. Midway between the boards, position the two 45-inch vertical bars. Measure and adjust, mark the correct positions, and tie the vertical bars tightly in place. Repeat for the remaining 36-inch vertical bars, positioning them so that their tops are 6 inches below the tops of the longer vertical bars.

5. Carefully carry the trellis to its site. Dig 12-inch deep holes for the board posts. Get a helper to hold the trellis as you set it in place and refill the holes, adjusting the position of the posts as you work to keep them straight. Firm in the soil around the board posts.

6. Blanket the area beneath the trellis with layers of compost, soil, leaf mold, and straw until it is 8 to 10 inches deep (see page 34 for more details on making a layered bed). Wait 2 weeks before planting the new bed with peas, pole beans, or another vining legume.

Do It Differently: Make It with Dowels

If you don't have bamboo, you can make a slightly smaller tie-together trellis using 6-foot-long 1-inch dowel rods for the horizontal crossbars, and ½-inch dowels for the vertical bars. Or, use string in place of the vertical bars. To do this, set the crossbars farther apart (12 and 36 inches from the tops of the posts), tie them in place, and install the trellis. Then weave cotton kite string up and down between the crossbars in a zigzag pattern. At the end of the season, snip the string and compost it along with the spent vines. Slip the crossbars out of the upright boards, pull up the boards, and store the pieces in a dry place until spring.

Build a Colorful Pyramid Pole

Flowers are the main source of color in a garden, but a painted trellis makes a valuable addition to any color scheme. This trellis raises color vertically, making nearby knee-high flowers appear even more bright and beautiful. If you decide to change your color scheme, a quick coat of paint will get your trellis ready for your garden's new look. Paint helps protect the wood from the elements, so you can use inexpensive pine lumber for this project. Turn the page for tips on choosing and using paint colors—and painterly plants—for this versatile trellis.

YOU WILL NEED

Tools: Fine-toothed handsaw, medium-grit sandpaper, paintbrush, tape measure, ruler, pencil, wood glue, hammer

Two 6-foot-long 1 x 2 pine boards

Two 8-foot-long 1 x 4 pine boards

Exterior-grade latex paint

Sixteen 2½-inch-long finishing nails

1. To make crossbars, use the saw to cut two 30-inch pieces from one of the 1 x 2 boards. Cut the other 1 x 2 into two 20-inch pieces and two 10-inch pieces. Remove 1 inch from one of the leftover pieces to make it 11 inches long.

2. Starting with one of the 10-inch pieces, saw one end to approximately a 30-degree angle. Use the cut end as a guide to mark cutting lines on the ends of the other pieces before cutting them to matching angles.

3. Lightly sand the cut pieces, as well as the 8-foot long 1 x 4s. Paint all pieces with a coat of paint, and allow to dry.

4. Lay one of the 1 x 4s on a flat surface. Starting at the top, measure and mark the following increments on the board: 11, 23, 35, 47, 59, and 71 inches from the top. Use a ruler to mark straight lines across the board at these points. Center one of the 10-inch crossbars at the top-most mark, followed by the five other increasingly longer crossbars, with the second 30-inch crossbar centered at the 71-inch line. Glue the pieces in place, and allow to dry for at least 2 hours. To make the top and bottom more solid, take the 11-inch piece of 1 x 2 and center it at the top of the 1 x 4. Center the remaining 12-inch piece of 1 x 2 to the bottom of the 1 x 4. Glue these pieces in place, too.

5. Place a small amount of glue on the center of each crossbar, and the 1 x 2 pieces at the top and bottom of the trellis. Lay the other 1 x 4 on top of the first 1 x 4, sandwiching the crossbars between them. Slightly to the left of center, hammer a nail at each place where a crossbar intersects so that it goes through all three layers. Also nail the trellis together near the top and bottom. Turn the trellis over, and again slightly to the left of center, hammer a second set of nails.

6. Apply a second coat of paint to the finished trellis, and allow to dry.

7. Set the pole trellis in the ground 18 inches deep. If needed, guy wires can be attached near the ends of the lowest crossbar (see page 79).

Keep It Natural

If you prefer the look of natural wood, use rot-resistant cedar and a combination water-seal-stain product in place of paint—a great idea if you want to use this trellis near a stained wood deck. Restain or reseal every 2 years, or allow the trellis to weather to a natural gray. You also can alter the shape of the trellis by changing the lengths of the crosspieces. Cutting them to a single length will create a strong columnar look. There are also creative possibilities at the top of the trellis, where you might install a reflective ball, a wind-driven whirligig, or a birdhouse for bug-eating wrens.

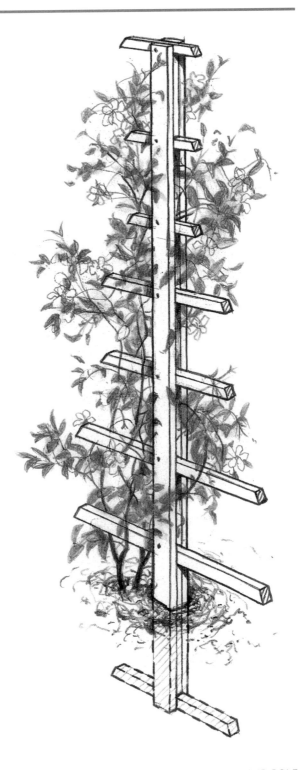

CREATIVE COLOR COMBOS

Some gardeners love to experiment with color in their gardens, while others find color so confusing that they opt to play it safe with traditional color combinations they have used before. If you're reluctant to take the bold step of painting a trellis a certain color, here are some things to think about as you envision perfect partnerships between plants and the trellises that support them. Basically, you have two ways to go. You can choose harmonious colors that quietly blend with colors provided by plants and their natural setting, or you can follow a planting scheme that helps opposites attract.

Happy Harmonies

Harmonious colors can be shades that vary slightly from those provided by the dominant flowers in your garden, or they can be so-called neutral colors that go with everything. For example, if you like your garden to glow in soft pastels, you might paint your trellis a smoky blue color, which will echo various blue hues and blend easily with pink, white, and pale yellow. Light pink or purple clematis are ideal vines for a gray trellis. In a garden where yellow reigns supreme, a trellis painted light yellow and planted with black-eyed Susan vine (*Thunbergia*) will create unity while flattering nearby flowers. If you love vivid red geraniums, salvias, or zinnias, a bright red trellis planted with ferny cypressvine morning glory will fit right in, and attract the interest of passing hummingbirds, too.

Painting your trellis dark green or black will transform it into a neutral element, which is often best in shady woodland gardens. These neutrals are not without contrast—envision a snow white clematis paired with a dark green or black trellis. If you want to paint your trellis only once and then use it in a variety of color schemes, sticking with a neutral color is the best choice. Don't feel that you're being unimaginative if you paint your trellis with paint leftover from the last time you painted your shutters, house trim, or front door. Repeating one of your house's accent colors in a trellis will make your landscape feel more unified, and won't detract from the color show being staged by your plants.

High-Contrast Complements

Color opposites, called complements, are high-energy combinations such as orange and blue, yellow and violet, and red and green. Working with complements can be tricky because there are so many different shades of common colors, but if you stick with a simple two-way combination, it's hard to go wrong. For example, you might use orange 'Profusion' zinnias to mask the base of a trellis planted with blue morning glories, or turn this combo upside-down by encircling a trellis that supports orange black-eyed Susan vine with blue 'Victoria' salvia. To play with yellow and violet, paint the trellis soft yellow, and set a pretty purple clematis at its base. A plain green trellis is an ideal support for red or deep pink sweet peas, or a red climbing rose.

Make a Window Frame Trellis

A discarded wooden window frame can easily be transformed into a time-hewn trellis. If a wall of your garage or other outbuilding gets plenty of sun, a window frame trellis will make it look like it has a real window. Check flea markets or salvage shops for a promising subject if you don't have an old window frame in your attic. Then use these techniques to get it ready for its new life.

1. Use a chisel to chip off old paint, and remove stray nails, glass, or bits of screen with a screwdriver. Sweep up and dispose of the debris, because very old window frames may have been painted with lead-based paint. If desired, paint the cleaned frame a new color.

2. On the back side of the frame, cut and nail pieces of 2-inch-wide molding just inside the outer edge to reinforce the joints.

3. Insert small screw eyes at 6-inch intervals on the back side of the frame, measuring to make sure the screws are opposite one another on both the horizontal and vertical inner edges.

4. String 20-gauge galvanized wire horizontally between facing eyehole screws, looping and then twisting the wire in each one to help it stay tight. When you're finished stringing the wire between the horizon-

tal eyehole screws, do the same with the vertical ones, weaving under and over the horizontal wires as you work. When you're done, the wires should cross at right angles, so they resemble windowpanes.

5. When installing the trellis, set its bottom edge on bricks or small stones to keep it from coming into direct contact with damp soil.

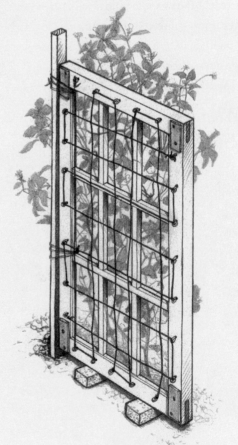

Build a Windproof Pillar

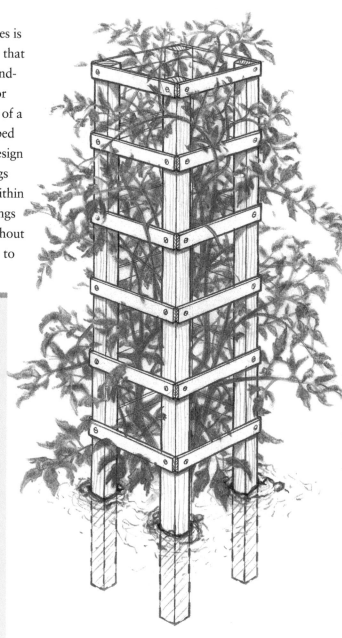

The number one enemy of garden trellises is wind, but this square pillar is so stable that it would take a hurricane to push it over. Standing 5 feet tall, its compact design is perfect for supporting clematis or sweet peas in the rear of a flower border, or you can use it for long-limbed tomatoes in a veggie garden. Its four-sided design makes great use of space, and roomy openings between the bars keep blossoms and fruits within easy reach. Extra space below the bottom rungs makes it possible to cultivate and replant without moving the pillar. You also can use this pillar to support a platform-type bird feeder.

What the Best-Dressed Trellises Are Wearing

Before you begin this project, visit a lumber or home supply store and look at decorative embossed moldings, many of which have botanical patterns cut into them. Embossed molding costs more than plain pine furring strips, but it's so pretty that your trellis will become a unique work of art. If you plan to paint your trellis, another time-saving option is to use molding that has already been given a white coat of sealant, which eliminates the need for the first coat of paint.

YOU WILL NEED

Tools: Ruler or tape measure, handsaw, medium-grit sandpaper, outdoor enamel paint or polyurethane stain, paintbrush, drill with ⅛-inch drill bit, screwdriver

Four 6-foot-long pieces of 1½-inch-wide pine furring strips

Four 6-foot-long pieces of 2 x 2 pine

Forty-eight 1¼-inch exterior (decking) screws

1 gallon of gravel or small stones

1. To make the horizontal bars, cut the furring strips into twenty-four 12-inch pieces. Sand the cut pieces and the 2 x 2s you will use for the uprights. Paint or stain all the pieces and allow them to dry.

2. Set two of the 2 x 2s on a flat surface, parallel with their outer edges 12 inches apart. Place one of the 12-inch horizontal pieces between the top edges of the 2 x 2s. Attach it with screws, which go in best when inserted into predrilled guide holes. Measure 10 inches down from the bottom edge of the first rung and install a second horizontal piece. Do the same with

4 more horizontals to create the pillar front.

3. Repeat Step 2 with the other two 2 x 2s and 6 horizontal pieces. Set the two assembled pillars on edge, 12 inches apart. Attach the remaining horizontal pieces at the same levels to form a sturdy box.

4. Apply a second coat of paint or stain to the assembled pillar and allow it to dry.

5. Dig a hole 14 inches deep and 18 inches wide. Place a 2-inch layer of gravel or stones in a 14-inch square in the bottom of the hole. Set the trellis in place, and add soil as necessary to make it level.

6. Use half of the excavated soil to refill the hole inside the legs of the trellis. Amend the remaining soil with compost or other organic matter before using it to refill the outer sections of the hole.

7. Plant the inside or perimeter of the trellis with your chosen seeds or plants. A tomato set inside the pillar will instantly receive support. If needed, lean small sticks against the lowest rungs to help vines find their way to the trellis. Or, use strips of soft, stretchy cloth to secure branches of tomatoes, roses, or other plants that must be tethered in place.

FINISHING TOUCHES

Let Your Tower Twinkle

To liven up your pillar in winter—or in summer, for that matter—drape it with a string or two of miniature outdoor white lights. With or without lights, you can stencil or paint designs on this trellis if you like, or simply paint it with dark green enamel if you want a classic look.

Make a Low-Maintenance Lattice Trellis

Preassembled lattice panels are classic materials for making trellises because they are sturdy, look great, and are the best type of trellis for screening out unsightly views. Wood lattice made from rot-resistant cedar or redwood is available in many areas, and every home supply center sells plastic lattice in a variety of colors. White is the most popular color, so white plastic lattice often is offered in more than one pattern. Whether you choose a diagonal pattern or a window-pane design, a trellis made from plastic lattice attached to a PVC pipe frame will go together in minutes and last for years. You will have the perfect trellis for training an espaliered pear or sweetly scented climbing rose. Use the small leftover piece of lattice as a trellis for a window box or other large container. To help harmonize the PVC pipe frame with lattice that is not white, paint the pipe and elbow connectors with spray enamel.

FINISHING TOUCHES

Add a Mirror

To help this trellis function as a wall for a garden room, furnish it with an oval mirror, hung in the center at eye level.

YOU WILL NEED

Tools: Wire snips or power saw with carbide-tipped blade, handsaw, drill, garden spade or trenching spade, hammer, level

One 2 x 8-foot plastic lattice panel

3 lengths of 2-inch PVC pipe, one 22 inches long and two 8 feet long

Two 2-inch PVC elbow connectors

PVC cement and applicator

20 to 30 ½-inch stainless steel screws

Two 4-foot-long pieces of ⅝-inch-diameter rebar

1. Use the wire snips or power saw to cut the 2 x 8-foot lattice panel to 2 x 6 feet. Saw the PVC pipe to the desired lengths with the handsaw or power saw.

2. To form the PVC-pipe frame that will support the lattice, lay the long pieces of PVC pipe 2 feet apart on a level surface. Attach the top piece to the side pieces with the elbow connectors. You may need to shorten the top piece to make the trellis the right width, so check to make sure the lattice fits properly before cementing the elbow connectors in place.

3. When the cement has dried, lay the plastic lattice over the frame, and drill guide holes before screwing the lattice onto the PVC pipe frame. The smaller the openings in the lattice, the more screws you will need. There should be 2 feet of free space at the bottom of the assembled panel.

4. In the garden, mark the locations for the sideposts. Dig narrow holes 12 inches deep for setting the PVC posts in place. Pound rebar stakes into the centers of the holes with the hammer. (Placing a small piece of scrap lumber atop the rebar stakes makes this easier). Use a level to make sure the rebar stakes are straight before pounding them as deep as they will go, or at least 18 inches. The tops do not have to be even.

5. Place the legs of the trellis over the rebar posts. Use the level to make sure the trellis is plumb, and then pack soil firmly around the PVC posts.

Working with Wood?

Panels of cedar or redwood lattice will make a beautiful trellis, but there is a knack to cutting them. Be sure to wear safety glasses in case you hit a staple while sawing, and find a helper to lend a hand. Measure carefully before you cut, allowing an extra margin if you are using molding in which the panel will fit into a precut groove.

Mark the cutting line in chalk, just below a line of staples. To hold the lattice sheet steady while you cut the lattice with a power saw—and to keep it from coming apart—sandwich it between two boards. Position the boards as close to the cutting line as possible. Weight the boards with a brick or concrete block at either end, and have your helper hold the boards firmly while you saw.

A Trellis That Suits to a "T"

The T-bar trellis offers grapes and other fruiting vines what they need for better health and higher yields—maximum exposure to light and a permanent place to ramble. You can use it for hardy kiwis or long-handled dipper gourds, too, or make a shorter version for raspberries. Consisting of two T-shaped posts set 12 feet apart and connected with three runs of galvanized wire, this trellis is meant to last for many years, so the posts are permanently set in concrete. This is a heavy trellis that requires the joint efforts of two people to build and install.

If you dream of a shady sitting place near a too-sunny garden, you can use two T-posts to support a small pergola. Set the posts 6 feet apart and top them with wood slats or a panel of cedar or redwood lattice, nailed into place.

T-trellises do not have to work in pairs. To use a single T-trellis to support a vigorous climbing rose, install diagonal wires between the ends of the crosspieces and the base of the post, and tie new canes to these wires with strips of soft, stretchy cloth. A single T-trellis also makes a great structure for supporting a collection of hanging baskets, which can be hung from the crosspieces as well as the main post.

YOU WILL NEED

Tools: Measuring tape, power saw, drill with ¼-inch extension bit, ratchet wrench, posthole digger, level, wheelbarrow, spade, wire snips

One 6-foot-long 4 x 4

Two 8-foot-long 4 x 6 posts of rot-resistant wood (cedar or locust)

Two 5-foot-long 4 x 6 crosspieces

Four 10-inch-long ⅜-inch-diameter lag screws

20 flat metal washers

Eight 5-inch-long ⅜-inch-diameter lag screws

Eight 7-inch-long ⅜-inch-diameter lag screws

6 large screw eyes

2 bags premixed concrete

42 feet of galvanized, high-tensile, 12-gauge wire

Three 5½-inch turnbuckles

1. To make the braces, measure and saw four 16-inch pieces from the 6-foot 4 x 4. Then cut 45-degree angles at the ends of each piece.

2. Lay the two 4 x 6 posts on a flat surface, broad sides down. Place 5-foot-long crosspieces at the tops of each post, measuring to make sure they are perfectly centered. Drill guide holes for two 10-inch lag screws 2 inches apart on the tops of the crosspieces. Thread washers onto the 10-inch lag screws. Use the ratchet wrench to attach the crosspieces to the posts with lag screws.

3. To attach braces to each T-post, position the braces and drill guide holes at each junction for one 5-inch and one 7-inch lag screw. Install the screws with washers as you did in Step 2, placing them at horizontal and vertical angles.

4. Mark the center of each crosspiece. Then mark spots 4 inches inside each outside edge. Drill guide holes for the screw eyes, and securely screw them into place.

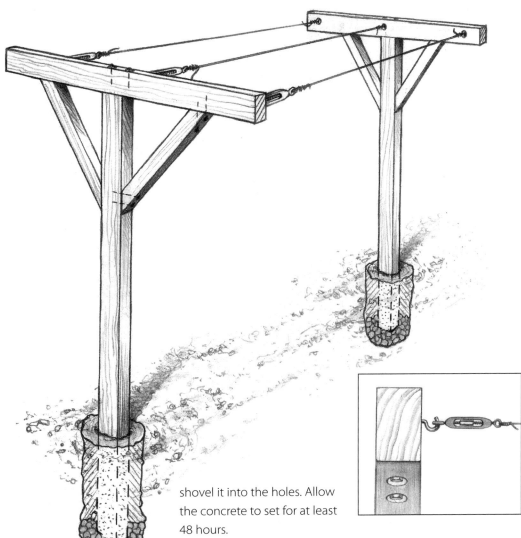

shovel it into the holes. Allow the concrete to set for at least 48 hours.

6. Cut three 14-foot lengths of the 12-gauge wire. Screw a turnbuckle to its maximum length, and hook one end into a screw eye. Thread the end of a piece of wire into the other end of the turnbuckle, loop the end through the eye twice, and then loop it around

5. Dig 24-inch-deep post-holes 12 feet apart. Set each assembled T-section in the holes, and use a level to make sure they are plumb. Mix concrete according to label directions (see page 80), and

itself. Attach the other end of the wire to the opposite T-post, stretching the wire as tightly as you can. Twist the turnbuckle to further tighten the wire. Cut off the excess wire, leaving a 3-inch long tail.

7. Repeat Step 6 to install the remaining 2 wires.

Make a Found-Wood Rustic Arbor

Some of the most rewarding building materials for trellises can be found in the woods, or you can scavenge them from brush piles after storms. Fashioned from found wood, this arbor can be made from anything from oak to maple, or even gnarled branches from dead rhododendrons or the trunks of discarded Christmas trees. Blemishes and knots make a rustic arbor more beautiful, whether it's clothed with clematis or standing bare against a winter landscape. Collect found wood whenever it is available, and set aside branches until you have enough for this garden showpiece. If you have flexible green willow branches (see "Seven Great Woods for Weaving" on page 253), use them for the arbor's curved top pieces.

Where should you put it? An arbor creates an instant feeling of enclosure, so it's a perfect way to frame the entryway to your flower garden, or you can use it to dramatize a simple walkway. In addition to using this arbor to support a pretty climbing vine, you can dress the base of your arbor with colorful little annuals or spring-flowering bulbs.

On a practical note, branches tend to roll when they are nailed, so it helps to partially drive nails into them before attaching them to other branches. As you attach the assembled side pieces to the posts (Step 2), try to recruit a helper who will hold the posts firmly as you nail into them. Wood stakes are used to help hold the trellis steady, but they may not be necessary if heavy posts are set into very firm soil.

YOU WILL NEED

Tools: Hammer, posthole digger, ladder, scissors

4 saplings, 8 feet long and 2 inches in diameter

Fifteen 2-inch finishing nails

6 branches, 3 feet long and 1½ inches in diameter

13 branches, 3 feet long and 1 inch in diameter (10 for sides, 3 for top)

10 branches, 5 feet long and 1 inch in diameter

About thirty 1-inch finishing nails

4 branches, 2 feet long and 1½ inches in diameter

About thirty 1½-inch finishing nails

3 curved branches, 4 feet long and 1½ inches in diameter

Four 18-inch-long wood stakes

Wire, jute, or hemp to bind the stakes to the arbor

1. Assemble the sides on a flat surface: Lay two 8-foot saplings 32 inches apart, and use the 2-inch nails to attach a 3-foot-long, 1½-inch diameter crosspiece 2 inches from the tops, and another

18 inches from the bottoms, with the ends of the crosspieces extending 2 inches beyond the posts. Repeat with the other two 8-foot branches.

2. Nail together the side grids before attaching them to the posts: Lay five 3-foot-long, 1-inch-diameter branches on a flat surface. Then lay five 5-foot-long branches across them, centered and about 6 inches apart. Nail together with the 1-inch nails. Repeat to create a grid for the other side. Nail the assembled grids to the sides.

3. Dig 18-inch-deep postholes, and set the sides in place at a slight angle, so they slant toward one another. Have a helper hold each side steady while you stand on a ladder to nail a 3-foot-long, 1½-inch-diameter branch between the sides near the top with 2-inch nails. Allow the ends of these "bridge" pieces to rest on the ends of the top crosspieces on each side.

4. Reinforce the top corners of the trellis by nailing a 2-foot-long branch diagonally across each corner with 1½-inch nails.

5. Assemble the top of the arbor by nailing three 3-foot-long, 1-inch-diameter branches across the tops of two 4-foot-long curved branches, spaced 2 feet apart. Add a third curved branch to the middle. Set the assembled top on the arbor, and nail it in place with the 1½-inch nails.

6. Pound stakes into the ground alongside the installed posts, and tie them in place with wire, jute, or hemp string.

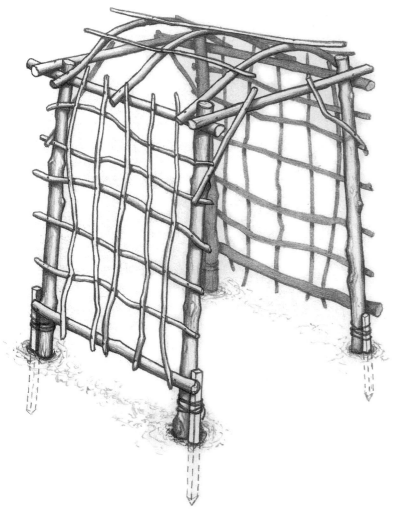

Make a Twig Tower in a Pot

In this project, the container is more than a place to grow plants. It also serves as a form for a tower trellis, in which the legs are held steady as they push against the inside of the pot. A low, broad half-barrel planter works best, but you also can use a large plastic or terra-cotta container.

Willow rods are the easiest wood to work with (see "Grow Great Wood for Weaving" on page 252), but you can use any type of sapling, including those pesky suckers you trim from hardwood stumps. One of the nicest things about this project is that you can make it neat and symmetrical, or weave the vines in whimsical patterns. If you like, add a decorative twig ball or other ornament to the top of the tower.

Once constructed in a pot, you can carefully move this tower to your garden if you prefer. Before lifting it from the pot, weave three or more lines of jute string through the upright branches just above the soil line, and tie them off tightly. Reset your twig tower in the garden at the same depth it stood in the container.

Wonder Wickets

While you're collecting long branches to make a twig tower, you will probably find shorter ones, too. Use them to make grow-through supports for bushy perennials such as peonies and black-eyed Susans. In spring, when the plants are only a few inches tall, push the ends of two pliable sticks into the ground to form parallel arches, like a pair of croquet wickets. Install a second set of arches across the first, at right angles. The plants will grow through the twig wickets, which will help hold them upright despite gusty winds from summer storms.

YOU WILL NEED

Tools: Pruning shears or loppers, wire cutters

One 6-foot-long flexible willow branch, about ¼ inch in diameter

One 4-foot-long flexible willow branch, about ¼ inch in diameter

Hemp or jute string

One 14-inch or larger pot, such as a half-barrel planter

One 20-pound bag of potting soil (more for larger containers)

Eight 6-foot-long flexible green sapling branches, about ¾ inch in diameter

Spool of floral wire

20 to 30 feet of fresh-cut vine such as grape, honeysuckle, or Virginia creeper

1. Use the pruning shears or loppers to cut the branches, choosing the straightest ones you can find. Trim off the weak tips, leaves, and small side branches.

2. Make two rings from the 6- and 4-foot-long willow branches. Make one 12 inches in diameter and one 8 inches in diameter. Bind the ends together with hemp or jute string. You'll slip these inside the tower to create a slightly outward bow in the vertical branches.

3. Fill the container with potting soil to 3 inches below the rim. Place the 12-inch ring on the surface of the soil.

4. Insert the 6-foot-long saplings into the container just inside the edge of the pot, pushing each branch all the way to the bottom of the pot. Tie the tops together, teepee style, with a 15-inch-long piece of floral wire.

5. Reach through the uprights and lift the 12-inch ring as high as it will go inside the tower. Crisscross a 4-inch piece of wire at each place where the ring meets a vertical branch to secure it in place.

6. Slip the 8-inch ring between the branches above the 12-inch ring, and slide it up until it fits snugly. Wire it into place.

7. Weave pieces of vine through the upright branches at the places where the rings are secured, tucking in the ends. If necessary, tie the ends

in place with hemp or jute string. Use small pieces of vine to cover the wire that secures the top of the tower.

8. Plant your tower with any type of flowering vine. Try cypressvine morning glory, which attracts hummingbirds with its bright red flowers.

Grow a Patio Climbing Rose

If your gardening space is limited to a deck or patio, you can still enjoy the beauty and fragrance of roses. Think small, that's all, and train a container-grown climbing miniature rose onto a pretty trellis.

Don't be misled by the delicate looks of miniature roses, because they are tough little plants that will grow for years with proper care. Miniature roses grow on their own roots, so they are cold-tolerant enough to stay outdoors all year. Like full-size roses, the minis love plenty of sun, water, and regular feeding. From late spring to fall, fertilize your rose with a liquid rose food, diluted to half the normal strength, every third time you water. Miniature roses become dormant in winter. In spring, prune the canes back by half their length to encourage the development of vigorous new branches.

Five Fine Miniature Climbers

- 'Rise 'N Shine' (Zones 6 to 9) grows to 2 feet tall and produces fragrant yellow blossoms that ripen to cream.
- 'Candy Cane' (Zones 5 to 9) is a taller variety that climbs to 4 feet or more. The pink blossoms have pretty white stripes.
- 'Love and Kisses' (Zones 5 to 9) produces vibrant red blossoms on tall, 6- to 7-foot canes, so it's a great choice for porch posts.
- 'Rainbow's End' (Zones 5 to 9) bears eye-catching blossoms comprised of yellow petals edged with red. Canes grow 5 to 6 feet tall.
- 'Work of Art' (Zones 5 to 9) bears soft salmon-orange blossoms on 5- to 6-foot canes.

YOU WILL NEED

Tools: Measuring tape, handsaw, hammer, strips of soft cloth

10 linear feet of ¾-inch-wide embossed wood molding

Six 1-inch brass nails

One 14-inch square planter box

1 can latex foam sealant

One 20-pound bag of commercial garden soil

1 miniature climbing rose

2 creeping thyme plants

1. To make the crossbars for the trellis, saw three 12-inch pieces from the piece of molding. Saw the remaining piece into two 40-inch pieces to form the uprights. Set aside the scrap piece for another use.

2. Lay the side pieces on a flat surface, with the decorative sides up. Position a crossbar between the top edges, and nail it in place. Nail the other two crossbars at 12-inch intervals from the top one.

3. Have a helper hold the trellis upright against the inside back side of the planter box.

Attach the trellis to the back of the box with the spray foam sealant (a little goes a long way). Hold the trellis still until the foam sets, about 3 minutes. Move the box to its permanent location.

4. Fill the planter box with soil, and plant the rose in the middle at the same depth it grew in its container. Plant the thyme just inside the edges of the box, and water well.

5. As the rose canes grow, tie them to the trellis with thin strips of stretchy cloth. In winter, move the planter to a protected spot against a wall of your house to shield it from strong winds.

Topple-Proof Trellised Containers

You can grow crunchy snap peas or salad-size cucumbers in containers, as well as flowering vines like sweet peas or morning glories. Whichever plants you choose, grow them in square or rectangular planters, which are much less likely to topple over than regular round flowerpots. You can attach a trellis to the inside or to the outside of a wood planter. Or, use string tied to stakes pushed into the pot to train vines over your porch or deck railings.

To balance the vertical lines of container-grown roses or vines, tuck a few cascading plants inside the edges of the planter. Creeping thyme pairs well with roses, or you can add trailing annual flowers such as petunias, lobelia, or moss verbena.

WORK WITH WHAT YOU HAVE

The projects in this chapter provide plenty of trellising ideas for different parts of your landscape, but you may already have posts or fences that can become plant supports with a little help. Use them to give your garden more vertical interest while making the most of limited space.

No More Plain-Jane Posts

The posts used to hold up your mailbox, bird feeder, or a panel of fence can easily be transformed into a hard-working trellis. Here are five easy ideas to try.

- Screw cup hooks into the upper part of the post, and run a fan of diagonal strings to stakes pounded into the ground.
- Tie short sticks together into a checkerboard square, and nail it onto the post to provide a climbing surface.
- Remove the tread from an old bicycle or tricycle wheel, and hang it on the post with a coat hook. You can do the same with an old oven rack, or three picture frames of different sizes.
- Cut an 18-inch-long piece of poultry netting or landscape fencing, bend it into a circle around the post, and secure the ends with short pieces of wire.
- Bend two equal-length pieces of willow or pliable green wood so they form the two halves of a heart (see "Seven Great Woods for Weaving" on page 253). Nail the heart to a wood post.

Retrofitting Fences

Fences make great plant supports as long as they don't block too much fresh air and light. This is not an issue with chain-link fences, which look more attractive if you paint them dark green or black. Picket fences shade the lower parts of plants, so it's best to pair them with tall plants that can make good use of the more abundant light at the fence's upper edge. Ideal candidates are perennials that tend to need staking, such as hollyhocks, delphiniums, and late-blooming asters. The fence will function as a row of stakes, so all you need to do is add a few stakes on the opposite side of the plants.

Wood privacy fences pose a greater challenge because they block light and air. A solid fence that faces north may be too shady for sun-loving flowers, so use its base for hardy ferns, hostas, and other plants that like moist shade. Solid fences or walls that face south or west are ideal for practicing the art of espalier. Try pruning and tying the branches of a fruit tree, climbing rose, or spring-blooming magnolia to wires or hooks. Plants handled this way have fine sculptural qualities and work wonders in tight, narrow spaces.

CHAPTER 4

Ingenious Ways to Water

Water adds beauty and
life to your garden, but
delivering it to your plants
can be tricky business.
This chapter reveals dozens
of clever ways to water,
making life easier for
you and for
your plants.

Thoughtful Watering

Water is elemental to plant life, and the presence of water in the garden can be as enjoyable as sharing company with beautiful flowers. Yet water is an increasingly precious commodity, so whether you are using it to nurture plants or treating yourself to the sound of a trickling fountain, water should be regarded as a natural treasure.

In most climates, a gardener's watering challenges change with the seasons. Sometimes there's too much water and other times there's not enough, so finding ways to even out your garden's water supply makes perfect sense. Several of the projects in this chapter, such as making a Working Rain Barrel (see page 132) or setting up a Bucket Drip System (see page 134), will do exactly that. There are also projects to help you alter your site to reduce your garden's water demands, and many more that will simply make handling water more fun. Whether you are cleaning up after a big day of weeding and mulching in an Outdoor Shower (see page 140) or relaxing on your deck as you listen to the gentle gurgle of a Terra-Cotta Fountain (see page 144), enjoying the pleasures of water is as rewarding as growing a water-wise garden.

Many of the projects here will require a trip to the plumbing section of a hardware or home supply store, which is strange territory to many gardeners. But rather than feeling intimidated by strange-sounding parts, do what plumbers do: Find the pieces you need, and check how they fit together before you leave the store. It's the best way to make sure your water-handling projects will proceed without a hitch.

WATERING YOUR GARDEN'S NEIGHBORHOODS

Smart gardeners understand that watering needs are rarely uniform from one end of their landscape to the other. Instead, most yards are comprised of ecological "neighborhoods"— some bright and sunny, some cool and shady. Some have rich, loamy soil that holds moisture well, while others are sandy and dry. Each district of a garden provides a suitable home for some plants, while others would feel out of place in the same spot. A good gardener is like a city planner who gets to know each neighborhood and delivers water services where they are needed most.

To promote harmony in your garden's neighborhoods, try to group plants with similar watering needs together—you'll save time and water this way, and the plants will appreciate it, too. The watering needs of vegetables should be addressed on a crop-by-crop basis in keeping with their growth cycles (see the "When They Need Water Most" chart on page 125). With flowers, use the plant lists at right to design a colorful landscape in which plants are matched to the naturally available water supply and the amount of water you are willing—and able—to provide.

30 Easy Flowers for Dry Sites

Anthemis (*Anthemis* spp.), perennial, Zones 4–9

Baby's Breath (*Gypsophila elegans*), annual, all zones

Black-Eyed Susan (*Rudbeckia* spp.), perennial, Zones 3–9

Blanket Flower (*Gaillardia pulchella*), annual, all zones

Blazing Star (*Liatris spicata*), perennial, Zones 3–10

Butterfly Weed (*Asclepias* spp.), perennial, Zones 3–10

California Poppy (*Eschscholzia californica*), annual, all zones

Candytuft (*Iberis sempervirens*), perennial, Zones 3–9

Coneflower (*Echinacea* spp.), perennial, Zones 3–9

Coreopsis (*Coreopsis* spp.), perennial, Zones 4–9

Cosmos (*Cosmos* spp.), annual, all zones

Crocus (*Crocus* spp.), perennial, Zones 3–9

Dusty Miller (*Senecio cineraria*), perennial grown as annual, all zones

Fleabane (*Erigeron* spp.), perennial, Zones 4–9

Gazania (*Gazania rigens*), perennial grown as annual, all zones

Grape Hyacinth (*Muscari* spp.), perennial, Zones 4–8

Ice Plant (*Delosperma* spp.), perennial, Zones 5–9

Lavender (*Lavandula* spp.), perennial, Zones 5–9

Mexican Sunflower (*Tithonia rotundifolia*), annual, all zones

Ornamental Grasses (Numerous species), Zones 3–10

Portulaca (*Portulaca grandiflora*), annual, all zones

Rosemary (*Rosmarinus officinalis*), perennial, Zones 7–10

Sanvitalia (*Sanvitalia procumbens*), annual, all zones

Sea Holly (*Eryngium* spp.), perennial, Zones 3–8

Sedum (*Sedum* spp.), perennial, Zones 3–9

Strawflower (*Helichrysum bracteatum*), annual, all zones

Sunflower (*Helianthus annuus*), annual, all zones

Verbena (*Verbena* spp.), perennials and annuals, all zones

Yarrow (*Achillea* spp.), perennial, Zones 3–9

Yucca (*Yucca filamentosa*), perennial, Zones 4–10

20 Easy Flowers for Moist Sites

Astilbe (*Astilbe* spp.), perennial, Zones 4–8

Bleeding Heart (*Dicentra spectabilis*), perennial, Zones 3–9

Browallia (*Browallia* spp.) perennials grown as annuals, all zones

Butterfly Flower (*Schizanthus pinnatus*), annual, all zones

Cardinal Flower (*Lobelia cardinalis*), perennial, Zones 2–9

Coral Bells (*Heuchera* spp.), perennial, Zones 3–9

Cup Flower (*Nierembergia caerulea*), annual, all zones

Foamflower (*Tiarella* spp.), perennial, Zones 3–8

Forget-Me-Not (*Myosotis* spp.), perennial, Zones 5–8

Hosta (*Hosta* spp.), perennial, Zones 3–9

Impatiens (*Impatiens walleriana*), annual, all zones

Iris (*Iris* spp.), perennial, Zones 5–9

Jacob's Ladder (*Polemonium* spp.), perennial, Zones 3–8

Lenten Rose (*Helleborus orientalis*), perennial, Zones 5–9

Lungwort (*Pulmonaria* spp.), perennial, Zones 3–9

Marsh Marigold (*Caltha palustris*), perennial, Zones 4–9

Meadow Rue (*Thalictrum* spp.), perennial, Zones 3–9

Monkshood (*Aconitum* spp.), perennial, Zones 3–8

Primrose (*Primula* spp.), perennial, Zones 3–9

Viola (*Viola* spp. and hybrids), annuals and perennials, all zones

Shaping Up a Water-Wise Garden

From the earliest days of agriculture, humankind has learned to shape the land into furrows, swales, and terraces to maximize the benefits of rainfall, minimize runoff, or channel away excess water when cloudbursts bring too much of a good thing. Shifting your garden's shape to help it handle water better requires a little forethought and spadework, but it doesn't have to cost a cent and is one of the simplest ways to satisfy plants' needs for moisture.

CONTOURS THAT CONSERVE WATER

If your garden tends to need more water than nature provides, there are several ways to add contours to help move water toward plant roots, and keep it there until plants have a chance to make use of it. Here are several approaches to consider.

- Plant vegetables in furrows or shallow trenches, and dam the ends with a mound of earth. This strategy turns planting rows into shallow moats. Should rain become abundant, simply make breaks in the sides of the furrows to allow excess water to drain away.

- In chronically dry climates, conserve scant water with sunken beds. To make a sunken bed, dig out the soil at least 12 inches deep, and set it aside. Mix half of the excavated soil with an equal amount of compost or other organic matter, and refill the pit with this mixture. Use the remaining soil to make wall-like mounds around the bed. In addition to channeling water toward thirsty plants, the walls above the bed will reduce water loss due to evaporation and wind.

- When setting out large plants, create a shallow basin over the root zone, enclosed by a raised ring of soil or mulch. Water will pool inside the basin and then seep down into the soil below. These basins can be 6 to 10 inches in diameter for tomatoes, roses, and small shrubs, or up to 3 feet across for larger shrubs and fruit trees.

- To slow the runoff down a slope, create natural barriers by hilling up berms across the slope. Plant them with densely rooted perennials such as daylilies or clump-forming ornamental grasses.

- Terrace hillside gardens to create a series of level tiers (see "Stack a Slope-Taming Terrace" on page 38). Each terrace will retain water that would otherwise rush down the slope.

FLOOD-PROOFING WET AREAS

In high rainfall areas, too much water causes as many problems as does too little water in other areas. Using raised beds will go a long way toward reducing damage to plants caused by waterlogged roots. You can also use large containers to grow plants that are sensitive to flooding. To carry away the torrents of water that flow from your gutters and then wash across your lawn, incorporate a Rock Swale into your landscape's design. Even when no water is present, a curving Rock Swale suggests the fluid presence of water.

Do make sure that the water that runs through the swale ends near a storm drain, or in some other place where it will not cause damage to your property, your garden beds, or a neighbor's property. And, in some instances, it's wise to check with local zoning authorities before installing a swale that will channel water toward roadways, sidewalks, and utility areas.

Build a Rock Swale

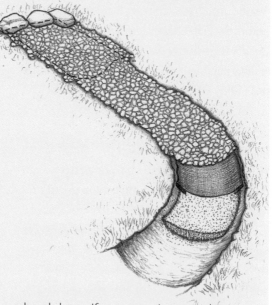

Any flood-prone site can be drained with a Rock Swale. A slight natural slope is ideal, but you can increase the slope of a nearly level site by moving soil dug from the far end of the swale to its point of origin. The materials given here will create a swale 2 feet wide and 20 feet long.

YOU WILL NEED

Tools: Garden hoses, level, shovel

Two 40-pound bags of sand

One 20-foot-long piece of 2- or 3-foot-wide landscape fabric

One 2 x 5-foot piece of flexible rubber pond liner

Several large rounded stones

12 cubic feet of cobbles (rounded river rock) or gravel

1. Use garden hoses to lay out the swale's path, keeping in mind that broad curves look more natural than straight lines. Use the level to make sure the swale slopes away from your house or other structures.

2. Dig the swale about 6 inches deep and 24 inches wide, curving the sides to create a bowl shape. If necessary, increase the slope of the swale by moving soil taken from high spots to the head of the swale.

3. Spread a 1-inch-deep layer of sand in the bottom of the swale. Line the swale with landscape fabric, folding under the edges if needed.

4. Cover the high end of the swale with the rubber pond liner. Anchor the top edge of the pond liner with several large stones.

5. Fill the swale with enough cobbles or gravel to hide the liners from view.

Keeping the Water You Have

Conserving water makes more sense than pouring it on, week after week. You'll save time and slash water bills if you take simple steps to minimize water loss due to evaporation. You can't control the weather factors that increase evaporation—intense sun and dry air—but you can reduce water loss by taming persistent wind and by using mulches and highly efficient watering methods such as soaker hoses or drip irrigation.

MOISTURE AND MULCH

Mulch forms a physical barrier between sun and soil, and the same mulches you use to prevent weeds and add organic matter to your soil can be strong allies in your quest to conserve water (see the "Seven Super Mulch Materials" chart on page 33). When water conservation is a priority, one of the smartest strategies is to layer coarse mulch materials over a base mulch of newspapers, as featured in the "Grow a Triple-Mulched Garden" project on page 34. By some estimates, a 3-inch layer of mulch reduces evaporation loss by 50 percent, and most mulches cool the soil, too. Mulch also traps and holds additional moisture from rain at the surface, which raises the humidity level around plants. In very dry weather, a slight increase in humidity can enhance pollination of corn, tomatoes, and several other vegetables.

If you are using a stationary watering system such as soaker hoses or the Bucket Drip System on page 134, wait until after the watering system is in place to pile on the mulch. That way, all of the water you provide will be insulated from surface evaporation, and the mulch will protect rubber or plastic drip lines from degrading due to exposure to strong sun.

Heavy mulching does sometimes have a drawback. Moist mulches create an ideal habitat for leaf-eating slugs and snails. Baited Slug Jugs and the other slug-fighting measures discussed on page 226 can control unexpected outbreaks, or you can simply wait until your drought season starts to begin generous mulching. If you don't have slug problems in your garden, have your mulches in place before your dry season begins.

WATER-SAVING WINDBREAKS

Wind pushes evaporation into high gear, so using windbreaks is a fundamental way to conserve water. Windbreaks can serve other purposes, too, such as reducing the physical torture plants endure as they struggle to stay upright. The windbreaks described in chapter 5 are designed to turn a wind-chilled garden into a warm oasis of calm, but when your goal is to conserve moisture, it helps if the windbreak also provides filtered shade to the root zones of plants. This is exactly what happens if you use a Snow Fence Windbreak, which has saved many a tomato patch from drying to a crisp in arid Southwest gardens.

Build a Snow Fence Windbreak

When the purpose of a windbreak is to conserve soil moisture, using a material that casts low shade while filtering wind is ideal. This simple version uses wood snow fencing, which is inexpensive, easy to install and remove, and may be attractive enough to leave up year-round.

Snow fencing is designed to let wind pass through it, and the openings between the slats also allow filtered sunlight to reach nearby plants. You can install a Snow Fence Windbreak for just the peak growing season or for high-wind periods, and put it to use again in winter to encourage snow to accumulate in places where you want it to melt in spring. Wood snow fencing, which is held together with wire, is the most attractive kind to use in your garden, but you can opt for lightweight, inexpensive plastic snow fencing if you prefer.

YOU WILL NEED

Tools: Measuring tape, sledgehammer, wire cutters, pliers

Enough 6-foot-tall steel fence posts to place a post every 8 feet along the fence

One 50-foot roll of 4-foot-tall wooden snow fencing

Plastic cable ties

1. Determine the location for your fence, which should be on the south or west side of the plants to be shaded, about 3 feet from the center of the row. Use a sledgehammer to drive posts into the ground at each end, and at any intermediate corners or bends. Install additional posts at 8-foot intervals.

2. Unroll the fencing and use the wire cutters to cut it to the length of your desired fence, allowing a few extra inches if the fence rounds a corner.

3. With the base of the fence resting on the ground, attach one end to a post with three plastic cable ties. Pull the fence tight and secure it to each successive post with zip ties.

4. Once the fence is attached to the final post, trim the excess with wire cutters and bend back any exposed wires with pliers. When it's time to remove the fencing, just snip off the plastic zip ties and roll up the fence for storage.

Ways to Water

There is no such thing as a garden that never needs its keeper to provide supplemental water. How much water plants need depends on soil, weather, and the plant itself. For example, established plants growing in porous, sandy soil usually need 1 inch of water per week in warm weather, while plants situated in moisture-retentive clay soils demand only half as much water. On the other hand, germinating seeds need constant moisture; shallow-rooted crops grow best when the soil never becomes truly dry; and tomatoes and some other vegetables develop physiological problems such as cracked fruits or blossom end rot when soil moisture fluctuates between wet and dry. Depending on the size of your garden, you may use one or several of the following four methods to deliver water to thirsty plants.

Hand watering is the most practical way to make sure germinating seeds and newly transplanted seedlings have adequate moisture, or to provide water to plants growing in containers, small raised beds, or other tight spots. Use adjustable nozzles to change the force of water when watering directly from a hose; a strong spray dislodges aphids and some other insects, but a softer shower is gentler to plant leaves. If you keep numerous containers, a Watering Wand (see page 130) is a valuable accessory when watering by hand.

Drip irrigation, in which small drips of water slowly ooze out of a drip hose or perforated container, is extremely efficient and effective when the drips are targeted to reach plant roots. If you install a large system, turn it on before you plant so you will know exactly where the puddles of moisture are located. Smaller drip buckets and bottles (see page 136) are an easy way to water widely spaced plants or closely planted beds. The Bucket Drip System (see page 134) is a great low-tech drip method that is used in many underdeveloped countries.

Soaker hoses weep moisture evenly along their length, and they can be curved if needed to match the contours of your beds. A soaker hose left on for several hours at very low pressure provides excellent deep penetration of water, yet the plants' leaves remain dry. Keep soaker hoses short, to less than 50 feet long, because long soaker hoses often release more water close to the water source, and noticeably less near the end of the hose. Soaker hoses work beautifully when used beneath mulch. You can buy soaker hoses made from recycled tires at most garden centers, or make your own Crybaby Soaker Hose (see page 139).

Sprinklers are much less efficient than other watering methods, yet they are a practical way to water large areas of lawn or expansive plantings of flowers or vegetables. It is best to use sprinklers in the morning, or early enough in the evening to allow time for foliage to dry before nightfall. Pulsing a sprinkler by running it for 15 to 20 minutes, interspersed with 10-minute breaks, helps water to penetrate deeply into the soil.

WHEN TO WATER

How can you tell when your plants need water? Wiggling your finger into the soil is a good test. If the soil feels dry knuckle-deep in containers or between shallow-rooted plants,

make plans to water. Checking the soil is often a more reliable method than simply watching your plants. Almost all vegetables and flowers wilt in the middle of a hot day, but midday wilting does not always tell a true story of what is going on below the ground. If the plants regain their perky posture by nightfall, they probably do not need supplemental water—unless they are at a life stage where any moisture shortage can lead to drought stress. The peculiar water needs of 18 popular home garden vegetables—and the best ways to satisfy those needs—are summarized below.

When They Need Water Most

CROP	CRUCIAL TIME	BEST METHODS
Beans and peas	Germination, flowering, and while pods are developing	Drip, soaker hoses, hand-watering provided foliage is kept dry
Cabbage, broccoli, cauliflower	For 2 weeks after transplanting, and while heads are developing	Drip, soaker hoses, hand-watering if aphids are present
Carrot, radish	Germination, and while roots are enlarging; excessive water at maturity can cause roots to crack	Hand-watering or sprinkler; allow time for foliage to dry before nightfall
Corn	Germination, and from tasseling to maturity	Soaker hoses, drip, sprinklers in dry climates to increase humidity during pollination period
Lettuce, other leafy greens	Shallow roots demand constant moisture throughout life cycle.	Hand-watering, sprinkler, light mulch
Melons	Germination, and during first 3 weeks following fruit set; moderate dryness enhances flavor of almost-ripe fruits	Soaker hoses, drip
Onions, garlic	While roots are enlarging and all leaves are still green; allow soil to become dry when leaves begin to brown	Soaker hoses, drip
Potatoes	Constant moderate moisture during last month of growth	Soaker hoses, drip, hand-watering if aphids are present
Squash, cucumbers	Germination and starting 1 week after the first flowers appear until fruit has set	Soaker hoses, drip
Tomatoes, peppers	For 2 weeks following transplanting, and continuously from first flowering to maturity	Soaker hoses, drip, hand-watering of containers

Working with Hoses

As time-consuming as watering with a hose can be, it's a mainstay of most gardens. When water is needed for a new planting—or to revive a plant that's unexpectedly run dry—turning on the faucet provides the fastest form of relief. The best-equipped gardeners own two types of hoses: high-quality, heavy-duty hoses that don't kink when moved around, and a comparatively inexpensive hose with thin walls that's easy to cut and splice. Set aside any buyer's remorse you may have after purchasing a cheap hose that's proven to be nothing but trouble. Instead, use it to make handy watering tools such as a Watering Wand (see page 130) or a Crybaby Soaker Hose (see page 139).

As for your good hoses, they will last for many years and be well worth their initial cost if you give them good care. Coil a hose when it is not in use, either by arranging it in a figure eight on the ground, or by winding it around a hose reel (see "Three Good Places to Coil a Hose"). Start with the female end (the larger fitting that screws on over a smaller one) when you coil a hose; that way, the male end (which attaches to nozzles, sprinklers, or soaker hoses) will be at the top when you need to use it. Drain hoses before storing them for winter. When storing a hose, connect the male and female ends together to keep insects or debris from getting inside.

Because bad things often happen to good hoses, it's wise to buy a few basic hose repair items when you purchase a hose. On the hose aisle at any hardware or home supply store you will also find male and female couplers, as well as splicing kits for repairing hoses that accidentally get chopped by mowers or spades. As long as these fittings match the diameter of your hose, installing them is a simple matter of trimming the hose end with a utility knife, soaking it in hot water for a few minutes to make it more pliable, and then screwing on the fittings.

HANDY HOSE ACCESSORIES

You can make life easier for yourself and increase the versatility and efficiency of a hose by installing various accessories.

- Save wear and tear on your faucet—and your back—by adding a 3- to 4-foot-long extension hose to your outdoor faucet. Then attach other hoses to this extension. To make an extension, use a utility knife to cut through the hose 4 feet from its female end, and install a male coupler to the cut end. If your outdoor faucet is hidden behind dense or prickly shrubs, add a second faucet mounted on a wood board to your hose extension, as is done in the "Extend a Hard-to-Reach Spigot" project on page 128.

- A splitter, often called a Y connector, allows two hoses to be attached to one faucet. With a splitter, you can keep a hose attached to one outlet and use the other for filling watering cans, rinsing produce, or washing your hands. Look for a splitter that has shut-off valves for each outlet. You also can buy four-way splitters, sometimes called gang connectors, that allow up to four hoses to run off of a single faucet. When doubling or quadrupling your outlets, bear in mind that the water pressure will be reduced by each hose you run simultaneously.

■ Snap connectors take the frustration out of screwing and unscrewing hose connectors, which have an uncanny talent for going on crooked, so you end up sprayed with water when you turn on the faucet. Snap connectors screw onto the end of a hose, and you put matching connectors on nozzles, sprinklers, or other water-handling hardware.

■ A simple mechanical or battery-operated timer between the faucet and the hose allows you to precisely control how long the water stays on, and makes it safe to forget that you left a sprinkler running. If you don't have a timer, other tricks to help you remember to turn off the water include using a kitchen timer, clipping a clothespin to your shirt, or slipping a hair scrunchie or big rubber band over your wrist. When you notice these odd accessories, you'll remember to turn off the water.

PLAY IT AGAIN

Three Good Places to Coil a Hose

You can hang a hose from a rack or buy a reel to coil it, but if you're looking for more resourceful (and less expensive) options, here are three ways to give cast-off items a second life bringing order to your hoses.

■ **Garbage can coil.** Cut down an old plastic trash can for a good hose-storage spot. Using a sharp, sturdy knife, carefully cut around the circumference of the can about 2 feet from the bottom. It may be easiest to do a rough cut first, and then go back and trim the edge. Turn the cut can over, and punch several drainage holes in the bottom with a hammer and large nail. Then coil your hose inside. In winter, you can drag the container and hose into your garage, basement, or shed for neat storage.

■ **Wheel rim coil.** An old automobile or truck wheel rim makes a good place to coil a garden hose. Spiff it up for garden use by sanding off any rust and then applying two coats of white, green, or black metal primer. Then simply lay the wheel on the ground and coil the hose around it.

■ **Big pot coil.** If you have a large terra-cotta pot that's lost its looks due to cracks and chips—or a half barrel planter that's become too fragile to hold plants—you have a great item for coiling your hose. Just turn the pot over, and coil your hose around the outside of the pot. Stow the male end, or nozzle, in the pot's drainage hole.

Extend a Hard-to-Reach Spigot

Tired of dodging spiders as you shimmy into the shrubs to turn on your faucet? Install a temporary twin faucet on the open side of the shrubs, which can be connected to the primary faucet with a short piece of hose. When winter comes, simply unscrew the hose, pull up the mounting board, and store the second spigot in your garage.

Don't be intimidated by the strange-sounding plumbing parts used to make this project. Any hardware store can provide you with the materials for a few dollars, and they will fit together like pieces of a puzzle.

YOU WILL NEED

Tools: Handsaw, drill with ⅞-inch bit, two adjustable wrenches, screwdriver, hammer

One 2-foot-long 1 x 4 pine or cedar board

1 tube of latex/silicone caulk

1 roll of Teflon plumber's tape

One ¾-inch x 1½-inch pipe nipple

One ¾-inch brass sillcock with threaded inlet (spigot made for mounting)

One ¾-inch lock washer

One ¾-inch male-female pipe-thread to hose-thread adapter

One 1½-inch-long wood screw

Small piece of scrap lumber

2 female hose couplers

Piece of ¾-inch garden hose long enough to reach between the two spigots

1. Use the handsaw to make two 45-degree cuts at one end of the 1 x 4 to form a rough V-shaped point.

2. At the other end of the board, 3 inches from the end, drill a ⅞-inch hole in the center of the board. Spread caulk around the hole on both sides.

3. Wrap a single thickness of Teflon tape around the threads on the pipe nipple, which will help to tightly seat the threads when the other pieces are screwed into place. Stretch the tape slightly as you wrap it around the pipe nipple.

4. Insert the nipple through the hole in the board. Using both wrenches, tighten the faucet into position on one end, leaving at least ½ inch of the pipe nipple exposed on the other side of the board.

5. On the back side of the board, place the lock washer over the end of the pipe nipple, and then screw on the pipe-thread to hose-thread adapter. Use two wrenches to firmly tighten the faucet and the adapter.

6. When the faucet is oriented correctly, position a wood screw in its retaining slot and screw it into the board. Place the piece of scrap lumber over the top of the mounting board, and drive the pointed end of the plank into the ground with a hammer.

7. Install female couplers onto both ends of the piece of hose. Connect the new spigot to the old one with the piece of garden hose.

Clever Ideas for Hose Guides

Instead of crushing plants or snagging on yard furniture as you drag your hose around your yard, install hose guides along the most-traveled routes between the faucet and your garden. One of the simplest of hose guides—a spinning pipe—begins with an 18-inch-long piece of rebar, pounded 10 inches into the ground. Then cover the top of the rebar stake with a piece of PVC or copper pipe. The pipe rotates as the hose rolls past, eliminating possible snags. Another option is to cover a rebar stake with two flowerpots, set bottom to bottom. As long as the drainage holes in the pots are big enough to fit over the stake, the pots will create an hourglass-shaped roller.

Want something prettier? Drive stout bamboo stakes or wood stairway spindles into the ground, and top them with decorative wood finials. You can leave them natural, or paint them dark green to help them disappear from view.

If you would rather pin a length of hose in place, do it with wickets—12-inch-long pieces of pliable green branches that are bent into arches and pushed into the ground over the hose. Wickets made from willow or other bendable wood (see "Seven Great Woods for Weaving" on page 253) will simply snap into pieces if they are accidentally caught in a moving mower blade.

Make a Long-Handled Watering Wand

YOU WILL NEED

Tools: Utility knife, measuring
    tape, handsaw, screwdriver

One 4-foot piece of garden
    hose

One male hose coupler

One female hose coupler

1 wood broom or mop
    handle, or a 30-inch-long
    ¾-inch wood dowel

Four #20 metal hose clamps

1 small roll of duct tape

1 adjustable spray nozzle
    with cut-off valve

After 10 minutes using a Long-Handled Watering Wand, you will feel as though your arms have grown 3 feet longer—a miraculous change that makes it much easier to water containers using a hose rather than a watering can. A Watering Wand also lengthens your reach in the garden, making the root zones of plants in the middle of a bed much more accessible. In a pinch, you can even let your watering wand do double duty as a sprinkler by slipping the end of the wood handle into a PVC pipe sleeve, such as those installed on the sides of the Easy-Does-It Raised Bed (see page 12). When adding water to a Combo Composter (see page 22), the end of the wand can slip into the bin's sides along with your turning fork.

1. If needed, trim the ends of the hose with the utility knife before installing the male hose coupler at one end, and the female coupler at the other.

2. Cut the broom handle or ¾-inch dowel to 30 inches long.

3. The male (small) end of the hose will be at the head of your wand, so line it up with the dowel until it is 1 inch beyond the end of the dowel. Install a hose clamp over the dowel and the hose, ½ inch from the end of the dowel. Tighten it firmly, but don't crimp the hose wall.

4. Space the other hose clamps at regular intervals, with the last clamp 1 to 2 inches from the end of the dowel.

5. In the spaces between the two lowest clamps, wrap the hose and dowel together with duct tape to create a hand grip.

6. Screw the nozzle onto the top of the wand.

PLAY IT AGAIN

New Lives for Old Hoses

A garden hose that develops leaks shouldn't be thrown on the trash heap. Once a hose is too stiff or cracked for watering, it may still serve the garden in other ways. In addition to using pieces to make a Watering Wand, Extend a Spigot (see page 128), make a Tube Hoop Cloche (see page 160), or create a Crybaby Soaker Hose (see page 139), here are some other ways to use bits and pieces of old hose.

■ Use 3-inch-long pieces to pad the top edges of a shovel. Slit the pieces down the side and slip them over the top edges, where you push with your foot. No more bruised feet from long digging sessions!

■ Pad an axe or hatchet handle, just under the head, with a 6-inch-long piece of hose, slit down the side. Squirt glue into the hose piece before popping it over the handle. The padding will help protect the handle from splintering in case of errant blows.

■ When staking newly transplanted trees, use a length of hose to pad the bark in places where guy wires might rub against the tree.

■ Slide a slit section of hose over the blade of an axe or saw as a blade guard—a wise safety precaution if children often go into areas where sharp tools are stored.

■ Use a 6-inch piece of hose to create self-opening pliers—or to keep old pruning shears that have lost their spring from locking up. Bend the hose so the ends fit over both handles of the pliers or shears. The springiness in the hose will open the handles unless you squeeze them closed.

Make a Working Rain Barrel

The basic idea behind rain barrels couldn't be simpler: Just put a barrel under a downspout, and every time it rains, you'll store up water. You can tap the full barrel by opening the spigot installed near the bottom, or by dipping water out with a pail or handled saucepan. If the barrel is higher than your garden, a hose can be attached to feed the water into a drip or soaker hose system.

Keep the following safety precautions in mind as you plan this project.

- Make sure the lid is completely childproof and mosquito-resistant. If mosquitoes do get into the water, keep them from breeding by adding a doughnut of *Bacillus thuringiensis israelensis*—a safe biological pesticide often used in water gardens.
- Find a barrel that was used to store food products or soap rather than chemicals. If you can't find a used barrel, buy a feed barrel at a farm supply store, or use a plastic garbage can.
- Never drink water from your rain barrel.

YOU WILL NEED

Tools: Level, screwdriver, hacksaw, saber saw or coping saw, drill with ⅝-inch bit, adjustable wrench

Gravel

2 concrete blocks

One 50-gallon or similar-size plastic barrel or sturdy plastic garbage can

2 downspout elbows

One piece of downspout long enough to connect the elbows to the existing downspout

Twelve ½-inch No. 8 self-tapping sheet-metal screws

1 square foot of window screen

One ½-inch boiler drain (downward-facing faucet)

1 tube of latex/silicone caulk

One 9/16-inch rubber O-ring

Two ½-inch plastic basin locknuts

6 feet of ½-inch-diameter vinyl tubing

One ½-inch-to-½-inch nylon barb adapter

1. Prepare the site by leveling the ground beneath the downspout, leaving a very gentle slope away from the foundation. Place 2 inches of gravel on the ground, and position the concrete blocks to support the barrel.

2. Find the seam in the downspout closest to 6 foot height. Remove the screws and then the downspout. Store these pieces so you can reinstall them in winter.

3. Assemble the downspout elbows and hold them over the barrel so the lower end is 2 inches above the barrel's top and the upper end is under the downspout. Measure and cut a piece of downspout to link the elbow assembly with the existing downspout. Screw the pieces into place.

4. Use the saber saw or coping saw to create a hole 6 inches in diameter in the top of the barrel beneath the downspout elbow. Screw the scrap of window screen over the hole to keep debris and

mosquitoes away from the standing water inside.

5. To install the spigot (boiler drain), drill a ⅝-inch diameter hole in the side of the barrel 2 inches above the bottom, or just above where the side straightens vertically. Drill a second ⅝-inch diameter hole 3 inches below the top rim of the barrel, about 8 inches to one side of the lower hole. This will be the outlet for the overflow pipe.

6. Coat outside of the lower hole with caulk. Slip the O-ring over the threads of the boiler drain, and then screw on one of the basin locknuts. Push the threaded pipe part of the boiler drain through the lower hole from the outside. On the inside of the barrel, coat the edges of the hole with caulk, and then screw the second basin locknut onto the back of the boiler drain. Use the adjustable wrench to tighten both of the locknuts.

7. Coat both sides of the upper hole with caulk. Push the vinyl tubing onto one end of the barb adapter, and push the other end into the

hole. Allow the sealants to dry overnight.

8. Use a hose to run several gallons of water through the gutter and into the barrel.

Check to make sure it is firmly seated, and also check for leaks around the spigot. Tuck the overflow pipe behind the barrel. When heavy rains fill the barrel, position the over-flow pipe to direct water away from the foundation of your house.

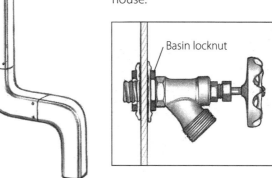

Basin locknut

Make a Bucket Drip System

This simple gravity drip irrigation system is comprised of a 5-gallon plastic bucket that is raised to chest height and then connected to two drip irrigation tapes. Similar systems are widely used in underdeveloped countries, and they have a proven track record of delivering enough water to grow excellent crops when no other water is available. In your garden, a bucket drip system can save hours of watering time over the course of a growing season. Hand-watering a 25-foot row with a watering can takes about 15 minutes, but you can refill the bucket reservoir in less than 5 minutes. In addition, none of the water is lost to evaporation, and the plants' leaves remain dry while their roots receive the moisture they need.

A Bucket Drip System also can solve the problem of maintaining moist soil conditions for newly planted seeds, and may mean the difference between success and failure when you are planting carrots or broccoli for fall harvest during the hot days of summer. And, during severe droughts when water use is restricted, you can fill the bucket reservoir with slightly used water saved from washing dishes.

Don't be discouraged by the length of the supplies list for this project. All are inexpensive to buy. If you can't find irrigation tape and fittings at a local farm supply store, you can order them by mail (see page 295). A 100-foot roll of irrigation tape (enough to make two bucket drip systems), plus fittings, costs only about $15. You also may want to innovate with the stand; any stand that lifts the reservoir pail at least 3 feet off the ground will work. At the end of the season, simply detach the irrigation tubes and rinse them off. When they are dry, roll them up and store them inside the bucket. With good care, they will last from 3 to 5 years.

YOU WILL NEED

Tools: Hammer, spade or post-hole digger, drill, utility knife

Two 5-foot-long wood posts or 2 x 4 pine boards

Two 16-inch-long pieces of 2 x 4 pine

Eight 3-inch nails

One 5-gallon plastic pail, preferably with lid

One 5-foot-long piece of garden hose

One female hose coupler

One 2-inch square of polyester window screening

One rubber band

1 small tube of latex/silicone caulk

One male hose coupler

1 hose splitter (Y connector)

50 feet of 10-mil polyethylene irrigation tape

2 irrigation tape end caps

2 irrigation hose starter fittings

1. To assemble the stand for the reservoir bucket, place the two 5-foot posts or boards on a level surface, 16 inches apart. Six inches from the tops of the posts, nail a 16-inch piece of 2 x 4 on the side of the posts. Flip the stand over, and nail a second 2 x 4 to the other side.

2. Dig postholes and set the stand at the end of a 30-inch-wide, 25-foot-long garden row. Ideally, the row should slope very slightly away from the stand.

3. Drill a hole in the bottom of the 5-gallon plastic pail. It should be only large enough

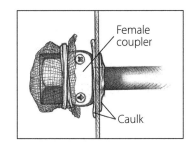

to allow the hose to pass through it.

4. Install a female coupler on one end of the hose. Place the piece of screening over the coupler opening, and secure it tightly with a rubber band.

5. Working inside the pail, pass the bare end of the hose through the hole in the bottom, and pull the hose through until the screen-covered end is just above the hole. Coat the inside and outside of the hole with silicone caulk, and seat the female coupler securely over the hole. Allow the caulk to dry.

6. Install the male coupler to the other end of the hose, and screw on the splitter. Place the bucket assembly on the stand.

7. Measure and cut two 25-foot-long pieces of irrigation tape. Place them in parallel lines down the length of the row, 10 inches apart. Install the two end caps at the far ends of the irrigation tape. Install the two hose starter fittings at the ends close to the reservoir, and attach them to the splitter.

8. Fill the reservoir pail with water, and cover it with a lid to keep out insects and debris. Observe where the water forms wet spots along the irrigation tapes. Plant seeds or plants in these wet spots. When the plants are established, weed the row and spread mulch over the irrigation tapes. Refill the reservoir pail whenever your plants need supplemental water.

Small-Scale Drippers

You can't beat the Bucket Drip System for watering closely spaced plants growing in a row, but there are other ways to drip water to widely spaced tomatoes and peppers, densely planted raised beds, or trees and shrubs scattered around your yard. Here are seven small-scale slow drippers that will save you watering time and make sure water reaches deep into the soil. When they're refilled with water from a hose or watering can, very little water will be lost to evaporation.

FLOWERPOT RESERVOIRS

Unglazed clay pots slowly lose moisture through their porous walls, and the least expensive clay pots are the most porous ones of all. To use clay pots as water reservoirs in raised beds, cover the drainage holes in several 4-inch pots with duct tape, and bury the pots almost to their rims among your plants. Fill the pots with water, and cover the tops with 4-inch-diameter disks of cardboard. The pots will empty slowly, over a period of 2 to 3 days, and are easily refilled with a hose or watering can.

LEAKY JUGS

Some of the most versatile water drippers can be made from plastic milk jugs or other large drink containers. Use a hammer and a thin finishing nail to tap two holes in one side of the jug or bottle, about 1 inch from the bottom. Fill the jug with water, cap it, and carry it up-side down to a plant that needs water. Place it on the ground right side up, with the holes facing the plant. You may need to loosen the cap a bit before it will start dripping. When most of the water has dripped into the soil below, the inch left behind will keep the jug or bottle from blowing away. If you live in a very windy area, you can drop several small rocks into your Leaky Jugs to give them extra weight.

DRIPPER PAILS

If you can't reach the root zones of some plants with Leaky Jugs, or you need to water plants growing in containers, try a Dripper Pail made by inserting narrow tubing into a hole drilled into the side of a plastic pail, about one inch from the bottom. For the tubing, try the inexpensive tubing used to repair window screens,

called spline. Insert the spline through the hole in the pail, caulk it into place on both sides of the pail, and place the end of the spline where you want the water to drip. As long as the pail is raised slightly higher than the outlet tube, it will slowly drip out water. If the water drips too fast, slow it down by placing a small piece of sponge over the end of the spline inside the pail.

SLOW SOAKER PIPES

Deep watering is sometimes a challenge, especially in clay soil. To make sure your plants receive water 12 inches below the surface, make Slow Soaker Pipes from 14-inch-long pieces of 2-inch-diameter PVC pipe. Drill several ¼-inch holes in one end of the pipe, and pound it into the soil around thirsty plants. Pull it back out, clear the plug of soil inside

the pipe, and pound it back into the ground. Then simply fill the pipe with water as you water your plants.

BURIED BOTTLES

If you know you will be faced with water shortages, plan ahead by including Buried Bottles in your planting rows. Cut the bottoms from 2-liter soda bottles or half-gallon plastic milk jugs, leaving about ½ inch of plastic intact on the "cutting" line so the bottoms form hinged lids that can be bent back. Bury the bottles spout side down between plants, with the open bottoms 2 inches above the soil line. Open the bottoms to fill the bottles, and let the water seep into the ground.

WINE BAG WATERER

The double plastic bags and attached spigots that come in boxed wine make great little water reservoirs. Cut the corner from the bag opposite the spigot, fill the bag with water, and loosely bind the cut edges together with a rubber band. Use a second rubber band to bind the top of the bag to a stake. Open the spigot very slightly, so a drip comes out every few seconds. If the bag has a push-button spigot, wedge a toothpick into the button to keep it partially depressed.

SEEPING COOLER

Put an old cooler to work as a movable drip irrigator. Place the cooler near plants that need water, fill it with a hose, and partially open the drain so that water dribbles out slowly. Meanwhile, you can move on to other tasks with the hose.

Using Soaker Hoses

Unlike drip watering devices, which often use gravity to move water from a reservoir into the soil, soaker hoses depend on low water pressure to push water through porous hose walls, or through small holes. Purchased soaker hoses can be snaked among plants and then covered with mulch, which makes them last longer by protecting them from sunlight. When buying a soaker hose, look for brands made from recycled materials. If you accidentally run over a soaker hose with your mower and need to repair it, the same couplers or other connecting hardware used for regular hoses can be used to fix a damaged soaker hose.

A slightly different type of soaker hose, called a sprinkler hose, has thousands of tiny holes or slits that emit a fine spray when turned hole-side-up, or work like soaker hoses when turned hole-side-down. A sprinkler hose is less efficient than a soaker hose, and may cause soil erosion around plants if the pressure is turned too high.

As long as you keep them short, homemade soaker hoses made by punching small holes into regular garden hoses will often do a good job. However, be prepared to see some holes emitting lots of water, while others weep very little. You can solve this problem by making a Crybaby Soaker Hose, or by wrapping your homemade soaker hose with strips of cloth, tightly tied in place. The fabric will help slow down water that moves through oversize holes a little too fast.

SMART SOAKING

How many soaker hoses do you need, and where should you put them? Soil is a big variable, because soil type affects how water soaks into it.

- In sandy soil, water moves downward quickly, so soaker hoses should be placed closer together and run for only 1 to 2 hours. For example, if you have sandy soil, you need 2 soaker hoses to thoroughly water one 14-inch-wide row. If no rain comes, you will need to run your watering system again in a few days.

- Loamy soil takes up water more evenly, so soaker hoses can be 12 inches apart and still give excellent penetration when turned on for about 3 hours every 4 to 5 days.

- Clay soils absorb water very slowly, so it's important to give soaker hoses plenty of time, at very low pressure, in order to deliver water deep into clay soil. When left on overnight, a single soaker hose will often rehydrate a 16-inch-wide band of clay soil. Depending on weather conditions, clay soil may retain enough moisture to keep plants happy for more than a week.

Keep in mind that soaker hoses begin putting out water in the section of hose closest to the water source, so there is often a big difference in water output between the head and tail ends of very long hoses. This is seldom a problem when soaker hoses are kept to less than 50 feet long.

Make a Crybaby Soaker Hose

You can have the advantages of a soaker hose without buying a thing by making a Crybaby Soaker Hose from an old garden hose and some plastic milk jugs. If too much water is pushed out through holes you make in the hose—a common problem with homemade soaker hoses—it is caught in the milk jugs and slowly drips into the soil below. The Crybaby Soaker Hose works best if turned on at low pressure for 1 to 2 hours.

YOU WILL NEED

Tools: Tape measure, utility knife, marker, ice pick or awl

One 15-foot-long piece of garden hose

4 to 6 half-gallon plastic milk jugs

1 female hose coupler

1 male hose coupler

1 end cap or metal clamp

1. Measure and cut a 15-foot piece of old garden hose. Lay it down the side of the row you want to water, or snake it among larger plants. Use the marker to mark places where you would like the hose to emit drips of water.

2. At each of the marked places, use an ice pick or awl to make three small holes in the hose, 2 inches apart.

3. Using the utility knife or another stout, sharp-tipped knife, cut a 1-inch-wide hole in the bottom

of the milk cartons. Then use an ice pick or awl to make three small holes in one side of each carton.

4. Thread the milk cartons over the hose, mouth first, and position them over the sets of holes you made in the hose.

5. Install the female hose coupler on the end of the hose closest to your water supply. Install the male coupler at the end of the hose, and close the end with the cap.

6. Connect the Crybaby Soaker Hose to your garden hose, and turn on the water at very low pressure. Adjust the positions of the milk cartons if needed so they collect water from the hose and then drip it into the soil in the right places.

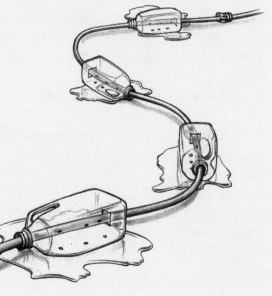

Make a Simple Outdoor Shower

When you've been working all afternoon in your garden—and picked up more mulch and compost than you want to trail inside—an outdoor shower offers a refreshing way to clean up. You can use it to rinse off veggies, too, and it can be a fun place for the kids to cool off on a hot day. Building a simple shower that connects to a faucet splitter is easy, too. This version is made by attaching a hose to a dowel that then slips into a flag bracket.

If possible, choose a location with some privacy for your outdoor shower, and keep a container of liquid soap within easy reach. If you'll be using the shower often, pave the ground beneath the shower with 3 inches of pea gravel, and then make a standing pad by nestling a wooden shipping pallet or concrete stepping-stone into the gravel. Perhaps you will even want to add hot water to your secret spot. This can be quite easy if your shower is close to a flat surface that bakes in the sun. Simply attach a long piece of dark-colored hose to your shower, coil it up in the sun, and fill it with water before you launch into the day's gardening tasks. The water will be pleasingly warm when you're ready to rinse off.

YOU WILL NEED

Tools: Screwdriver, handsaw

One flagpole bracket

One male coupler

One 3-foot-long piece of garden hose

One female coupler

One hose shut-off valve

One 24-inch-long ¾-inch or 1-inch wood dowel (size to fit flag bracket)

Three 2-inch hose clamps

One plastic garden shower head

One 14-inch piece of flexible wire

1. Using the supplied screws (or appropriate-size wood screws if none are supplied), mount the flag bracket to a wall or post about 6 feet above the ground.

2. Install a male coupler at one end of the piece of hose, and a female coupler at the other end. Screw the hose shut-off valve into the female end.

3. Attach the hose to the dowel by slipping hose clamps over both the hose and the dowel and tightening them snugly with the screwdriver. Allow the male end of the hose to project 10 inches beyond the top end of the dowel, and leave about 6 inches of bare dowel (with no hose attached) at the bottom end.

4. Screw the shower head onto the male end of the hose. Insert the free end of the dowel into the flagpole bracket.

5. Connect the shower to your garden hose, open the shut-off valve, turn on the water, and check to see if it sprays where you want it to spray. If necessary, bend the shower head into position, and secure it in place by attaching it to the dowel assembly with the wire.

Plan for Easy Cleanup

Gardening can be a dirty business, but you can keep garden debris outdoors—where it belongs—with these time-tested tips.

- On days when your garden is bursting with good things to gather, use a plastic laundry basket like a giant colander. Collect your veggies, give them a cool rinse with your hose, and then move to a shady spot to sort them before their final cleaning.
- When you have a lot of repotting to do, fill a wheelbarrow, large tub, or plastic storage bin with warm, soapy water before you get started. You can use the water to rinse your hands between projects. Toss dirty pots into the water to soak, too.
- Save small pieces of bath soap, as well as empty dishwashing detergent bottles. Use a knife to cut the soap into pieces small enough to fit through the top of the bottle. Add warm water, shake well, and you'll have a handy container of liquid soap to keep near your outdoor faucet.
- When mowing sections of your lawn near entryways, collect the clippings in your mower's bag attachment. Far fewer clippings will get tracked into the house as you come and go from your garden, and you can use the clippings as mulch.
- Make a boot scraper by nailing, screwing, or gluing a stiff-bristled brush to a sturdy board. Station it near your compost area or outside your back door, and use it to remove mud from your shoes.

Grow a Potted Lotus

Water isn't just essential for plants in your garden—it also adds beauty to your outdoor living space. You can build a Pocket Pond (see page 202) as a permanent feature in your landscape, or enjoy the company of water on your deck or patio by installing a Terra-Cotta Fountain (see page 144). Regardless of its size, any water feature brings a cool touch to the landscape, and it also can expand your gardening horizons by creating good growing space for aquatic plants.

Because they aggressively claim space with their spreading, tuberous roots, water lotus (*Nelumbo* spp.) often are not welcome in water gardens. Yet they are truly spectacular plants that thrive when grown in large containers. Early in the season, the rounded leaves rest on the water's surface. Then, as temperatures rise, so do the lotus stems, and many grow to 3 feet tall—or taller—by the time blooming begins in midsummer. Lotus blooms are beautiful, but you also should expect to be spellbound by the way raindrops form beads on the smooth leaves, and then roll about like crystal balls before plopping into the water below. A hardy lotus grown in a weather-resistant container can be left outdoors through winter to Zone 6. Farther north, simply move the container to an unheated garage or other protected place where the roots will not freeze solid.

The goldfish that live in the lotus container also are surprisingly winter hardy. If you become attached to them as pets, you can keep them indoors from late fall to spring in a goldfish bowl. During the summer, it is not necessary to feed the goldfish, which eat pondweed (buy a few sprigs when you get your fish at any aquarium shop) as well as mosquitoes and other insects. If you do feed your fish, give them no more than a pinch of fish food every 2 to 3 days.

Lotus benefit from monthly feeding from spring to fall. This is easily done by placing a teaspoon of granular or powdered organic fertilizer in a 4-inch square piece of paper towel, folding it into a packet, and slipping it onto the soil's surface. Every other spring, divide and replant your lotus by pulling up the roots, breaking them into 12-inch-long pieces, and replanting them in fresh soil. Do not use potting soil when planting your lotus. Because they are native to the mucky bottoms of ponds and slow-moving rivers, lotus prefer heavy clay soil, which you can probably dig right out of your yard.

YOU WILL NEED

Tools: Hand trowel, garden hose

One 40-quart or larger plastic storage bin or tub

2 gallons of small rocks, pebbles, or gravel

4 gallons of garden soil

1 dormant water lotus

4 or 5 pieces of pondweed

2 small comets (goldfish)

1. Place the storage bin or tub where you want to grow your lotus. Choose a warm spot on your deck or patio that receives at least 6 hours of sun each day.

2. Place half of the rocks in the bottom of the container. Spread the soil over the rocks, and dampen well.

3. Handling the lotus tuber gently to avoid breaking it, plant it in the muddy soil 2 inches deep. Position the tuber so the growing tip faces the center of the container. Cover the soil's surface with the remaining rocks.

4. Add water to bring the water level 4 inches above the soil line. Place the pondweed on the surface of the rocks, and hold it in place with some of the rocks and gravel.

5. Allow the water to settle for 1 week before introducing the goldfish. To reduce possible trauma, add fish when the water temperature is above 60 degrees.

Picking Aquatic Plants

Water lotus is the most dramatic blooming plant to grow in a still-water container, but there are many more choices to consider. The leaves of hardy water lilies (*Nymphaea* spp.) hug the water's surface, yet they are as easy to grow as lotus and come in a range of colors. To add a bit of vertical interest, add an upright plant to the rear of a container planted with water lilies. Dwarf cattail (*Typha minima*) and flag iris (*Iris* spp.) are hardy enough to be left in the container year-round, or you can use tropical plants such as dwarf papyrus (*Cyperus isocladus*) or aquatic cannas (*Canna* spp.) as temporary summer plants.

Make a Terra-Cotta Fountain

Who doesn't love the sound of trickling water from a small fountain? Fountains are surprisingly easy to make, and you can find the hardware you will need at most home supply stores. The actual design of your fountain is limited only by your imagination. If you like, you can attach ½-inch-diameter tubing to the outlet on the pump and send water coursing through hollow pieces of bamboo, artistically twisted copper pipe, or a nicely figured piece of drift-wood with a hole bored through it for the tubing.

This simple terra-cotta fountain will appear perfectly at home when set among other containers on your deck or patio. Other types of containers will work, too, including those made from plastic, fiberglass, or even concrete. Be sure that the inside of the container is sealed against moisture loss and that a hole can be made in the bottom large enough to pass the plug through it.

To keep the water in your fountain crystal clear, drain, scrub clean, and refill the container every 2 to 3 weeks. You can use the water in your garden beds, or you can use it to water nearby container-grown plants. Water that is slightly green is rich with algae, which provide nutrients that are easily taken up by thirsty plants. Before freezing weather arrives, drain, clean, and store your fountain. If left out in freezing weather, the container is likely to chip or crack.

YOU WILL NEED

Tools: Paintbrush, knife, rubber gloves

One 20-inch or larger terra-cotta pot with a large drainage hole in the bottom

1 quart of acrylic sealant

1 small submersible pump rated at 60 GPH (gallons per hour) or higher

1 cork

1 tube of latex/silicone caulk

2 brick pavers

3 bricks

1. Working outdoors or in a well-ventilated place, coat the inside of the pot with acrylic sealant. Allow the sealant to dry thoroughly, and apply a second coat.

2. When the sealant is dry, lay the container on its side. Place the pump inside the container, and thread the plug out through the drainage hole. Leave 10 inches of electrical cord inside the container.

3. Trim the cork if needed with the knife, and wedge it into the drainage hole next to the cord. Wearing rubber gloves, fill the crevices on both sides of the plugged drainage hole with caulk. Allow the caulk to dry overnight.

4. Place the pavers on the ground, and position the container over them, making sure it is level. Place the bricks inside the pot, and place the pump on top of the bricks. Adjust the height of the bricks as needed so that the top of the pump is no more than 10 inches below the top of the container.

5. Fill the container with water, and turn on the pump. If needed, adjust the height of the bricks, or the flow rate of the pump, to create the look and sound you find most pleasing.

Going Solar

The most affordable pumps for garden fountains run on electricity, and most have 6-foot-long cords. This means they must be located less than 5 feet from an electrical outlet. Finding a good place for a Terra-Cotta Fountain may not be a problem if your deck or patio has plenty of outlets. But out in your garden, you will need a weatherproof electrical outlet, called a ground fault interruptor (GFI) outlet, to power up the pump. Installation of such an outlet can be costly, but there is an alternative: a solar-powered pump. Solar-powered pumps cost more than electric ones, and most work only when the sun is shining. However, you can get a solar pump with built-in rechargeable batteries that will continue to pump at night and on cloudy days. Compared to the cost of hiring an electrician—and the fact that solar pumps generate their own free power—you may decide that buying one is a good investment. To lead the way to a fountain tucked away in a remote corner of your landscape, you might even add a few low-wattage solar-powered lights.

Watering Thirsty Containers

Everyone enjoys the close company of container-grown plants kept on a deck or patio, but keeping those containers watered can be a time-consuming chore. Large containers usually retain water longer than small ones, but in hot weather even large pots may need daily watering. Why not set up a drip system for your potted beauties similar to one you might use in your garden? Which type you choose will depend on how your containers are arranged. A row of containers is easiest to water with a Drip Pipe, but if your containers are positioned in groups, make a Taped Tube system instead.

DRIP PIPE

Measure the distance spanned by your row of containers, and buy that many feet of 2-inch-wide PVC pipe, along with a T connector and two end caps. It doesn't matter if the containers are of different heights, as long as two or more of the highest pots are of equal height. Cut the pipe in half, and install the T in the middle and the caps on the ends. Lay the pipe across the containers, and mark 3 small dots on the pipe above each container. Drill 1/8-inch holes at each mark. Store the prepared pipe behind the containers or in another safe place, and when it's time to water, just position the pipe over the containers, fill it with water through the open end of the T, and let the drips fall into all of the containers. Repeat if needed to thoroughly water your plants. It's a good idea to mark where the pipe should be positioned over the first container so you can find the right place to put it every time.

TAPED TUBE

Use a piece of string threaded over the tops of your pots to determine how much tubing you will need to drip water to your plants. Buy a piece of 1/2-inch vinyl tubing of this length, along with a roll of colored duct tape, a clamp to close down the end of the tubing, and a 1/2-inch female coupler. Install the clamp at one end of the tubing and the coupler at the other, and arrange the tubing across the tops of the containers you want to water. Wrap a small piece of tape around the hose above each container, and then puncture the hose next to the tape two or three times with an ice pick or sharp awl. Keep the holes as small as you can make them and still penetrate the hose wall. When you're ready to water, stretch your drip hose over the containers, lining up each tape mark above a container. Attach the female coupler to a hose, and turn it on at very low pressure. If the hose spurts too much water or sprays into the air, turn down the water pressure at the faucet.

Make a Rain Chain

Although you may hear the faint trickle of rainwater as it gushes through your gutter's downspouts, the visual excitement of its downward movement is hidden from view. In Japanese gardens, rain chains, called *kusari doi*, are used to guide water from the roof to the ground, where it can then be captured in pails or watering cans.

Japanese rain chains come in many styles, and they are traditionally made from copper. Weight can be a limiting factor if you install an ornate rain chain to your house's gutters, but it's easy to translate the concept of a rain chain into a pretty, practical way to gather rainwater for container-grown plants.

YOU WILL NEED

Tools: Ladder, hammer and nail or drill, wire cutters, utility knife

1 wire clothes hanger

One 8-inch-long piece of flexible wire

8 feet of decorative brass or copper-plated chain

One 2-inch snap ring

1 watering can

1 roof shingle

1 tube of latex/silicone caulk

1. Locate a section of gutter near your deck or patio where you would like to install a rain chain, and use a hammer and nail to make a ¼-inch-wide hole. If you have vinyl gutters, make the hole with a drill.

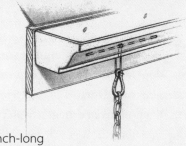

2. Cut a 6-inch-long piece of wire from the clothes hanger, and lay it across the hole inside the gutter. Working from below, thread the flexible wire through the hole, loop it around the piece of clothes hanger twice, and then bring the end back out through the hole. Secure the ends of the wire together to form a 1-inch-wide loop beneath the hole.

3. Attach the wire loop and chain together with the snap ring. Place the watering can beneath the chain, and shorten the chain if needed so that the end of the chain is about 3 inches above the watering can.

4. In winter, remove and store your rain chain, and patch the hole in the gutter with a 2-inch square of roof shingle held in place with caulk. In spring, pop off the patch with the tip of a knife, and reinstall your rain chain.

Dealing with Drought

Gardeners in dry climates are always looking for ways to conserve precious water, but no garden is immune from the effects of a prolonged drought. Watering restrictions may limit how much outdoor watering you can do, but even if you have access to unlimited water, it's important to make good use of every drop.

- **Harvest rain.** Rainwater is better for plants than water from the tap anytime—it has no chlorine or other chemical treatments, it's usually softer, and it's often warmer than water from your faucet. To make good use of rain, place small pails in places where runoff is common, such as around parked vehicles or under leaks in gutters.
- **Collect wasted water.** Keep a plastic milk jug near each faucet in your house, and collect the water you run as you wait for hot water. Keep a bucket in the bathroom and put it in the shower while you wait for the water to warm up, too. You also may be able to harvest condensation that drips from air conditioners, or use the water collected by dehumidifiers.
- **Use safe gray water.** Household water that has been lightly used can easily be recycled to plants. Safe gray water includes water used for rinsing off after showering, as well as water used to wash fruits and vegetables. Water used to boil or steam vegetables also can be used to water plants once it has cooled off.
- **Prevent weedy thieves.** Get rid of weeds that steal moisture needed by your vegetables and flowers, but instead of pulling them up, use pruning shears to clip them off at the soil line. The disturbed area left open after weeds are pulled loses water more rapidly than undisturbed soil.
- **Add more mulch.** Leave no soil unmulched during a drought. Use anything you can get your hands on, including newspapers, scrap lumber, or pieces of old carpeting.
- **Hold the fertilizer.** Plants that are stressed by drought should not be encouraged to make new growth, so wait until the drought passes to provide supplemental nutrition.
- **Coddle containers.** Set up an outdoor emergency room for plants growing in containers. Place a kiddie pool in a shady spot and line the bottom with a half-inch-thick layer of damp newspapers. If you have some old towels, wind them around and between the containers, and dampen them, too. They will slow water loss from the sides of the containers. When the drought ends, tear the newspaper into strips and add it to your compost.
- **Water at night.** Nighttime watering is often discouraged because it can increase problems with fungal diseases and slugs. Yet night is the most efficient time to dispense water to plants. Use methods that keep leaves dry, such as using a Watering Wand (see page 130), a Bucket Drip System (see page 134), or Small-Scale Drippers (see page 136).

Stretching Every Season

Making full use of the gardening year brings more food, more flowers, and more fun. Keep your garden growing in all kinds of weather with these easy projects and techniques.

Thinking Like a Plant

When you awaken in the morning, perhaps you spend a few minutes thinking of what should happen to make this day as close to perfect as it can possibly be. You can use a similar approach to stretch the seasons in your garden, only instead of thinking like a gardener, you think like a plant. What small changes could make the garden a kinder, more nurturing place for your plants? Depending on the season, the answer might be raising or lowering the soil temperature, increasing or decreasing light, or perhaps taking the sting out of blustery winds. The projects in this chapter will help you simulate or prolong the best aspects of spring, summer, and fall, and show you ways to shave several weeks off of winter. Along the way, you will discover easy ways to tame common weather factors that create tortuous conditions for plants.

CREATING MINOR MIRACLES

Harvesting the first tomatoes in your neighborhood may be your biggest reason to use season-stretching methods, but the benefits of cloches, cold frames, and shade covers go far beyond getting a head start in spring. Depending on your climate, using smart season-stretching devices may make it possible to grow a crop you've only dreamed about, whether that crop is heat-loving eggplant (a challenge in a cold climate) or crunchy lettuce (always iffy in hot climates where spring quickly gives way to summer). If certain crops simply don't seem to fit into the weather cycles that rule your garden, season-stretching tricks can help you conjure up a few extra weeks of warm or cool conditions, depending on the needs of the crop.

Flower gardeners can make great use of season-stretching strategies, too, which translates into more color over a much longer period of time. Cold-climate gardeners, for example, might use a plastic-covered tunnel (see page 174) to grow pansies, poppies, and other hardy annuals through winter, while flower lovers in warm climates can grow cool-natured calendulas or sweet peas by sowing seeds beneath a Tube Hoop Cloche (see page 160) in late winter.

Getting planting times right is something most gardeners learn through trial and error, yet quirky weather patterns have a way of turning the best-learned planting schedules into mere fantasies. The flexibility gained through using season-stretching techniques gives you at least some control over otherwise uncontrollable weather factors. For example, a Mini-Greenhouse (see page 158) can take much of the risk out of hardening off seedlings during the topsy-turvy days of spring. If you live in a windy area, you can set up Sheet Windbreaks (see page 166) each time you make a new planting. Choose projects that address the most pressing weather-related issues in your garden, and you will soon wonder how you ever gardened without them.

UNDERSTANDING THE SEASONS

By the time you started first grade, you had learned that there are four seasons in every year: spring, summer, fall, and winter. Yet as a gardener, you quickly discover that making use of the in-between seasons, such as mid-spring and late summer, is crucial to growing a healthy, productive garden. The reasons go far beyond changes in the day's high and low temperatures. If you think like a plant, several other major seasonal changes will capture your attention.

■ In late winter, days steadily become longer. Despite continuing cold temperatures, hardy perennials and shrubs often respond to lengthening days by sending energy to new buds aboveground, and to new root buds below the surface.

■ In early spring, warming soil temperatures trigger many plants to emerge from dormancy, including the ultimate form of dormancy, which we call seeds. Seeds that are coaxed to germinate ahead of schedule, and are then given protection from cold winds, will hasten the arrival of spring in the garden.

■ In mid- to late spring, as the last frost passes, warmer soil temperatures open the door to a huge range of productive plants. Days are continuing to get longer, too, which spurs many plants to race toward maturity.

■ The long days and intense light levels of summer create a dream world for plants whose ancestors came from tropical regions, such as tomatoes, peppers, and sweet potatoes. Modifying strong sun with shade covers can prevent sun-related damage and make it possible to continue planting through the hottest season.

■ Nights become longer in late summer, which is a cue for many plants to flower and set fruit while they can. For others, a shrinking quota of daylight causes their growth to slow down and reduces their motivation to develop flowers and seeds. You can use these factors to your advantage by planting a "second spring" garden in late summer that includes lettuce, broccoli, and other cool-season plants.

■ Fall is most often used as a season of ripening, but it also can be a season of new beginnings. Hardy plants such as spinach and garlic often survive winter when planted in the fall, and it's also a great time to begin preparing space for your next year's garden. And, by filling your garden with plants that flourish in the cold, short days of early winter—and providing them with protective covers—you can easily have garden-grown goodies to enjoy at your Thanksgiving table.

The projects in this chapter are arranged in approximate seasonal order, with more projects to choose from in spring—the season when all gardeners are eager to get started. Some of the projects, such as growing Perpetual Potatoes (see page 164), are designed to help you discover the season-stretching potential of certain plants, while others involve building covers or structures you can reuse for several years. After all, discovering ways to make the most of every season in your garden is a process that will continue for many years to come.

USING SEASON-STRETCHING PLANTS

It's important to remember that life goes on in the garden year-round, not just during the days between the last frost in spring and the first frost in fall. Many plants are well equipped to grow beyond these frost dates, so making use of season-stretching plants is a basic strategy for extending your garden's performance. Several talented season-stretching crops are described in the "Eight Great Season-Stretching Vegetables" chart, but these plants are only the beginning of growing a super-productive garden. Four other variables—variety selection, timed planting, the ability of plants to withstand extreme temperatures, and long storage potential—can make a huge difference in how much you harvest from your garden, and when.

Diversified Varieties

If there are certain crops you like so much that you would love to have them ready to pick for months rather than weeks, simply sow varieties that mature at different times. For example, you might indulge a passion for peas by planting a compact, fast-maturing pea at the same time you plant a long-vined variety that matures 2 or 3 weeks later. The same strategy can be used with beans, sweet corn, and even tomatoes. Along with diversifying your choices based on each variety's days to maturity, you often can choose varieties that are particularly well adapted to stressful weather. For example, most lettuce varieties with "oak leaf" in their name stand up well to heat; those described as "crisp heads," however, perform best with consistently cool temperatures.

Smart Successions

A second option is to make several small plantings of a favorite crop, which is called succession planting. In addition to extending the harvest time of fast-growing veggies such as lettuce or cucumbers, succession planting can help you avoid the feast-or-famine syndrome that often happens with extremely productive crops like summer squash or bush beans. Allow at least 3 weeks between plantings, especially in spring, when days that are becoming longer and warmer tend to speed up the growth of most vegetables.

Built for Extremes

If some parts of your gardening year can only be described as extreme, you are wise to stick with plants that know what to do when faced with frigid cold or scorching heat. With protection from a winter tunnel (see page 174), kale, spinach, and a few other vegetables can be grown through cold winters. Gardeners in hot climates can have cooking greens through summer by growing heat-tolerant Swiss chard.

Long-Storing Standouts

Growing vegetables that naturally store well for weeks or even months is tremendously satisfying, and it's an excellent reason to make room in your garden for potatoes, sweet potatoes, carrots, winter squash, onions, and garlic. While it's true that the first salad greens of the season always seem quite precious, prepare to be delighted by the aroma of a garden-grown butternut squash baking in your oven on a cold winter day.

Eight Great Season-Stretching Vegetables

NAME	TYPES	SPECIAL TALENTS	CULTURAL TIPS
Carrot (*Daucus carota*)	Root size, shape, and color vary with variety.	Sow a spring crop for harvest in summer. Carrots sown in late summer and mulched in fall will keep in the ground well into winter.	Carrots need fertile, well-worked soil. Weed early and often. In summer, use shade covers to keep soil moist until seeds germinate.
Garlic (*Allium sativum, A. ophioscorodon*)	Softneck (best in mild winter climates), hardneck (extremely cold-hardy)	Extremely cold-hardy; produces three edible crops—young greens, curved seedscapes, and long-storing bulbs	Plant cloves in fall. Keep planting free of weeds. In early summer, dig and dry bulbs when half of the leaves fade from green to brown.
Kale (*Brassica oleracea*)	Traditional (curly leaves) and "dinosaur" (ribbed leaves with blistered texture)	Extremely cold-hardy. Grow baby greens in spring; sow main crop in mid- to late summer for harvest in late fall and winter. Immature blossoms edible, too.	Grow in rich soil, or feed often with an organic, water-soluble plant food. Regular harvesting of outer leaves encourages growth of new leaves.
Onion (*Allium cepa*)	Bunch-forming scallions, bulb-forming types	All onions are edible as young scallions (green onions). Cured bulb onions keep for months in cool storage. Bunch-forming scallions are very cold-hardy.	Plant sets or seedlings of bulb onions in spring, 1 inch apart, and pull every other one to eat as scallions. Grow bunching onions as perennials, dividing and replanting in spring or fall.
Peas (*Pisum sativum*)	Shell (English), snow, snap	Seeds germinate in cold soil; young seedlings tolerate frost.	Plant in early spring. In areas with cool summer nights, a fall crop can be sown in midsummer. Extend harvest by planting various types that mature at different times.
Spinach (*Spinacia oleracea*)	Smooth leaf, savoy leaf	Grow smooth-leafed types as baby spinach in spring. Sow hardy savoyed-leaf types in late summer or early fall. Fall sowings survive winter and regrow in spring.	Plant in very rich, fertile soil or feed often with a water-soluble organic fertilizer. Pick individual leaves frequently to encourage growth of new leaves.
Swiss chard (*Beta vulgaris*)	Rib color varies with variety; may be white, red, or shades of yellow, orange, or purple	May be harvested young as baby greens, or allowed to grow into large, heat-tolerant plants. Best cooking greens for warm weather. Plants often survive winter in Zones 7 to 9.	Seed capsules contain two seeds. If both germinate, nip out one with a small pair of scissors. Twist off old leaves to encourage development of new ones.
Winter squash, butternut type (*Cucurbita moschata*)	Tan bulb-shaped (traditional) or ribbed "cheese" pumpkins	Young fruits can be eaten like summer squash; extremely nutritious mature fruits store for 4 months or more at room temperature.	Direct seed in late spring or early summer. Vines are resistant to squash vine borers. Choose mildew-resistant varieties whenever possible.

Build a Sliding Window Bed Topper

The type of structure commonly called a cold frame is one of the most versatile season-stretching devices you can have in your garden. You can use a cold frame, which is comprised of a frame with a translucent top, to harden off seedlings before planting them out; give cool-season plants such as broccoli, cabbage, lettuce, pansies, and spinach an extra-early start; or shelter tender perennials from fickle spring weather. While spring is prime cold-frame time, the protection provided by a cold frame can keep late-season greens going a few weeks longer in the fall, too. Through the winter months, a cold frame makes a great place to overwinter rooted cuttings or containers of hardy spring-flowering bulbs.

This project makes it possible to turn a Propagation Bed (see page 68) into a cold frame by outfitting it with a removable top. You also can use the Sliding Window Bed Topper to protect direct-seeded crops by simply placing it on the ground. Just as you open and close your windows to fine-tune the temperature in your house, you can slide the vinyl panel open to vent out hot air, and keep it closed to retain warmth. Increase ventilation even more by propping up the base of the Bed Topper with the scrap pieces of wood left over from trimming the sides to diagonal angles. In summer, you can remove the vinyl panel altogether, and replace it with wire screening or cloth if you need to protect plants from animal pests or hot midday sun.

Late winter and early spring are often breezy seasons, and strong winds are the worst enemy of any type of cold frame. To prevent possible wind damage, install two sets of hook-and-eye latches to fasten the back of your Bed Topper to your Propagation Bed.

YOU WILL NEED

Tools: Tape measure, marking pencil, electric saw (jigsaw or rotary saw), hammer, screwdriver, utility knife

Two 4-foot-long pieces of 1 x 6 pine lumber

Two 2-foot-long pieces of 1 x 6 pine lumber

Four 21-inch-long pieces of quarter-round molding

One 6-foot-long 1 x 2 furring strip

Twelve 1-inch-long finishing nails

Twenty-five 2-inch-long wood screws

One 2 x 4-foot piece of ⅛-inch-thick clear sheet vinyl

1. To make the back and side pieces, cut the 1 x 6 lumber to the proper lengths.

2. Make a mark 3 inches from the long outside edge on one of the 2-foot-long side pieces. Draw a diagonal line from the mark to the opposite corner. Saw along this line to make the side piece 6 inches wide at one end and 3 inches wide at the other end. Repeat with the other side piece.

3. To make runners for the sliding top, saw the quarter-round molding into four 21-inch-long pieces. Center one of the pieces of molding just inside the long diagonal edge of a side piece. Secure in place with 3 finishing nails. Nail a second piece of molding ¼ inch from the first piece to form a channel for the sheet vinyl. Repeat this step with the other side piece.

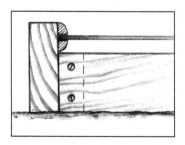

4. Saw one 4-foot-long piece (for the front of the frame) from the 1 x 2. To make corner reinforcement blocks for the topper, cut two 4-inch pieces and two 2-inch pieces from the 1 x 2.

5. Position the top, sides, and front of the topper frame together on a flat surface. Butt the ends of the back and front pieces against the ends of the side pieces (the inside width of the Topper should be 48 inches). Screw the corners of the frame together with the wood screws. Set the reinforcement blocks in each corner, with the base of each block flush with the ground. Screw the back, sides, and front of the topper to the rein-forcement blocks.

6. Set the frame up on its back, and slide the sheet vinyl into the runners. On sunny days, slide the sheet vinyl forward to create a vent at the top of the Bed Topper.

Build a Lean-To Greenhouse

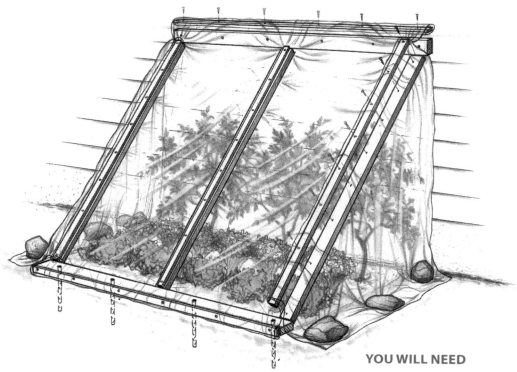

A lean-to is one of the oldest types of shelter in the world, and a lean-to covered with plastic makes a primitive yet effective greenhouse. All you need is a south-facing wall with at least 6 feet of vertical clearance that receives full sun for most of the day. It can be the wall of your house, garage, or other structure. Even a tall wood privacy fence will work as long as it's sturdy and solid enough to block cold north winds. This version is 6 feet tall at its peak, and extends outward 5 feet from the wall. That gives you about 30 square feet of growing space, or even more if you add a shelf or table to raise some plants up off the ground.

YOU WILL NEED

Tools: Tape measure, marking pencil, level, ladder, hammer, drill with ⅝-inch expansion bit, screwdriver

Five 8-foot-long 2 x 4s

1 box of 10d 3-inch nails

Four 12-inch-long pieces of ½-inch rebar (or ½-inch-diameter metal pipe)

1 piece of 4- to 6-mil opaque plastic sheeting, 10 feet wide and 25 feet long

Five 8-foot-long 1 x 2 furring strips

Forty 1¼-inch galvanized decking screws

Cross section of rafters.

1. On a south-facing wall, measure 6 feet up from the ground and mark the spot. Use a level to make an 8-foot-long horizontal line on the wall.

2. With two people, one working on the stepladder and one on the ground, lift an 8-foot-long 2 x 4 up to the mark on the wall. Lay the wide side of the 2 x 4 flat against the wall to form the header of your lean-to. Drive a nail through the end of the board into the wall. Move your ladder to the other end, check to make sure the board is level, and nail the other end in place. Secure the header to the wall by nailing every 18 inches.

3. To create the footer of your lean-to, measure and mark a spot 4 inches from the end of another 8-foot-long 2 x 4. Drill a ⅝-inch hole through the marked spot. Repeat on the opposite end of the board. Measure 2 feet in from each hole and drill two more holes.

4. On the ground, measure and mark a parallel line 5 feet from the base of the wall, exactly opposite the header. Place the prepared footer along this line. Peg the footer firmly into the ground by hammering the rebar stakes through the holes.

5. Position the three remaining 2 x 4s as evenly spaced rafters, flat sides down, with one end resting against the front edge of the header and the other end pushing against the inside edge of the footer. Place one rafter in the middle, and align the outside rafters with the outer edges of the header and footer. Nail the rafters to the header and footer by hammering nails in diagonally from the outside edges of the rafters into the header and footer.

6. Drape the plastic over the lean-to frame, leaving equal overhangs on each side. Make sure the overhanging plastic is long enough to reach the supporting wall and the ground.

7. Pull the top edge of the plastic 6 inches above the top edge of the header. Wrap the edge of the plastic around one furring strip, wedge the plastic-wrapped strip onto the top of the header, and screw it into place.

8. On one side of the lean-to, smooth the plastic from top to bottom. Lay a furring strip on top of the end rafter, sandwiching the plastic in between. Fasten the furring strip to the rafter with a screw every foot along its length. Repeat the process on the middle and end rafters. Place another furring strip over the plastic along the footer and attach it with screws.

9. Pull the ends of the plastic against the wall. You can open or close these flaps as needed to ventilate or seal the lean-to. Secure the flaps to the ground with pieces of scrap lumber, bricks, or heavy stones.

Build a Mini-Greenhouse from a Box

Today, nearly 75 percent of all cardboard boxes are recycled, but one type of box—the moisture-resistant waxed cardboard boxes used to ship produce and live plants—still gives the recycling industry fits. While recycling programs do reclaim some waxed boxes (which are often turned into artificial fireplace logs), waxed boxes often pose a disposal problem for grocers and florist shops. Ask, and you can likely get all the waxed boxes you can use. They make a great raw material for garden projects, including this Mini-Greenhouse. It's a great place for tomato seedlings that have outgrown a Drawer Light Box (see page 50), yet it's small enough to keep on your deck or patio.

For this project you will need two boxes— one for the Mini-Greenhouse itself, and another slightly larger one from which you will cut out one side to use as a hinged cover. With a few straight cuts, a little duct tape, and a scrap of plastic, you will have a Mini-Greenhouse that will stand up to wet weather for several months.

YOU WILL NEED

Tools: Utility knife, yardstick or ruler, grease pencil or crayon, scissors

2 waxed cardboard boxes of slightly different sizes

Heavy-duty aluminum foil

Duct tape

One 2-foot square piece of 4- to 6-mil clear or opaque plastic

2 wood or plastic clothespins

1. Set the smaller box on a flat surface, open end up. Use the utility knife to remove the flaps from the front and sides of the top of the box. Leave the rear flap attached. It will become the hinge for the Mini-Greenhouse cover.

2. Measure and mark points on the two front edges of the box 4 inches from the top. Draw a straight horizontal line across the front of the box between the two marks. On the sides, draw a diagonal line between the two marks and the top back edges of the box (not including the flap).

3. Use the utility knife to carefully cut along the marked lines on the front and sides of the box. To get a clean cut, score the cutting lines on the outside of the box, and then cut along the lines on the inside of the box.

4. To increase the amount of light that reaches the plants inside, line the back and sides of the box with heavy-duty aluminum foil. Tape it in place with duct tape.

5. To make a cover for your Mini-Greenhouse, cut out one large side, with its flap attached, from the larger box. Lay this panel on a flat surface, and carefully cut out the center, leaving a margin at least 2 inches wide around the edges. Do not cut into the flap.

6. Place plastic over the cover's window, and trim it to fit. Attach it at all sides with duct tape.

7. Place the cover over the sloping top of the smaller box, with the two box flaps together. Adjust how the flaps meet so the translucent top is centered over the box. Fasten the two flaps together by wrapping them several times with duct tape.

8. Place the assembled Mini-Greenhouse in a protected, sunny location. On sunny days, use clothespins to hold the cover open for ventilation.

Make Sun-Dried Veggies

When you're finished using your Mini-Greenhouse in spring, keep it in a dry place until summer, and then use it as a solar food dehydrator. Place empty food cans in the bottom, and set a baker's rack over the cans. Arrange thin zucchini slices, cherry tomato halves, or anything else you'd like to dry on the rack. Fold back the top of the box, drape a double thickness of cheesecloth over the top edges of the box to keep out insects, and then return the top to its closed position. Place the box in a sunny spot, and turn the veggies twice a day. In warm, dry weather, you should have home-dried veggies within a few days. If the weather turns rainy, shift your veggies to a 150°F oven to finish the drying process. An hour in a 150°F oven also will kill any unwanted visitors. Store your dried veggies in airtight containers in your freezer.

Make a Tube Hoop Cloche

If you want to get a head start growing widely spaced hills of potatoes, squash, or melons, or protect a drift of flowers from late freezes, you need a cloche that can cover some ground. A Tube Hoop Cloche covers a 20-inch-diameter circle, and it's easy to move from place to place. Made from easily scavenged materials, this cloche looks like a giant shower cap. An opening in the top makes it easy to vent on sunny days, or you can close it up tight when the weather turns cold. When the vent is open, a coat hanger attached to the stake keeps the plastic from falling down onto the plants below.

Get Creative with Cloches

The historical version of a garden cloche was a glass bell jar, but in more recent times, resourceful gardeners turned to cloches made from plastic milk jugs with their bottoms removed. To help hold a milk carton cloche steady in the wind, push a stick through a V-shaped cut made in the top of the handle. Leaving the top off of a milk jug cloche creates an instant vent.

To cloche a plant that's too big for a milk carton, use bubble wrap to make an insulated teepee. Place four or more 24-inch-long sticks around a plant, tie them together at the top, and enclose the base of the teepee with a 16-inch-wide band of bubble wrap (available in the office supply section at discount stores). Secure the wrapping in place with clothespins, and be sure to leave an opening at the top through which hot air can escape.

YOU WILL NEED

Tools: Heavy-duty scissors, measuring tape, utility knife, office stapler, felt-tip marker, pliers

1 bicycle inner tube

One 7-foot-long piece of old garden hose

One 4-foot-square piece of 4- or 6-mil clear plastic

1 wire coat hanger

One 20-inch-long piece of ½-inch PVC pipe

2 thick rubber bands

1. Use the scissors to remove the air valve from the inner tube by cutting across the tube on either side of the valve. Use the utility knife to trim the garden hose to 2 inches shorter than the length of the tube, or about 70 inches.

2. Slip the hose inside the tube. Overlap the ends of the tube about ½ inch. Pinch together the overlapped edges of the tube on the outside of the hoop, and staple them together.

3. Spread out the plastic, and lay the prepared tube on top.

Use the scissors to cut a circle of plastic 12 inches wider than the hoop on all sides (about 46 inches in diameter). Make 8 equally spaced marks along the outside edge of the plastic circle with a felt-tip marker.

4. Pull the loose plastic up through the center of the hoop, and staple the edge of the plastic to the outside of the hoop at equal intervals by pinching the inner tube, folding the edge of the plastic over the pinched rubber, and stapling it in place. Using the marks on the plastic as guides, begin by stapling 4 opposite points around the edge of the tube. Then install staples at midpoints between the first 4 staples. Between the 8 stapled points, gather the loose edges of plastic into pleats. Fold the pleats over and staple them to the tube.

5. Use the pliers to bend down the hook of the coat hanger. Hang the coat hanger in the top of the stake, and secure it in place with a rubber band. Push the PVC pipe stake into the ground near the plant you want to protect, and center the Tube Hoop Cloche over the stake.

6. Use scissors to cut a 6-inch-wide X in the top of the plastic. Hold the cut edges together above the top of the stake and secure them with a rubber band. On sunny days, remove the rubber band so hot air can vent out of the top of the cloche. When open, the top edges of the plastic will be supported by the clothes hanger.

7. To move the cloche, secure the top edges of the plastic to the top of the pipe with a rubber band, grasp the pipe firmly just above the coat hanger, and pull it up. Place the cloche in its new place, and push the pipe into the ground.

Ways to Warm Soil

In early spring and late fall, anything you can do to help warm up the top few inches of soil will help your plants grow faster. Plants have an easier time taking up nutrients in warm soil, and on cold nights, warmth from the soil radiates upward to give plants a few degrees of protection from extreme cold.

The most common way to warm soil is to cover it with black plastic or black fabric weed barrier. Both methods work, but why not add these two projects to your soil-warming bag of tricks? Your Solar Snake can slither among germinating seeds, and Ladybug Rocks can help keep containers warm on cold nights.

Make a Solar Snake Bed Warmer

Any bicyclist or bike shop will happily give you leaky inner tubes, which you can quickly transform into versatile bed warmers. The black rubber absorbs solar heat, which is retained by wet sand inside the tube. Unlike black plastic, Solar Snakes can be reused again and again for many years.

YOU WILL NEED

Tools: Scissors, funnel, small soda bottle
1 bicycle inner tube
4 wood clothespins
1 quart dry sand

1. Use the scissors to cut across the inner tube on either side of the valve. Fold over 2 inches on one end of the tube and secure it with 2 clothespins.

2. Hold the other end of the tube open, and slip the funnel into the opening. Slowly add about 5 handfuls of dry sand. If the funnel clogs, use a small stick to open it.

3. Remove the funnel, shake down the sand, and pour about ½ cup of water into the tube.

4. Repeat Steps 2 and 3 until the tube is full to within 3 inches of the top. Fold over the end and secure it with 2 clothespins.

5. Coil the Solar Snake over the root zone of transplants, or let it slither over a newly seeded bed.

Paint Some Ladybug Rocks

The newest ladybugs to welcome to your garden don't prey on aphids, but they can help keep plants a bit warmer in chilly weather, and double as garden ornaments during the summer months. Easy to make and great to give as gifts, Ladybug Rocks are fun to use in beds and containers, or you can let them come indoors in winter to bask in a sunny window. When using your Ladybug Rocks as bed warmers, turn them over so that their black undersides face the sun.

YOU WILL NEED

Tools: Scrub brush, newspapers, small paintbrushes

Several hand-size smooth stones

1 can flat black spray paint

1 small container red acrylic paint

1 small container white acrylic paint

1 small container blue acrylic paint

1 can semigloss polyurethane varnish

1. Use the scrub brush to thoroughly clean the stones to remove rough edges and loose bits of soil. Allow to dry thoroughly.

2. Working outdoors or in a well-ventilated place, arrange the stones on several folds of newspaper. Paint the top sides with black paint and allow it to dry. Turn the stones over and paint the other sides.

3. Paint two red wings on the back of each ladybug, following the pattern shown. Then add a smiling mouth. When the red paint is dry, add black dots to the wings. Use white paint to make eyes. When the eyes are dry, paint blue pupils inside the white ovals. Finally, use a very small brush to make a series of small white dots for antennae. Add a white dot to the center of each eye.

4. When the Ladybug Rocks are completely dry, arrange them on newspaper and spray lightly with polyurethane. Allow it to dry, turn the bugs over, and spray the other sides.

Use the heat-absorbing power of the color black to make other low-tech soil warmers from items rescued from the recycling bin. Fill clear soda bottles with stale coffee, strong tea, or another dark-colored liquid, and lay the filled bottles on their sides between plants. To keep plants beneath a plastic tunnel warm through cold nights, paint liquid laundry detergent bottles flat black, fill them with water, and set them inside the tunnel.

Grow Perpetual Potatoes

Most people eat more potatoes than any other vegetable, so it makes perfect sense to grow them every chance you get. Fortunately, potatoes are easy to grow, and if you save a few small tubers from each crop, you can keep a strain going for many seasons, just as South American gardeners have been doing for thousands of years.

In this project, regular potates are joined by sweet potatoes, which are equally fun and rewarding to grow. Regular potatoes grow best in cool weather, while sweet potatoes thrive when summer gets cooking. Long, warm summers are needed to grow heavy-yielding sweet potatoes, but anyone can grow ornamental sweet potatoes as perpetual plants. Even when grown in containers, ornamental sweet potatoes produce tuberous roots you can save and replant from year to year.

Follow these eight easy steps to grow two crops of regular potatoes, and one crop of either edible or ornamental sweet potatoes in your garden. As long as you save and replant only perfect, blemish-free tubers, you can grow, harvest, and replant your own home-grown potatoes for many satisfying seasons.

1. BEGIN WITH THE BEST

Get your start in early spring by taste-testing several types of potatoes that produce small tubers. You can use gourmet potatoes you buy to eat, or get organically grown seed potatoes from specialty producers. The small red-skinned potatoes often sold as new potatoes are a good choice, as are elongated fingerling potatoes. Set aside 1-inch-diameter potatoes, which are the best size for planting.

A month before your last spring frost is expected, place your planting potatoes in a warm windowsill. They will turn green and begin to sprout, and they'll be ready to plant in weeks. Plant small potatoes whole, or cut larger ones into chunks. Plant them as soon as the soil is dry enough to work. Use cloches if necessary to protect plants from late frosts.

2. DOUBLE YOUR FUN

As spring gets under way, either buy a tasty sweet potato at the market or pick up a potted ornamental sweet potato at a garden center. To induce an edible sweet potato to sprout, push four toothpicks into the tuber and suspend it in a jar of water, pointed end down, so that one-third of the potato is submerged. Keep your forced tuber, or your purchased plant, in a warm, sunny windowsill.

3. ADJUST THE TEMPERATURE

As soil temperatures rise in early summer, hill up an extra inch of soil over the root zones of your potatoes, and then add 2 inches of mulch to keep the soil cool and moist. It's also time to break off the leafy stems that have grown from your forced sweet potato, and transplant them to warm, sunny soil. Break off the "slips" as close to the mother potato as possible, and set them in diagonal holes so that only the topmost two leaves show at the surface. If you are growing an ornamental sweet potato, transplant it to your garden, or shift it to a large, 12-inch-wide pot.

4. MAKE YOUR FIRST HARVEST

When your potato plants begin to die back, gently harvest your first crop. Pull up the plants, and use your fingers to find all of the hidden potatoes. Wash them in cool water, pat dry, and store them in your refrigerator or another cool place. Set aside small potatoes less than 1 inch in diameter, as well as any that have turned green from contact with strong sunlight. Place these in the bottom of a 6-inch flowerpot, cover with 3 inches of lightly moist soil, and set it aside in a cool, shady place.

5. INCREASE YOUR SUPPLY

Once you see how sweet potatoes form a lush groundcover or tumble over the sides of a planter, perhaps you will want more plants. Both edible and ornamental types can be propagated by taking 4-inch-long stem tip cuttings, pinching off the lowest leaves, and planting the groomed cuttings in a container of damp potting soil. Keep the cuttings in a shady place, and they will be rooted and ready to move or transplant in only 2 weeks.

6. STAGE A COMEBACK

After resting for 3 to 4 weeks, the little potatoes saved from your spring crop will be ready to grow. Plant them 2 inches deep in a sunny, well-drained bed, and mulch immediately to insulate the roots from heat and drought.

7. DIG YOUR SWEETS

As soil temperatures begin to cool in early fall, dig and cure your sweet potatoes. The tubers often do not form right under the plants' crowns, so it's best to begin digging 3 feet away from the main growing point and work your way inward. Cure the unwashed tubers in a very warm place, such as atop your refrigerator or hot water heater, for 7 to 10 days. After this curing period, store the sweet potatoes you plan to eat in a cool, dry place where temperatures range between 55°F and 70°F.

Set aside small tubers that are less than 1½ inches in diameter for replanting, as well as roots produced by ornamental sweet potatoes. Layer the tubers in a roomy, clean flowerpot filled with a half-and-half mixture of peat moss and sand. To keep them from drying out, dribble ¼ to ½ cup of water onto the pot every 2 weeks through the winter months.

8. PULL YOUR SECOND SEASON SPUDS

Those little green potatoes you planted in late summer won't produce as heavily as your spring crop, but beneath each plant you should find several nice potatoes for eating—plus a few small ones to replant in spring. Harvest them soon after the first frost has passed. Store your extra eating potatoes in your refrigerator or another cool place where they will be well protected from sunlight. Save small 1-inch-diameter potatoes for replanting in spring. If you have no room for them in your refrigerator, keep them in a pest-proof container in your basement or garage.

Make a Sheet Windbreak

YOU WILL NEED

Tools: Tape measure, staple gun, mallet or sledgehammer

1 cup of flour or cornmeal

1 old sheet or 3 yards of 45-inch-wide fabric

Four 5- or 6-foot-long wood tomato stakes

1. Determine the direction the wind is coming from as it assails your garden, and select a place for your windbreak 3 feet on the windward side of the plants you want to protect. Measure a 7-foot-long line, and mark the two endpoints with a small amount of flour or cornmeal. Measure 22 inches inward from the end marks, and mark these two points.

2. Fold the sheet or fabric in half lengthwise, and lay it on a flat surface. Lay 2 tomato stakes along opposite edges of the folded sheet or fabric, so that the two hemmed sheet edges or selvage edges are 14 inches from the bottom tips of the stakes.

W hen cold spring winds make it tough for tender transplants and newly emerged seedlings to get growing in your garden, install an instant windbreak to give them some relief from the blustery blows. This quick-and-easy windbreak works equally well when hot summer wind threatens to bake your garden to a crisp.

This 7-foot-long Sheet Windbreak uses wooden tomato stakes and an old bed sheet. Either a twin- or full-size sheet, folded in half lengthwise, is the ideal size, or you can check fabric stores for a 45-inch-wide fabric remnant about 3 yards long. In between uses, simply pull up the windbreak, roll it up, and stow it away until your garden is again in need of its calming influence.

3. Fold the outside of each edge of the folded sheet or fabric around the two stakes, and staple them in place at 3 points along the stakes. Turn the stakes over toward the middle of the folded sheet or fabric, and staple the sheet or fabric to other sides of the stakes.

4. At the site of your windbreak, pound the two remaining stakes 12 inches into the ground at each of the two marked spots in the middle.

5. With one end stake and the attached sheet or fabric resting on the ground, pound the other end stake 12 inches into the ground at one of the marked spots at the end. Stretch the windbreak out along its length, with all stakes on the lee (garden) side of the cloth. Lightly pound the second end stake 3 inches into the ground at the opposite end.

6. Go back to the second stake, and stretch the sheet or fabric taut before stapling it to the stake. Repeat with the third stake. Pull the shallowly set end stake from the ground, stretch the sheet or fabric taut, and pound it back into the ground 12 inches deep.

7. Don't worry if wind and weather make the cloth sag slightly after a few days; it will still do a good job of blocking wind. Following heavy rain, give each stake a few sound blows to further anchor your windbreak in place.

Grow a Single-Season Windbreak

Prettier and more interesting than a cloth windbreak, a living windbreak of tall, sturdy plants is an ideal way to tame wind all season long if you garden in a windswept site. You can use a single type of plant, such as branching sunflowers, but why not mix things up by including grain-bearing plants like broomcorn (sorghum), millet, or amaranth? At the end of the summer, when their windbreak chores are done, you can harvest and eat the seeds, use the dried seed heads to make attractive wreaths and arrangements, or save them as treats for winter birds. See "Grow Gifted Grains" on page 260 for more ideas for growing and using grain-bearing plants.

When growing any plants as living windbreaks, keep in mind that a thick planting comprised of two or three closely spaced rows gives the best wind protection. For example, you might plant 10-foot-tall broomcorn on the windward side of your windbreak, with shorter millet, amaranth, and branching sunflowers on the garden side. Choosing eye-pleasing plants for the innermost layer will help your living windbreak look as good as it works. 'Italian White' sunflowers mixed with 'Purple Majesty' ornamental millet make a great high-contrast combination.

Make a Convertible Wheeled Crate

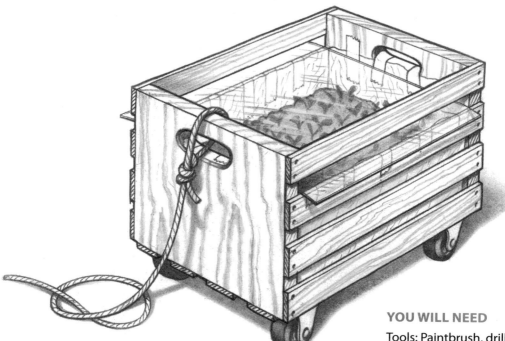

One of the tricks of keeping plants happy in spring and fall is toning down the changes that happen when the weather swings back and forth between cold and warm. If your garden is small, an excellent alternative to a cold frame is a Convertible Wheeled Crate that can be moved indoors and then back outside in a matter of minutes.

The Convertible Crate has two "convertible" features—wheels on its base, and a removable translucent top. Remove the top on warm, sunny days, but leave it on when you want the crate to work like a cold frame on wheels.

YOU WILL NEED

Tools: Paintbrush, drill, screwdriver, tape, ice pick, office stapler, yardstick, marking pen, utility knife

1 wood crate, about 24 inches long and 14 inches wide

1 small container wood sealant

4 casters with mounting screws

One 3-foot-long piece of rope or chain

1 heavy-duty black plastic garbage bag

One 40-pound bag of potting soil (more for a larger crate)

One 1/8-inch-thick piece of clear vinyl, slightly larger than the top of the crate

1. Working outdoors or in a well-ventilated place, paint all surfaces of the crate with a sealant to keep the wood from absorbing water when the crate is placed outdoors. Allow it to dry thoroughly.

2. Turn the crate upside down, and use the drill to make guide holes for the mounting screws for the casters at each corner. Install the casters.

3. Turn the crate right-side up. Attach the rope or chain to the handle on the end of the crate.

4. Keeping the garbage bag folded into a double thickness, arrange it in the center of the crate. Fold ½ inch of the long edges of the garbage bag over the next-to-the-top side slats of the crate, and use small pieces of tape to tack them in place. Tack inner corner folds with tape, too. Don't try to do a perfectly neat job, because as the crate is filled with soil, the weight of the potting soil will pull down the edges of the plastic. Between the bottom rungs of the crate, use an ice pick to poke a few drainage holes in the plastic liner.

5. Place the crate near where you plan to use it. Fill the crate two-thirds full of potting soil. You can then add more soil and plant directly into the crate, or nestle containers into the soil. Open the stapler and use it to tack the edges of the plastic bag to the inside of the crate.

6. To make a top, measure the inside dimensions of the crate. Subtract 1 inch from the length, and add 8 inches to the width. Use the yardstick and marker to draw a rectangle with these dimensions on the clear vinyl. Score the marked lines with the utility knife, flip over the vinyl, and score the marked lines on the other side. Gently bend the vinyl until it breaks along the lines. Slip the vinyl through one side of the crate so the edges rest on the next-to-the-top slats of the crate.

Grow Tender Tropicals in a Convertible Crate

If your summers are warm enough to please tropical plants like cannas and caladiums, but you don't want to have to dig and store the roots through winter, grow them in a Convertible Crate. Simply add board slats to the sides of the crate to use it as a planter, or grow your plants in large containers nestled inside the crate. Wheel the Convertible Crate indoors when temperatures drop in the fall, and move it back outdoors when the weather warms in spring. Through winter, the crate can double as a storage box for the dormant tubers provided you keep it in a place where temperatures stay well above freezing. A Convertible Crate is also perfect for growing dwarf citrus trees (like calamondin orange or 'Meyer' lemon), which love to spend summer outside and winter indoors.

Make a Movable Sun Shade

Step into the shade after spending even a few minutes under the sizzling sun on a cloudless July afternoon and you'll instantly understand the relief your seedlings will feel if you finish off the transplanting process with a Movable Sun Shade. If you're faced with a serious drought, and you can only offer selected plants enough water to keep them alive, using a Sun Shade also can reduce evaporation, so the plants can make use of every precious drop.

This simple project creates a portable shade panel that can be set up or taken down quickly, so you will always have easy access to garden beds for weeding, mulching, and watering. Hooks and eyes are used to attach the shade screen to stakes, so it can be suspended over a newly planted row and you won't need to worry that a sudden thunderstorm will send it crashing down onto your plants. If you want higher shade, simply attach the Sun Shade to taller stakes. Providing modest midsummer shade often improves summer fruit set of tomatoes and peppers, which often bloom but set no fruit under very hot conditions. To use your Sun Shade to keep newly seeded beds moist in hot weather, or to cool down the root zones of drought-stressed plants, you can install your shade panel lengthwise on the south side of your plants, with one long edge resting on the ground. Then attach the Sun Shade to stakes installed at either end. The Sun Shade also makes a handy sunscreen for newly divided perennials being grown in a Propagation Bed (see page 68).

YOU WILL NEED

Tools: Measuring tape, pencil, handsaw, drill, screwdriver, scissors, staple gun

Two 8-foot-long 1 x 2 furring strips

Sixteen 1¼-inch decking screws

4 hook-and-eye latches

Four 24-inch-long wood stakes

2 yards of 45-inch-wide lightweight muslin fabric

1. Measure, mark, and cut each of the furring strips into two pieces: one 6 feet long and one 2 feet long.

2. On a flat surface, lay the long pieces parallel to each other, broad sides down. Lay the short pieces over the ends of the long pieces to form a rectangle. Tack each corner together with one decking screw. Check to make sure the frame is square, and add a second screw at each corner. Gently flip the frame over on the other side. Secure each corner with two more screws to increase the frame's stability.

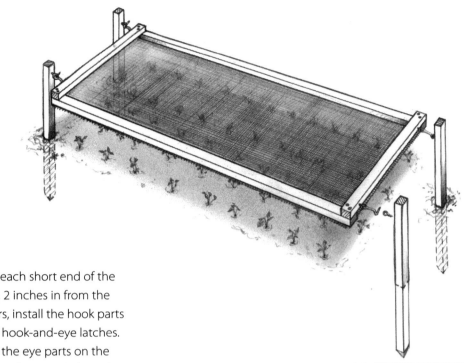

3. On each short end of the frame, 2 inches in from the corners, install the hook parts of the hook-and-eye latches. Install the eye parts on the wood stakes, 1 inch from the tops of the stakes.

4. Lay the fabric out on a flat surface, and measure, mark, and cut it into a 6-foot-long by 26-inch-wide rectangle. Starting with the long edges of the frame, fold under 1 inch along the edge of the fabric, and staple the fabric to the frame. Do the same with the short edges.

5. To install the shade panel, push or pound two stakes into the ground, 20 inches apart. Attach one end of the frame to the stakes, and then install the stakes for the other end.

More Easy Ways to Make Shade

Almost all vegetables—and many flowers—require abundant sunshine to flourish, but that does not mean that they need full sun all the time. Plants especially appreciate a bit of relief during their first week or two in the garden, when their main task is to grow dependable roots. Shade covers for tender transplants are helpful in spring, but in late summer, when you are setting out seedlings for your fall garden, they are essential. To provide short-term shade to individual plants, simply cover them with upturned flowerpots or small cardboard boxes for a few days after transplanting. Don't worry that the darkness will hurt your plants. They will make use of their shade break by spending their time settling in to their new life in the garden.

Making the Most of Fall

Most of us can't wait to get our hands in the dirt in spring, and as the season winds down in late summer, so do we. But why let a perfectly good mini-season pass you by? Fall weather is ideal for growing vegetables that like cool conditions, and it's the perfect time to get started with a few special flowers, too. You can even use the fall season to get a head start on planting projects, such as creating a special compost heap (see "Make a Cucurbit Compost Pile" on page 28) or sowing a patch of hairy vetch for No-Work Tomatoes (see page 18).

FINE FALL VEGGIES

The Asian Stir-Fry Garden (at right) can help you fill vacant spaces in your vegetable garden, or you can stick with more traditional fall crops such as broccoli, cauliflower, collards, mustard, and kale. Lettuce, spinach, arugula, radishes, and other salad crops grow beautifully in the fall, too, and some will even grow through winter with good protection (see "Make a Winter Tunnel" on page 174).

The list gets even longer if you plan ahead and manage to get carrots, beets, cabbage, and slow-growing Brussels sprouts into the ground in late summer. Whatever you do, don't miss the many opportunities for gardening in the fall. In addition to eating from your garden longer, you will find that you are also eating better because the quality of many vegetables improves when they mature in cool autumn weather.

FALL-TO-SPRING FLOWERS

The planting of pansies has become a familiar ritual for flower lovers because cold-tolerant pansies often survive winter as far north as Zone 4. But many of us have yet to discover the early rewards that result from scattering seeds of hardy annual and biennial flowers in our gardens every fall. If you sow seeds of the five flowers listed below in the fall, you will find that some germinate right away, others come to life in winter (often beneath snow), and still others emerge as seedlings in spring. Another surprise to look for when working with these fall-to-spring flowers is their ability to self-sow when grown in a place that pleases them.

- Cornflower (*Centaurea cyanus*), also called bachelor button. Colors include blue, pink, white, and wine red. Hardy to Zone 6.
- Foxglove (*Digitalis purpurea*) bears tall spikes studded with pink, white, or purple-throated bells. Hardy to Zone 4.
- Lunaria (*Lunaria annua*), also called Honesty. Pretty pink flowers give way to pretty coin-shaped seedpods. Hardy to Zone 5.
- Rose Campion (*Lychnis coronaria*). Felted gray foliage looks great in partial shade; flowers range from white to magenta. Hardy to Zone 3.
- Sweet William (*Dianthus barbatus*). Rounded pink, white, red, or bicolored flower clusters are often fragrant. Hardy to Zone 3.

GROW AN ASIAN STIR-FRY GARDEN

If you love Asian food, fall is the time to celebrate your passion in your garden. All you will need is a patch of rich soil, a handy water supply, and an assortment of seeds.

When should you get started? Count back 45 days from your area's average first frost date, and you will know the perfect time to plant your Asian Stir-Fry Garden. The four vegetables listed here grow fast and tolerate light frost. You can start thinning your planting—and eating the baby plants you pull—only 3 weeks after planting. And, if you cover your Stir-Fry Garden during fall's first cold spells (see "Great Garden Cover-Ups" on page 176), you can continue harvesting nutritious veggies as fall turns to winter.

Depending on your climate, you may need to use special techniques to keep your Asian Stir-Fry Garden on track. If hot, dry weather prevails at planting time, use a Movable Sun Shade to help keep the soil moist until the seeds germinate. Leaf-eating flea beetles and aphids sometimes attack young plants, but they won't have a chance if you cover your bed with a fabric rowcover. These Asian vegetables also need moist soil to support strong, steady growth, which is easily provided with a Watering Wand (see page 130).

DECIDING WHAT TO GROW

The vegetables listed in the "Four Stir-Fry Standouts" chart represent four very different vegetables that belong to a single species—*Brassica rapa*. The original wild strain is thought to be native to Southern Europe, but over a period of 500 years, gardeners in China and Japan developed numerous subspecies, or groups. Some produce thick stems, others feature delectable leaves, and the type we call turnip is prized for its round, crunchy root. Exploring the differences between each type of vegetable makes great garden fun, and great eating, too.

Four Stir-Fry Standouts

NAME	DAYS TO MATURITY	GROWING TIPS	SPACING
Broccoli Raab (*Brassica rapa* var. *ruvo*)	40 days	Cut 6-inch-long bud-bearing stems just before yellow flowers open. Steam or stir-fry before eating.	Space seeds 2 inches apart; thin plants to 4 inches apart.
Chinese Cabbage (*Brassica rapa* var. *pekinensis*)	50 days	Crisp stems and lettucelike leaves make a great slaw. Pull whole plants, and eat raw or cooked.	Space seeds 2 inches apart; gradually thin to 8 inches apart.
Pac Choi (*Brassica rapa* var. *chinensis*)	50 days	Thick, crisp stems form a tight head. Pull whole plants and lightly steam or stir-fry.	Space seeds 2 inches apart; gradually thin to 8 inches apart.
Turnip (*Brassica rapa* var. *rapifera*)	45 days	Young leaves make great stir-fry greens. Pull bulbs when young and tender, and enjoy them raw or cooked.	Space seeds 1 inch apart; gradually thin to 3 inches apart.

Make a Winter Tunnel

The end of summer doesn't have to mean the end of enjoying freshly harvested food from your garden. With the help of a plastic-covered tunnel, you can enjoy a home-grown salad with your Thanksgiving dinner—and maybe even with your New Year's Day brunch! This project makes a low tunnel that's 5 feet long and 3 feet wide—a good size for growing compact salad crops, but not so large that it is likely to be torn apart by strong winter winds.

Ice and snow are likely features of winter weather, so it's essential that the tunnel be very well supported. This is easily accomplished by using welded wire, bent into an arch, as the support structure for the tunnel.

In mild winter areas, be sure to open the ends of the tunnel to provide ventilation on sunny winter days, and monitor the soil beneath the tunnel to make sure it does not become extremely dry. In all climates, expect the growth of your under-cover crops to be slow in December and January, when short days and limited sunshine often cause plants to stop producing new leaves. Wait for a mild day in February or early March to open your tunnel, drench the plants with a water-soluble organic fertilizer, and then cover it up again. Within weeks, you will be picking plenty of fresh salad greens from your over-wintered plants.

YOU WILL NEED

Tools: Measuring tape, garden spade, heavy-duty wire snips or bolt cutters, hammer, wheelbarrow, scissors, staple gun

One 6-foot-long piece of 5-foot-wide concrete reinforcing wire

Four 18-inch-long wood or rebar stakes

One 25 x 10-foot sheet of clear 4 or 6-mil plastic

One 5-foot-long piece of 2 x 4 lumber

Several large rocks or heavy pieces of firewood

Wood or plastic clothespins

1. In September (or October in Zones 7 and 8), prepare a 5 x 3-foot bed in a fertile, sunny spot. Plant the bed with cold-hardy salad vegetables including spinach, kale, butter-head lettuce, chicory, mache, arugula, and endive. Plug a few green onions into the middle of the bed. Water every few days until the plants are up and growing.

2. Two weeks before your first frost is expected, install the tunnel. Use the wire snips or bolt cutters to cut the concrete reinforcing wire to length, and bend it into an arch over the bed. At each corner of the bed, pound a rebar stake into the ground diagonally to help hold the arch in place.

3. Dig a 4-inch-deep trench along the outside of one long side of the bed, and place the excavated soil in a wheelbarrow. Lay the sheet of plastic over the arch so that 4 feet of plastic (or more) extends from each end of the tunnel. Align one side edge so it extends 2 inches beyond the outside

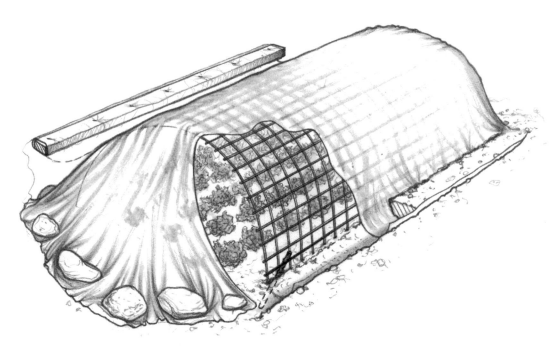

of the trench. Refill the trench with soil, covering the plastic. You should still be able to see the edge of the plastic.

4. Pull the plastic over the arch to the opposite side. Trim off excess plastic, leaving about 12 inches extra. Place the 2 x 4 over the edge of the plastic and staple the plastic to the wood. Roll the 2 x 4 over until the plastic is tight, and staple the plastic in place again.

5. Gather the plastic on the ends of the tunnel into folds, pull the folds taut to the ground, and weight the ends with several large rocks, or wrap them around heavy pieces of firewood.

6. Open the ends of the tunnel on mild days, and secure the bunched plastic with clothespins. Water your crops as often as needed to keep the soil moist. To weed and harvest, open the ends and the side attached to the board. Before periods of cold, windy weather, check your tunnel to make sure all of the edges are secured.

Curl Up a Cage

In summer, you can take the same piece of welded wire you use for your winter tunnel to make a sturdy tomato cage. Simply curl the arch into a cylinder, wire or tie the ends together, and place it around your tomatoes. Be sure to include diagonal stakes to help anchor the cage in place. Guy wires also may be needed as robust tomatoes become top-heavy with fruit.

Great Garden Cover-Ups

Weather can change fast, but it's easy to be prepared for plunging temperatures, heat waves, or even leaf-shredding hailstorms. Just as you cover yourself with jackets, sunscreen, or a sturdy umbrella, plan in advance to protect your plants from the elements with appropriate outerwear.

HANDY HARD HATS

In spring, when every gardener plays hide-and-seek with late frosts, you can win the game every time with the help of hard hats—flowerpots, buckets, and cardboard boxes that can be popped over plants in minutes, and removed with equal ease when mild weather returns. It's ideal to have a number of pots or pails that can be stacked together. The stack can be left at the garden's edge, safe from strong wind. Hard hats usually need to be weighted with a brick or stone, but don't bother to lug these back and forth from a storage place. Instead, simply leave them on the ground near your plants, or arrange them into a temporary edging along the side of a bed.

Big plants need larger hats, and it's hard to beat bushel baskets if you need to protect robust plants from hail or extreme sun. Baskets also make fine temporary shade covers for plants that must be set out in hot weather. Cardboard boxes don't last as long as baskets, but they're more trustworthy in strong wind when the flaps are weighted with bricks or stones.

LOFTY LINENS

Any type of blanket that you drape over your plants will give them several extra degrees of warmth on a cold night, but the best ones are lightweight insulated blankets that tend to shed water instead of absorbing it. Bedspreads, comforters, sleeping bags, or mattress pads that include a puffy layer of polyester filling are perfect, and the bigger the better. To keep blankets from rubbing against the growing tips of your plants, support them with several stakes, or cover plants with hard hats before adding a blanket. In fall, you can drape blankets right over beans, peppers, and frost-sensitive flowers. The weight of a blanket may flatten the plants a little, but they will regain their shape as the leaves and stems are warmed by the sun.

CAGES STUFFED WITH FLUFF

One of the basic ways to enhance the cold-hardiness of plants is to pile on plenty of winter mulch, yet doing so can set the scene for disease complications due to damp conditions over the plant's crown. You can get the insulating advantages of mulch without this unwanted side effect by surrounding plants with wire cages that can then be stuffed with a light, fluffy material such as wheat straw or pine needles. Another option is to cover resting plants with a coarse layer of evergreen boughs before moving in with mulch. The boughs form a cushion that prevents suffocation of shallow buds.

CHAPTER 6

Attracting Wildlife to Your Garden

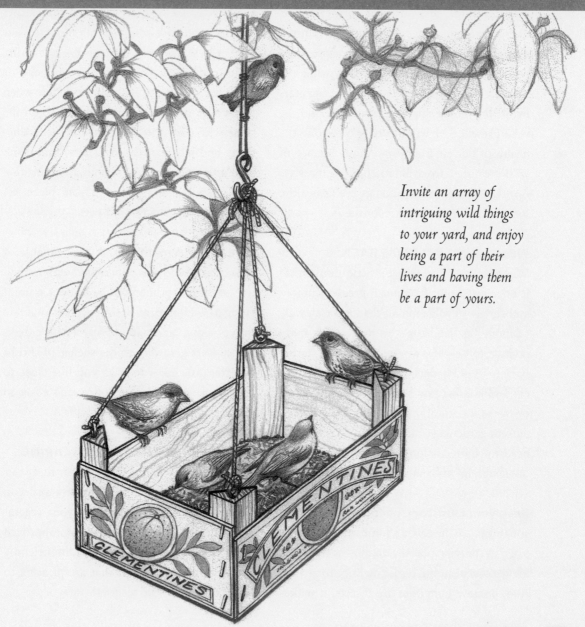

Invite an array of intriguing wild things to your yard, and enjoy being a part of their lives and having them be a part of yours.

Why Welcome Wildlife?

From the buzz of insects to the trill of bird songs, wild creatures of all shapes and sizes help connect us to the natural world. Their natural rhythms—migrating, hibernating, raising young—help free us from the unnatural rhythms our own lives sometimes follow. Their beauty rests our eyes, while the intricate behaviors of wild things are as amazing as the most complex technology. And the very presence of wildlife tells us about the health of our environment. An abundance of wild creatures, from microscopic to massive, is a sign that our surroundings are as healthy for our families as they are for theirs.

WELCOMING WILDLIFE BACK

Wherever you live, there's little doubt that it once was home to a much greater number and variety of wild animals than it is today. By adapting our landscapes to make them more inviting to wildlife, we are welcoming nature back to its old haunts. Before you set out feeders and houses, sow butterfly-magnet plants, or install a natural pond, take a look at your current gardening practices. Some things may need to change before your yard is ready to host buntings and bunnies.

Keep your landscape pesticide-free. Most songbirds eat insects at some stage in their lives, so spraying poisons on bugs is like feeding it to the beautiful birds you hope to attract. And, because butterflies *are* insects, it makes little sense to spray pesticides if you enjoy seeing butterflies flutter through your yard.

Curb your pets. Even well-fed house cats love to hunt, so if you're luring birds to your yard with food, make sure you're not luring them to their deaths. Keep Kitty indoors, or make her wear a bell that warns wildlife when she is near, and ask your neighbors to do the same with their cats. Dogs also hunt instinctively and will harass any critters that catch their attention. If you're serious about making wild animals feel at home at your place, set some boundaries with your pets.

Give up your manicure. A bare expanse of closely cropped grass punctuated with a small tree and tightly pruned shrubs is about as uninviting to wildlife as an acre of asphalt. Wildlife thrives along landscape edges, where grasses and flowers give way to the shelter of shrubs and trees. Be as orderly as you like close to your house, but enhance your yard's edges to make it more hospitable to wildlife.

WILDLIFE-FRIENDLY LANDSCAPING

As you lure in wildlife, don't worry that your yard will turn into a wild jungle—and you certainly don't have to sacrifice your vegetable garden. Instead, take a positive approach by stocking your yard with wildlife-friendly plants, arranged in ways that are pleasing to you and to your wild visitors.

- Look for ways to create pathways for wildlife to travel through your landscape.
- Plant a hedge that includes berry-producing shrubs and evergreens for year-round shelter and winter food.
- Work with your neighbors to form connected greenways for birds and animals.

BALANCING BENEFITS

It's natural that the pleasure you find in gardening should lead you to an interest in your landscape's wild side. Yet when it comes to wildlife, cute is in the eye of the beholder. Chipmunks are fun to watch until they uproot an entire planter full of pansies while digging for seeds. Deer appear elegant until they eat a patch of expensive tulips you've waited all winter to see bloom.

Gardening to attract wildlife is a balancing act between your commitment to preserve and protect nature and your desire to create a landscape that satisfies your family's needs for food, recreation, and beauty. You can achieve both goals by taking a strategic approach to sharing your landscape with wildlife.

SUCCESSFUL SHARING

The old saying about good fences making good neighbors is practical guidance when it comes to sharing your landscape with wildlife. As much as human development allows, wildlife live, roam, and eat according to their instincts. Most of the wild creatures that enter your domain will show little interest in your gardens, but it takes only one or two troublemakers to take the pleasure out of playing host to your wild neighbors. A little planning—and some sturdy fencing—can help keep wildlife from raiding your garden and spoiling your fun.

- Place feeding stations away from your vegetable garden, fruit trees, and berry patch.
- Provide desirable alternatives. Plant a mulberry tree to give fruit-eating birds something other than your blueberries and cherries to dine on; sow a patch of "bunny" lettuce far from your garden and close to sheltering shrubbery.
- Use fences, netting, rowcovers, passive scare devices, and other techniques to keep your food from becoming their food. See Chapter 7, "Solving Pest Problems in Earth-Safe Ways," for proven methods and projects that will keep unwanted critters out of your garden.

Who's at Home in Your 'Hood?

Where you live determines, in large part, what species of wildlife are likely to appear in your yard. A visiting armadillo is an improbable (at best) guest in a Minnesota garden, and a Stellar's jay (a western species) would be a surprising rarity in South Carolina. Visit your local library, talk to wildlife-minded neighbors, or join a bird-watching group to learn more about what kinds of birds, reptiles, and mammals call your region home. Then take steps to provide the types of food and shelter that will make them feel welcome in your landscape.

Give 'Em Shelter

Providing shelter is the best way to attract different kinds of wild creatures to your landscape. Every creature needs a place to hide from predators, rest, and perhaps raise their young. More than shortages of natural food or water, a scant supply of suitable habitat is responsible for the shrinking populations of many wild species. Giving wildlife a place to live and reproduce in your landscape can be a treat for you, too. You'll have the chance to see species that don't visit feeders, and you may enjoy the rare pleasure of watching fledgling birds testing their wings in first flight, or the remarkable sight of a mother opossum with her babies clinging to her back.

HEDGE YOUR BETS

Creating shelter for wildlife is relatively simple. While you might think first about building houses for birds and animals, most wild animals—even the cavity-nesters that houses are meant for—prefer natural sites for nesting and cover. With a little planning, your landscape can include the sorts of natural shelter that wild birds and animals like best and need most. A well-placed evergreen windbreak, for example, can help lower your heating costs by sheltering your house from winter winds, and at the same time provide roosting and nesting places for birds, as well as cover for many small mammals.

Like an evergreen windbreak, a hedge of mixed evergreen or deciduous shrubs creates superb shelter for wildlife. By providing a long row of unbroken shelter, a hedge lets small animals move through their habitat unseen by predators. It offers safe nesting spots for songbirds, and a place where they can dash for cover when a hawk flies overhead. Hedges that include fruit-producing plants serve as a food supply, too.

A wildlife hedge need not be carefully pruned, and will probably be more attractive to you, and to wildlife, if it is comprised of a tangle of evergreen and berry-bearing deciduous shrubs. The plants listed below are easy to grow and can be woven into a wildlife-friendly hedge. If you don't have room for a long hedge, try mixing shelter and food shrubs together by grouping several together along the outer edge of your landscape.

12 TERRIFIC SHELTER AND FOOD SHRUBS

Barberries (*Berberis* spp.)

Bayberries, wax myrtles (*Myrica* spp.)

Cranberry bush (*Viburnum trilobum*)

Elderberries (*Sambucus* spp.)

Hollies (*Ilex* spp.)

Junipers (*Juniperus* spp.)

Lilacs (*Syringa* spp.)

Mahonia (*Mahonia aquifolium*)

Manzanitas (*Arctostaphylos* spp.)

Ninebark (*Physocarpus* spp.)

Rugosa rose (*Rosa rugosa*)

Yews (*Taxus* spp.)

STAND UP FOR SNAGS

A dead, decaying tree, which is called a snag, may not fit your vision of landscape loveliness, but it's an ideal home for many cavity-nesting birds and animals. The most adorable birdhouse you can imagine won't get a second look from chickadees, nuthatches, titmice, woodpeckers, and wrens if there's snag space available. Kestrels and owls often move into holes created by woodpeckers, as do squirrels and raccoons. In addition to spaces for nesting and roosting, snags often host wood-eating insects, so they are also a food source for insect-eating birds and mammals.

Whenever possible, leave room in your landscape for this perfect wildlife refuge. If you find yourself confronted by a landscape tree that is dead or dying, consider your options before firing up the chain saw.

- Is it a hazard to people or property? Sometimes trimming off a few limbs reduces the likelihood that the tree might cause damage.
- Can you leave a significant part of it? A 12- to 20-foot trunk is better than no snag at all.
- Is it attractive? With the addition of plants, feeders, or drilled nesting holes, a dead tree may become the liveliest focal point in a wildlife lover's landscape.

If the top of the remaining trunk is at a reasonably accessible height (for you, not for the birds), top it with a birdbath or a hopper feeder. Drill holes into the trunk and stuff them with suet or peanut butter. Drive a few long nails into the trunk and use them to serve halves of apples or oranges. Mount a hanger

Lay Down the Log

If a standing snag isn't feasible in your landscape, consider a log instead. You can turn a section of a fallen tree trunk or even a substantial branch into a "horizontal snag" by simply placing it on the ground. Once it's in place, wildlife will discover the log and move in. Small mammals like chipmunks and rabbits will nest under it, as will toads, snakes, salamanders, and lizards. Woodpeckers will fly in to hunt for insects during the day, and skunks may make nighttime visits for the same reason. To find a suitable piece of deadwood, ask permission to search in local woods, particularly after a storm has moved through the area. Utility companies, tree services, and parks departments are other potential sources for a nice log.

arm and hang a tube feeder from it. Birds will flock in to enjoy the treats you provide.

Don't worry, by the way, about the insects that arrive to chomp and chew through the decaying wood of a dead tree—they're not about to attack other plants in your landscape. The insects that feast on dead trees are specifically there for that purpose, and healthy landscape plants are not their cup of tea.

However, insect-eating birds regard wood-chomping insects as a delicacy. Snags often attract woodpeckers and other birds for whom wood-eating insects are dietary staples.

Make a Cagey Fruit and Suet Feeder

Serving fruit to tempt orioles, mockingbirds, catbirds, house finches, Carolina wrens, thrashers, and other fruit-loving birds is as easy as impaling an orange half on a sturdy nail and waiting to see who flies in for a sweet meal. Unfortunately, the birds may lose out on this treat when squirrels, raccoons, and other varmints discover that they can make off with the fruit. Capable of doing double duty as a box for purchased suet cakes, this simple feeder lets birds enjoy halves of oranges or apples while deterring greedy starlings, raccoons, and squirrels.

YOU WILL NEED

Tools: Measuring tape, pencil, saw, drill with ¼-inch bit, wire cutters, hammer, screwdriver

One 22-inch-long piece of 1 x 2 furring strip

1 wire clothes hanger

Eight 2-inch nails

1 scrap board or shingle, 8 to 12 inches long and 6 to 8 inches wide

One 6-inch-square piece of wire hardware cloth with ½-inch mesh

One 2-inch-long piece of thin scrap wood or wood craft stick

One 3-inch nail

2 screws

1. Saw the furring strip into two 6-inch pieces and two 5-inch pieces. Lay them on a flat surface to form a square frame. Use the drill to make matching holes through the lower sides of the frame 1 inch from the bottom of the side pieces. Use the wire cutters to cut the straight bottom from the clothes hanger, and check to see that it easily passes through the drilled holes in the sides. Set the hanger wire aside.

2. Use 6 of the 2-inch nails to nail the frame pieces into a square on the scrap board or shingle base.

3. Cut a square of hardware cloth to match the size of the frame. Weave the hanger wire through the bottom of the hardware cloth, and then push the ends through the holes in the sides of the frame. Use wire cutters to bend them back toward the base.

4. Turn the feeder over, and drive a 2-inch nail through the back of the baseboard, so that its tip protrudes through the center of the wooden frame.

5. Loosely nail the 2-inch-long piece of scrap wood or craft stick to the top of the frame to hold the hardware cloth door closed. Drive a 3-inch nail into the base of the frame to serve as a perch.

6. Drill guide holes for the mounting screws, and securely attach the feeder to a sturdy post or dead tree. Stock it with a halved apple, orange, or a cake of suet.

Setting the Table for Birds

Just like relatives, birds and other wild creatures will beat a path to your garden if they can find a free meal there. Many songbirds love sunflower and other seeds, while woodpeckers and nuthatches prefer a high-fat diet of nuts and suet. Several of the showiest birds prefer fruit. To attract the widest variety of birds, provide special feeders stocked with different foods in different parts of your yard. In addition to the fruit feeder, you can make a "Goldfinch-Getter" tube feeder (see page 186), turn a fruit box into a tray feeder (see page 184), or make a stone landing trimmed with fragrant herbs for the area where you offer tempting seeds (see page 188).

If you're just getting started feeding birds and other wildlife, do a little research to see who's likely to visit, and at what time of year. Check with your neighbors or your local cooperative extension office to get the scoop on the birds and other critters that live in or migrate through your area. Then set the table accordingly, putting out only a little food at first, so there's less wasted if it goes uneaten. When you start to get takers, increase the supply to match the demand. With a little patience, you'll be amazed at the variety of wildlife that shows up looking for breakfast in your yard. Different species may show up at dusk for an early dinner.

Make an "Oh My Darling" Tray Feeder

Providing meals for birds and other wildlife doesn't have to be a budget-buster—and your wild guests won't groan "not this again" like your family does when they find leftovers on the table. Foods such as bread or pizza crusts, crushed crackers, leftover pasta, fruit pieces, and crumbled suet work best when offered on a tray feeder's flat feeding surface. In addition, these freebies can help to draw bossy crows, jays, magpies, pigeons, and starlings away from your seed feeders, reducing your seed bill and giving your favorite songbirds a chance to enjoy their preferred foods in peace.

Tray feeders are a handy way to offer all sorts of foods that don't lend themselves to other types of feeders, so they're the perfect place to serve bird-friendly leftovers. A tray with a wire mesh bottom will let some crumbs sift through, but it also lets water drain away, so foods on the tray don't get soggy (and moldy) if they sit for a couple of days. Even so, keep an eye on treats that you put on your tray feeder. If birds don't gobble them up in a day or two, empty the tray and try offering your feathered friends something else.

Making a tray feeder is easy. Treat yourself to a box of the sweet little oranges known as clementines, and then transform the lightweight wooden box into a feeder. If you don't have a fruit box, use an old picture frame with its back removed as a tray feeder frame.

YOU WILL NEED

Tools: Tin snips, staple gun, drill

One 24-inch-square piece of aluminum screening

1 open-topped fruit box

4 small screw eyes

4 yards of nylon cord or lightweight chain

One 12- to 18-inch piece of wire

1 S hook

1. Cut a piece of aluminum screening to match the outside dimensions of your wooden box. Staple the aluminum screening to the bottom of the box to keep feeder foods from falling through the cracks and corner holes.

2. Drill a small pilot hole at each corner of the top (open side) of the box and insert a screw eye in each hole. Fasten a piece of cord to each screw eye. Join the other ends at the top, so the feeder hangs parallel to the ground.

3. Loop the wire over a tree limb, fasten the ends securely, and use the S hook to attach the feeder to the wire.

Whooo's There?

Birds and squirrels will visit a tray feeder by day, but after dark, your tray feeder may host a different clientele, including some who come to dine on the other diners!

Flying squirrels are seed-eaters like their chipmunk and squirrel cousins, but they're active at night. Just because you don't see them doesn't mean they aren't around. Feeders that seem to empty overnight are a clue that these small squirrels are gliding into your feeding station while you sleep.

Mice are quick to find seeds and other morsels on the ground below bird feeders, and they'll quickly adopt a routine of visiting your feeding station for a nightly buffet. Keep the area around your feeders tidy to avoid attracting mice (and their larger rodent relatives).

Opossums eat a wide range of foods, and these curious-looking marsupials may stop by your feeders after dark for a late-night snack. Splay-footed star-shaped tracks around your feeders may be the first sign you see of opossums in your yard.

Owls don't eat seeds, but these efficient predators may fly in on muffled wings to hunt mice that are feasting on fallen bits of food. Since people rarely get to see these carnivorous cavity-nesters, owls can be a good reason to tolerate mice around your feeders.

Raccoons may become nightly regulars, especially if you have a water source nearby for their well-known "washing" rituals. Intelligent and persistent, raccoons can become unwelcome garden raiders, so locate feeders as far as possible from your cultivated crops.

Make a Goldfinch-Getter Tube Feeder

This easy homemade feeder serves up the shard-shaped seeds known as nyjer, niger, or (inaccurately) thistle seed to beautiful goldfinches, redpolls, and siskins while protecting the expensive seed from raids by seed-gobbling starlings and squirrels. Because this feeder has no perches, greedy house finches can't pig out on the nyjer it holds. Goldfinches and pine siskins, meanwhile, will cling to the screen wire and enjoy a feast of their favorite feeder food.

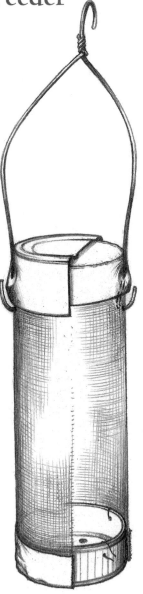

YOU WILL NEED

Tools: Sturdy gloves, tin snips, drill with small (1/16-inch) bit, hammer, needle-nose pliers

One 12-inch-square piece of aluminum screening

1 plastic jar lid (from a peanut butter or mayonnaise jar)

1 tuna can

Thin flexible wire, such as florist's wire, cut into 4-inch pieces

Duct tape or electrical tape

1 large nail

1 wire pants hanger, with cardboard removed

Nyjer seeds

1. Wearing gloves to protect your hands, use the tin snips to cut an 11- by 12-inch rectangle of aluminum screening.

2. Roll the screening into a 12-inch-tall tube, overlapping the ends as needed to make a diameter that fits snugly around the outside of the plastic jar lid (the feeder's bottom), and the inside of the tuna can (the feeder's top). Secure the edges with short pieces of wire in 3 or 4 places along the tube's length.

3. Drill 4 evenly spaced holes into the side of the jar lid. Then drill 3 more holes through the top of the lid for drainage. Make sure these holes are smaller than the diameter of nyjer seeds.

4. Slip the jar lid inside the bottom of your tube, open side up, and thread florist's wire through the screening and the drilled holes in the sides of the lid to fasten it securely in place. Wrap the outside of the base of the tube with electrical tape or duct tape to further secure the tube to the jar lid, and to cover any protruding pieces of wire.

5. Using the nail and hammer, make two opposing holes in the sides of the tuna can. The holes should be large enough so that the clothes hanger wire will pass through them easily.

6. Use the pliers to straighten the ends of the two corners of the hanger, but leave the hooked hanging part intact. Then bend the ends inward, so that the hanger forms a long triangle. Push the ends of the wire through the holes in the can from the outside.

7. Reinforce the top of the screen tube with a band of duct tape. Poke the ends of the wire into the tube, through the tape and then outward through the screening.

8. Use the pliers to bend and shape the hanger wire as needed so the lid will slide up for filling the feeder.

9. To make it easy to collect spillage, place the finished feeder on a piece of news- paper before filling it with nyjer seeds. Hang your feeder from a branch or sturdy hook and watch for the cheery flashes of yellow that tell you goldfinches have discovered this special treat.

Grow a Blooming Birdseed Garden

Goldfinches and other seed-loving birds will enjoy the flowers listed below, not for their colorful blossoms but for the bounty of seeds that those flowers produce. Until the seeds ripen, butterflies will visit these flowers to collect nectar, and bees will gather pollen. Allow some of the blossoms to remain on the plants until they begin to shatter, and watch the show as birds enjoy snapping them up.

Bachelor buttons (*Centaurea cyanus*), annual, all Zones
Black-eyed Susan (*Rudbeckia* spp.), perennial or annual, all Zones
Coreopsis (*Coreopsis lanceolata*), perennial, Zones 4–9
Cosmos (*Cosmos bipinnatus, C. sulphureus*), annual, all Zones
Globe thistle (*Echinops ritro*), perennial, Zones 3–9
Goldenrods (*Solidago* spp.), perennial, Zones 3–9
Marigolds (*Tagetes* spp.), annual, all Zones
Purple coneflower (*Echinacea purpurea*), perennial, Zones 3–9
Sunflower (*Helianthus annuus*), annual, all Zones
Zinnias (*Zinnia* spp.), annual, all Zones

Pave the Way to Bird-Feeding Ease

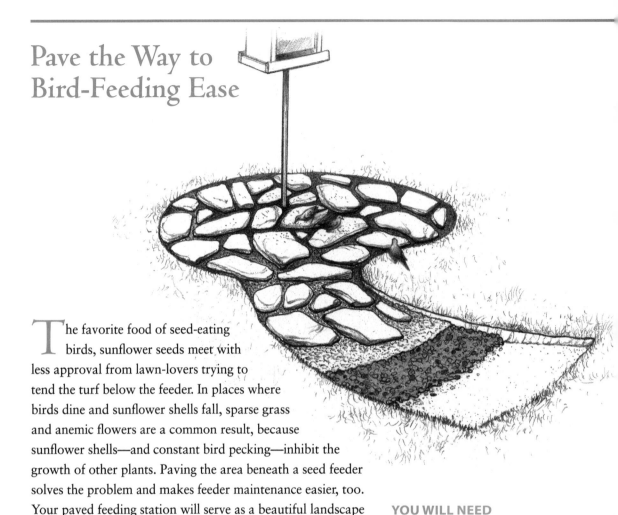

The favorite food of seed-eating birds, sunflower seeds meet with less approval from lawn-lovers trying to tend the turf below the feeder. In places where birds dine and sunflower shells fall, sparse grass and anemic flowers are a common result, because sunflower shells—and constant bird pecking—inhibit the growth of other plants. Paving the area beneath a seed feeder solves the problem and makes feeder maintenance easier, too. Your paved feeding station will serve as a beautiful landscape focal point even when no birds are present.

Installing pavers involves a bit of heavy lifting, but it's an otherwise easy project that produces long-lasting results. Doing the math to figure out how many flagstones or pavers you need is simple multiplication, but you may get confused when estimating how much paver base and sand to buy. These materials are sold in 40- to 60-pound bags, which contain a specified measurement in cubic feet (this information is printed on the label). One cubic foot is 12 inches wide and deep, so a cubic foot of crushed stone will cover 6 square feet when spread 2 inches deep (12 divided by 2 equals 6).

YOU WILL NEED

Tools: Stakes and string, shovel, wheelbarrow, tamping tool, carpenter's level, mallet, broom

Flagstones or brick pavers

Crushed stone, sometimes called paver base

Coarse sand, also called builder's sand

1. Mark off the area you wish to pave. For straight-edged shapes, use stakes and string to mark the space; for irregular or curved shapes, mark the border with flour, flexible garden hose, or rope.

2. Measure the space you've marked, then dust off your math skills and determine its area by multiplying its length by its width. Get enough pavers or flat flagstones to cover the area.

3. Shovel out the soil to a depth of 4 inches. Use the excavated soil to fill raised beds or for other garden projects. To improve drainage, dig the foundation so that it has a very slight slope of about ¼ inch per 2 feet of space, slanted downward to the edges.

4. Fill the excavated area with 2 inches of crushed stone. Tamp it down firmly with a flat tamping tool or with the end of a 4 x 4 landscaping timber.

5. Top the crushed stone with a 1-inch layer of coarse sand. Tamp it down firmly.

6. Starting with the straightest edge, lay your stones or pavers in place, leaving ¼ inch between them. Leave larger crevices near edges where you'd like to grow herbs or other crevice plants. Use the carpenter's level to make sure adjoining stones or pavers are even.

7. Take a moment to look at the layout of your pavers. If you're happy with how things look, use the mallet to tap each paver into its spot. If your pavers appear uneven or crooked, remove them and re-level the crushed stone and sand base.

8. Toss sand onto the paved area and sweep it into the spaces between the pavers. Sprinkle the area lightly with a hose to help settle the sand into the joints, and add more sand if needed to fill in the crevices.

Big Benefits from Crevice Plants

Tuck low-growing herbs like creeping thymes (*Thymus* spp.), Corsican mint (*Mentha requienii*), or Roman chamomile (*Chamaemelum nobile*) into the spaces between pavers to help connect your feeding station with the rest of your landscape, and to prevent problems with weeds. Sprinkle seeds into cracks and cover them lightly with sand, or install small plants in planting pockets between the pavers. Water regularly until seedlings or plants are well established. In addition to softening the hard edges of the paving, these herbs will release their sweet scents when you step on them while tending your feeders. Their small flowers will provide food for bees and numerous tiny beneficial insects, too, and some of the insects that visit the flowers will become food for insect-eating birds.

Open a Circus for Squirrels

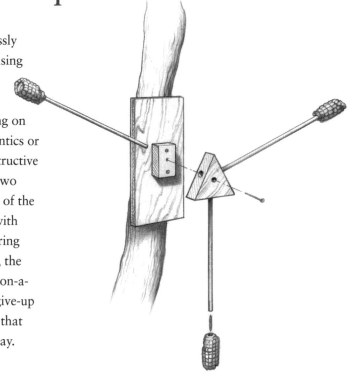

Intelligent, acrobatic, and endlessly persistent, squirrels can be amusing or aggravating. If you enjoy feeding wild birds, your feelings about squirrels will vary, depending on whether you're laughing at their antics or cursing their greedy and often destructive raids on your bird feeders. These two squirrel feeders will help put some of the humor back in your relationship with those bushy-tailed raiders. By offering dried corn, a true squirrel favorite, the Squirrel Spinner and the Squirrels-on-a-Spring transform squirrels' never-give-up attitude into a circuslike sideshow that can brighten the dreariest winter day.

Make a Squirrel Spinner

Dizzy squirrels are a frequent result of this simple spinner that holds three ears of dried corn at the end of its wooden spokes. The fun usually lasts until the squirrels manage to pull the corn free of the spinner and make off with them.

YOU WILL NEED

Tools: Drill with ³⁄₁₆- and ¾-inch bits, pliers, hammer, screwdriver

3 wooden dowels, 24 inches long and ¾ inch in diameter

Three ¼ x 3-inch hanger bolts

1 wood triangle, 2 inches thick, with 4-inch sides

Glue

Three ¾-inch nails or brads

1 piece of scrap wood, 10 to 12 inches long and 4 inches wide

1 block of wood, approximately 2 inches thick and 4 inches square

Two 2-inch finishing nails

One 3-inch nail with head

Two 2-inch wood screws

1. Using a ³⁄₁₆-inch bit, drill guide holes into the ends of the dowels. Use pliers to screw the bolts into the guide holes, so that the pointed screw ends (for mounting ears of corn) point outward.

2. Drill three 1-inch-deep, ¾-inch-diameter holes into the center of each side of the wood triangle. Then use a ³⁄₁₆-inch drill bit to drill a hole through the center of the triangle.

3. Put a few drops of glue into each ¾-inch hole and on the screw-free end of each dowel. Insert the dowels into the holes. For added stability, tap a small nail or brad through the back of the triangle and into each dowel. Wait for the glue to dry.

4. Set the scrap wood on a level surface, and place the 4-inch-square block of wood in the center. Nail them together with the finishing nails. Then set the wood triangle with attached dowels on top. Partially drive the 3-inch nail through the hole in the middle of the wood triangle and into the block of wood until it's about ¾-inch deep—deep enough to secure the triangle while letting it turn freely on the nail.

5. Use wood screws to mount the spinner on a post or dead tree, about 5 feet above the ground.

6. Twist an ear of corn onto the screw at the end of each dowel, and wait for the fun to begin.

Watch Squirrels-on-a-Spring

A testament to the lengths squirrels will go to in order to get at an ear of corn, this bouncy device made from an elastic bungee cord (tie-down) attached to a length of chain gives any squirrel that manages to mount it a first-rate ride.

YOU WILL NEED
Tools: Pliers, ladder
1 large screw eye
One 18-inch bungee cord
One 24-inch length of lightweight chain
One 12-inch piece of split garden hose or bicycle inner tube

1. Use pliers to fasten a screw eye to one end of the bungee cord, and the chain to the other end, by squeezing the end hooks closed.

2. Loop the end of the chain around a horizontal tree branch about 6 feet from the ground. Cushion the chain with a split section of garden hose or bicycle inner tube to keep it from injuring the bark before fastening it in place.

3. Twist an ear of dried corn onto the screw eye so that it dangles about 3 feet above the ground. Enjoy watching squirrels bungee jump to the corn, and the speed with which they solve this puzzle.

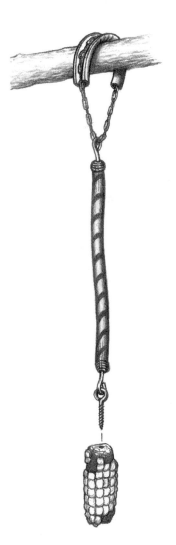

Make a Gourd Birdhouse

Bulb-shaped hard-shell gourds are fun and easy to grow (see page 280), and they make wonderful houses for birds. Birds don't mind if their house has a natural finish, or you can scrub the gourd with a copper dish scrubber, allow it to dry, and then paint it to create a birdhouse that's pretty and functional. Do be careful to gauge the size of the entry hole to the type of bird you hope to attract, because birds prefer a hole that's so small that predators can't get in to rob the cradle. Some of the most common birds that like gourd houses—and living near people—include wrens, chickadees, titmice, and sparrows. Tailor the house to suit wrens or chickadees by making the entry hole only 1 to 1⅛ inch wide. Titmice and sparrows prefer a 1½-inch-wide entry hole.

YOU WILL NEED

Tools: Disposable dust mask, drill with ⅛-inch bit, keyhole saw, long-handled fork or spoon

1 dry gourd, 8 to 10 inches in diameter

2 feet of sturdy, flexible wire

1. Shake the gourd to loosen the seeds inside it. Put on a dust mask (many people are allergic to gourd dust). Holding the gourd on a steady surface, use the drill to start the entry hole: Drill 3 small holes, ¼ inch apart, just above the widest part of the gourd. Enlarge the hole to its finished size with the keyhole saw.

2. Turn the gourd upside-down, and make three small holes in the bottom. Should rain blow into the house, it will drain out through these holes.

3. Shake the loose seeds and membranes out through the entry hole. Then use the fork or spoon to scrape out any remaining loose material. If desired, sand the gourd and then paint it with light-colored exterior enamel paint (dark colors will cause the house to overheat on hot days).

4. Drill 2 small holes on either side of the stem, 1½ inches from the top. Run flexible wire through the holes and twist it over the top of the gourd to form a hanger.

5. Choose a spot to hang the house where your new tenants will be in plain view, but far enough from open windows so you won't be bothered by the chirping of hungry chicks.

Be a Good Landlord

Providing housing for birds, and watching their private lives, can make it difficult to leave home. Whether you make gourd houses, supply custom nesting boxes, or put up purchased birdhouses, consider these guidelines to make sure that your tenants are safe and satisfied.

Go with quiet colors. Beware of brightly painted, overly decorated birdhouses. Birds care little for exterior décor, and bright colors may attract unwanted visits from bees and hummingbirds.

No perch, please. Cavity-nesting birds have strong feet and good gripping abilities. A perch on the front of a house gives less agile starlings or other pushy birds something to hold onto as they try to take over a smaller bird's nest.

Choose quality construction. Birdhouses assembled with screws last longer than those built with nails. Nest boxes made of wood are more durable and better insulated against heat and cold than those made of cardboard, plastic, or metal.

Not too tight. A roof that keeps out rain is essential, but ventilation and drainage are also necessary features of a good birdhouse. Holes for ventilation keep young birds from overheating on sunny days, and drainage holes allow any water that gets into the house to escape.

Location matters. Attracting the occupants you want involves putting the right house in the right place. When choosing a site, consider a bird's preferred habitat over your own. Putting the right box in the wrong spot usually results in an empty house.

Provide a security system. Nest boxes mounted on trees or wooden posts are more accessible to climbing predators, including squirrels, raccoons, snakes, and cats. Smooth metal or PVC poles offer the greatest security to nest box occupants because they are impossible to climb.

Create a Hummingbird Haven

Hummingbirds don't eat seeds, suet, or fruit, but a combination of resting places, red flowers, and nectar feeders makes an inviting haven for jewel-like hummingbirds. A single sugar-water feeder will attract these zippy flyers to your yard, but they're more likely to stick around your landscape if they also find plenty of tubular flowers to supply them with natural nectar. Fortunately, many of the same flowers that attract hummingbirds also attract butterflies, and the two creatures coexist quite peaceably. See "Favored Flowers for Natural Nectar" on page 196 for a list of top hummingbird plants.

Meanwhile, use a feeder stocked with sugar water to lure hummingbirds close enough so you can see them easily by looking out of your windows. Wait until mid-spring or later, because hummingbirds migrate south in the winter. Setting up an appealing hummingbird site is remarkably simple, and once the tiny birds make a habit of visiting, they will return daily until nature calls them to fly to the tropics in fall.

1. Stretch a thin wire between two posts—such as on a porch or beneath an arbor—and hang one or more nectar feeders from it. Decorate the wire with a few red ribbons or red silk flowers to get the hummers' attention and to keep unsuspecting humans from accidentally running into it. Hummingbirds will sometimes perch on the wire between visits to feeders and flowers.

2. Include flowers that bloom red, and others with tubular blossoms, in your garden, or in pots or hanging baskets. Red petunias, impatiens, or geraniums will attract hungry hummers, as will any color of salvia or lantana. Grow beautiful blue morning glories up the support posts next to the feeders. Hummingbirds find the color red irresistible, but you will often see them sipping nectar from lavender hostas or pink geraniums. Hummingbirds don't read plant lists, and once they find a flower they like, they will return to it again and again.

FEEDER FEATURES AND FILLING

Hummingbird feeders are easily found in supermarkets, chain drugstores, hardware stores, and specialty bird centers. They come in a wide range of prices and styles. Choose a feeder that suits your needs, as well as the birds'. It should be easy to clean and refill, and have a translucent nectar reservoir that lets you see when it needs cleaning or refilling. Also look for guards over the feeding ports, which keep wasps and bees from becoming a nuisance. If the feeder you like best is not made of bright red plastic—the color that catches a hummingbird's eye—just fasten a red artificial flower to it the first few times you put it out. Hummingbirds will quickly figure out that it's the feeder, not the flower, that merits their attention.

Perches aren't necessary on a hummingbird feeder, because these tiny dynamos hover while they drink by lapping with their long tongues. But hummers sometimes will use perches between sips, as will woodpeckers and songbirds that discover the sweet treat. If the competition for nectar at your hummingbird feeder becomes too intense, consider removing the perches or switching to a perchless model.

There's no need to spend money on commercial nectar mixes. To make nectar for your feeder, combine 1 part sugar with 4 parts water—for example, ¼ cup of sugar to 1 cup of water—and bring the mixture to a boil. Do not add red food coloring, and don't use honey in place of sugar. Food coloring is unnecessary, and honey poses a hazard to hummingbirds' health. Let the "nectar" cool, then fill your feeder. Store any extra nectar in the refrigerator for up to a week. To keep mold from growing in the feeder, clean out any remaining nectar every 2 or 3 days, wash the reservoir and feeding ports, and refill it with fresh sugar water.

Best in the West

While bird watching is generally an equal-opportunity activity across North America, with each region having its fair share of species to enjoy, that's not the case with hummingbirds. A nectar feeder in Nashville may fairly hum with hummers all summer long, but it stands almost no chance of hosting anything like the variety of hummingbirds that may appear at a nectar feeder in Tucson. With the exception of the coastal areas of Louisiana, Mississippi, and Alabama, North America east of the Mississippi River plays host to just one species— the ruby-throated hummingbird. Over 20 more species make their way north from Mexico and Central America each summer to feed on flower nectar in the west.

Favored Flowers for Natural Nectar

PLANT NAME	LIFE CYCLE	DESCRIPTION	SITE
Bee balm (*Monarda didyma*)	Hardy perennial, Zones 4–9	Red or pink flowers in midsummer attract hummingbirds, butterflies, and bees. Leaves used to make tea.	Rich, moist soil in partial shade
Cardinal flower (*Lobelia cardinalis*)	Hardy perennial, Zones 5–9	Deep red flowers cover tall stems from midsummer into fall, welcoming hummingbirds and butterflies. Good for damp sites.	Average to wet soil in partial shade
Cleome, spiderflower (*Cleome hassleriana*)	Annual	Airy clusters of fragrant pink, white, or purple flowers top 4- to 5-foot-tall stems from midsummer to fall. Often reseeds.	Average to dry soil in sun or partial shade
Columbines (*Aquilegia* spp.)	Hardy perennial, Zones 3–9	Elegant spurred flowers, in many colors and bicolors, appear in spring and early summer. Often reseeds.	Rich, well-drained soil in partial shade
Coral bells (*Heuchera* spp. and hybrids)	Hardy perennial, Zones 4–10	Vertical stalks studded with tubular red, pink, or white flowers rise above neat mounds of rounded, often variegated leaves.	Moist, well-drained soil in partial shade
Four-o'clocks (*Mirabilis jalapa*)	Perennial in Zones 7–9; annual elsewhere	Fragrant tubular flowers in red, pink, yellow, or white open in late afternoon from midsummer to frost. Often reseeds.	Average soil in sun or partial shade
Impatiens (*Impatiens walleriana*)	Tropical perennial grown as an annual	Jewel-toned flowers in a rainbow of reds, oranges, pinks, purples, white, and bicolor combinations tempt hummingbirds from late spring until frost.	Evenly moist, well-drained soil or containers in sun to shade
Nasturtium (*Tropaeolum majus*)	Annual	Single, funnel-shaped flowers bloom through summer in shades of red, orange, yellow, and white. Flowers and leaves are edible.	Average to dry soil or containers in full sun
Nicotiana, flowering tobacco (*Nicotiana* spp.)	Tender perennial grown as an annual	Fragrant trumpet-shaped flowers of red, white, pink, purple, yellow-green, or white rise above broad, fuzzy leaves. Good for an evening garden.	Moist, rich soil or containers in sun to partial shade
Petunias (*Petunia* spp. and hybrids)	Annual	Bright funnel-shaped flowers come in a huge range of colors and bicolor combinations. Many are fragrant at night.	Average to rich soil or containers in sun to partial shade
Salvia, pineapple sage (*Salvia elegans*)	Tender perennial grown as an annual	Upright spikes of sweet-smelling, tubular flowers from early summer to frost. Red varieties attract the most hummingbirds.	Moist, fertile soil or containers in sun or partial shade
Sunflower, Mexican (*Tithonia rotundifolia*)	Annual	Red-orange daisies bloom on bushy, 3- to 6-foot-tall plants from midsummer into fall. Excellent cut flowers.	Average, well-drained soil in full sun

Best Bloomers for Butterflies

PLANT NAME	LIFE CYCLE	DESCRIPTION	SITE
Asters (native *Aster* spp.)	Hardy perennial, Zones 4–8	Late-blooming plants produce a profusion of small daisylike blooms in late summer or fall, much loved by migrating monarchs.	Moist, moderately rich soil in full sun to shade, depending on species
Blazing star (native *Liatris* spp.)	Hardy perennial, Zones 4–9	Fuzzy spikes of purple-pink flowers welcome swallowtails and other butterflies from midsummer to early fall.	Moist but well-drained soil in full sun
Butterfly bush (*Buddleia davidii*)	Deciduous shrub, Zones 6–9	Elongated purple, pink, or white flower spikes lure butterflies from summer to fall. Remove faded flowers to prolong bloom time and limit reseeding.	Average, well-drained soil in full sun
Butterfly weed (*Asclepias tuberosa*)	Hardy perennial, Zones 3–10	Bright clusters of orange, red, yellow, or pink flowers in midsummer. Often used as a food plant by butterfly larvae.	Well-drained soil in full sun
Coneflower, purple (*Echinacea purpurea*)	Hardy perennial, Zones 3–10	Purple, white, or orange daisies with orange-brown centers produce nectar for butterflies and seeds for birds. Roots used medicinally.	Rich, well-drained soil in full sun or partial shade
Daylilies (*Hemerocallis* hybrids)	Hardy perennial, Zones 4–10	Large trumpet-shaped blooms in endless shades of orange, yellow, and red. Many newer varieties rebloom with good care.	Average soil in full sun to partial shade
Goldenrods (*Solidago* cultivars)	Hardy perennial, Zones 5–9	Golden plumes of tiny flowers top bushy plants in late summer and fall. Named cultivars are prettier and less invasive than wild species.	Average soil in full sun to partial shade
Joe-Pye weed (*Eupatorium* spp.)	Hardy perennial, Zones 3–9	Sturdy, statuesque plants grow up to 7 feet tall, topped by rounded clusters of pink, purple, or white flowers in late summer.	Moist soil in full sun to partial shade
Lantana (*Lantana* hybrids)	Perennial in Zones 8–10; annual elsewhere	Clusters of small flowers bloom from late spring to fall in a range of colors. Can be invasive in warm climates.	Moist, well-drained soil in full sun
Phlox, garden (*Phlox paniculata*)	Hardy perennial, Zones 4–8	Clusters of pink, purple, white, blue, or red flowers top 3- to 4-foot stems from summer to fall. Deadhead to prolong bloom time.	Moist, rich soil in full sun to partial shade
Verbena, garden (*Verbena* x *hybrida*)	Perennial in Zones 7–9; annual elsewhere	Low-growing spreader produces clusters of small purple, red, pink, white, or peach flowers from summer to frost.	Moist, well-drained soil in full sun
Zinnia (*Zinnia elegans*)	Annual	Single daisy-flowered varieties with prominent yellow florets in the centers are best for butterflies. Deadhead to prolong bloom time.	Average soil in full sun

Three Great Ways to Beckon Butterflies

You will see plenty of butterflies flitting through your garden if you grow some of the flowers described in the "Best Bloomers for Butterflies" chart on the previous page, but why not go a step further by providing "flying flowers" with more things they like? All summer long, fruit that's no longer fit for humans can be set out on a Butterfly Fruit Plate, and

Put a Fruit Plate on the Menu

Instead of a sundial, gazing ball, or other garden ornament that butterflies will ignore, put a fruit plate on a pedestal in your garden to serve butterflies a tasty (to them) treat. Using two sturdy plastic picnic-style plates makes it easy to clean up leftovers and to replenish the feeder. Keep in mind that butterflies like their fruit overripe (to the point of liquefaction) because they drink their meals through their strawlike tongues.

1. Select a spot in your garden and install a suitable pedestal. The base of a ceramic birdbath will work nicely, as will a 4 x 4 inch wooden post.

2. Attach a plastic plate to the top of your pedestal. If you have a ceramic base, use a bead of caulk or all-purpose glue to attach the plate; if you have a wooden post, nail the plate to the top of the post.

3. Put a second plate on top of the first one and secure it with two or three spring-type clothespins around the rim.

4. Put a few pieces of very ripe fruit on the plate and wait to see who flutters in to dine. Cut the fruit into halves or chunks, so butterflies can get to the softest parts. Be patient—you may have to wait a day or two for the fruit to become mushy enough and for butterflies to discover this treat.

5. When the fruit becomes so rotten that even the butterflies can no longer bear it, unclip the top plate and scrape the remains into your compost bin. Clean the plate and fill it with another round of overripe fruit.

Make a Pebble Puddle

Moisture and mud may seem like unusual butterfly attractants, but butterflies love to stand on a pebble and sip muddy water. Male butterflies often gather to drink together, so they are the most common visitors at a Pebble Puddle. To dress up your butterfly watering hole, place a few broad, flat stones nearby in a spot that gets morning sun. On cool mornings, butterflies will use them as basking spots, where they can warm up in preparation for their day's work.

1. Fill a shallow container, such as a plant saucer, garbage can lid, or a shallow food storage box, with pebbles.

2. Select a sunny spot in your garden, and bury the container almost to the rim. Leave 2 inches of bare soil around the outside of the container.

3. Add water to within ¼ inch of the tops of the pebbles. After filling the container, soak the surrounding soil until it's muddy.

4. Watch for butterflies stopping in to take a sip. If butterflies visit the mud but not the dish of pebbles, add a handful of soil to the pebbles to increase the salts in the water. Make it a regular habit—daily during the hot days of summer—to visit the area to moisten the pebbles and the mud.

thirsty butterflies will pause to sip mineral-rich water from a Pebble Puddle.

But there still may be a missing piece needed to turn your yard into a good butterfly habitat: plants that larval butterflies (caterpillars) like to eat. Most caterpillars grow up on a diet of wild tree, shrub, or weed leaves, but a few prefer herbs and other garden plants. Plant a few extra carrot family herbs, and you can watch the drama as tiny green and black-striped caterpillars gain size daily, and eventually become black swallowtail butterflies.

The small, fragrant flowers of many herbs also attract wild and domestic bees, which provide their pollination services free of charge.

Also expect to see a huge range of beneficial buzzers that help keep peskier insects under control. In addition to the nine butterfly (and beneficial insect) beckoning herbs listed here, you will find more ideas for growing, eating, and crafting with herbs on page 266.

Chives (*Allium schoenoprasum*)
Garlic chives (*Allium tuberosum*)
Dill (*Anethum graveolens*)
Lavender (*Lavandula* spp.)
Oregano (*Origanum* spp.)
Parsley (*Petroselinum crispum*)
Rosemary (*Rosmarinus* spp.)
Pineapple sage (*Salvia elegans*)
Creeping thyme (*Thymus serpyllum*)

Build a Toad Palace

When you're creating homes and hangouts for fast-moving wild things, don't forget a gardener's favorite slug-muncher, the humble toad. Contrary to old beliefs, toads are not slimy, nor do they give you warts if you touch them. Toads are able to emit a toxic fluid when they're threatened, but it's meant to get them out of a predator's mouth before it's too late. It won't harm you at all, unless you get it in your eyes.

If you have rock piles, a dry streambed, or a stone wall in your yard, chances are good that toads have already taken up residence in the cool, moist shelter beneath the stones. But why not give them a special place of their own? A small stone cavern that stays cool and moist will give garden toads a place to rest during the day, so they can emerge refreshed at nightfall, ready to patrol for tasty insects.

YOU WILL NEED

Tools: Shovel, carpenter's level, handsaw

1 gallon of play sand

One 4-inch-long piece of 3-inch-diameter PVC pipe

30 assorted flat stones, 2 to 4 inches in diameter

2 sturdy sticks, 12 inches long and 1 inch in diameter

3 or 4 flat stones, 8 inches in diameter

Shade-tolerant foliage plants, such as hostas, heucheras, or hardy ferns

1. In a shady spot in your yard, dig a square hole 8 inches deep and 10 inches across. Use the level to make sure the edges of the hole are level. Cover the bottom of the hole with 1 inch of sand, and dampen it well.

2. Use the saw to cut the PVC pipe to length, cutting one end at a diagonal angle. Decide where you want the entrance to be, and dig a diagonal trench for the pipe, which will be the entrance tunnel. Position the pipe so that the angled end protrudes just above the soil line, with the long edge on top.

3. Line the sides of the hole with the small flat stones. Place the sticks across the top of the hole, and then install a roof made of the larger flat stones. If needed, add more small stones around the edges of the roof, and pile a few on top of the entrance pipe, too.

4. Set a few shade-tolerant plants around the entrance and edges of your Toad Palace.

Other Toad-Tempting Tactics

If you don't "dig" the idea of excavating a hole for toads, a large upended clay pot with an entryway chipped into the rim works reasonably well. Tuck a flowerpot toad house into a damp, shady spot in the garden.

In addition to providing housing and hiding places, you can add other features that will make your landscape more inviting to toads and small frogs.

- Go organic. Most gardens have insects in profusion, but remember that toads like their meals clean and green. Chemical applications to eliminate insects will eliminate your toad population, too. Let toads take care of pests such as slugs, earwigs, sowbugs, cutworms, and gypsy moths—a single toad will gobble up 10,000 or more in a single season.
- Give them a drink—or a swimming pool. A shallow container of water, such as a plant saucer or a birdbath basin, set into the soil in your garden will supply toads with necessary moisture during the growing season. But if you want to be sure that your garden will benefit from the insect-eating prowess of toads, give them a shallow garden pond such as the Goldfish Pocket Pond on page 202, where they can lay their eggs and you can watch little tadpoles grow to maturity.
- Turn on a light. If you've ever startled a toad while it was dining beneath your porch light on a summer evening, you know that toads seek out places where nocturnal creepy-crawlies tend to congregate. Give them their very own night-light, mounted no higher than 3 feet off the ground and located at the edge of a garden area, and toads will quickly adopt it as their favorite nightspot for grabbing their evening grub.

Create a Pocket Pond for Goldfish

Installing a pond requires quite a bit of digging, but it has big payoffs for you and many insects and animals. Toads and frogs, newts and salamanders, dragonflies and water striders will set up residence in and around a small pond, while birds of all types will come to drink and bathe in the shallow water at its edge. At night, raccoons may find the pond's edge to be the perfect place for a quick cleanup.

Flexible liners let you design a pond in almost any shape you can think of, but it's best to start small with a pond that is not outfitted with pumps and filters, which require special electrical wiring. In a small pocket pond, aquatic plants will keep the water nicely oxygenated, and goldfish will snap up any mosquitoes that dare to enter. The fish will get most of the food they need from the plants. You can feed your fish for pleasure, but not out of necessity.

Goldfish are surprisingly cold tolerant, though they move very little when water temperatures are below 50 degrees. In climates where ice less than 3 inches thick is likely to form in winter, the goldfish can stay in the pond year-round. In colder climates, keep them indoors in a goldfish bowl in winter.

The Sound of Falling Water

Larger ponds require electric pumps, which usually entail the installation of a weather-proof outlet, called a ground fault interrupter. However, several companies sell small solar-powered fountains, which run on energy from the sun. They won't pump a large volume of water, but if you simply want to enjoy the sound of gently falling water in your pocket pond, solar is the way to go.

YOU WILL NEED

Tools: Shovel, wheelbarrow, carpenter's level, garden hose, utility knife

2 cups of all-purpose flour

One 4-foot-long piece of scrap lumber

One 50-pound bag of play sand, or a 4 x 7-foot piece of scrap carpeting

One 10 x 10-foot piece of fish-safe pond liner

One 2-ton pallet of attractive stone, or any type of found stone

One 50-pound bag of round river rocks

Aquatic plants of your choice

4 plain pet shop goldfish (comets)

1. Choose a site that receives at least a half day of sun that is also easily viewed from your favorite sitting area. Use the flour to mark an oval or kidney-shaped outline 4 x 3 feet in size.

2. Dig out the soil, sloping the sides of the pond down from the edges to a maximum depth of 18 inches. Use the soil you've removed for other garden projects.

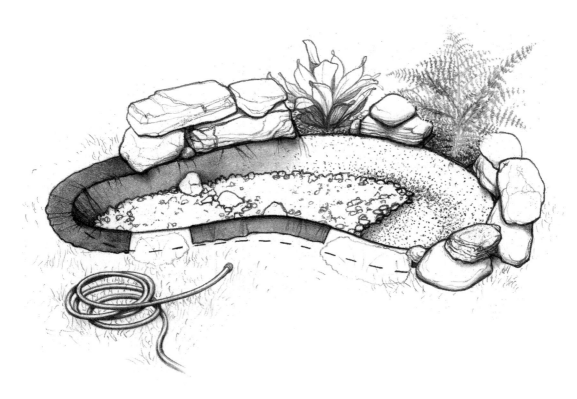

3. Place the carpenter's level on a board resting across the hole and make sure that all edges of the pond are level. Adjust the height of the edges as necessary to make them perfectly level.

4. Cover the bottom and sides of the hole with a 1-inch layer of sand, or line it with a piece of scrap carpeting.

5. On a warm, sunny day, lay the liner in the hole and smooth it into place. Fill the pond with about 6 inches of water, smoothing wrinkles as the weight of the water pushes on the liner. Don't worry if the water gets dirty, because this is a natural pond.

6. Use the utility knife to trim away excess liner, but leave at least 8 inches extending beyond the edges of the pond. Place stones around the edges, and fill a few pockets between stones with soil to create planting places for pondside plants. Line the bottom of the pond with river rocks and more stones.

7. Fill the pond with water, and wait 1 week before introducing plants such as parrot's feather, water lettuce, hardy water lilies (grown in submerged pots), or elodea (green pond weed). Wait another week to add fish. Don't worry if one fish dies. Comets that survive their first day will likely be with you for several years.

MORE WILDLIFE-FRIENDLY WATER FEATURES

Not everyone wants or needs a pond in the yard, and there are plenty of simple ways to give wild visitors a drink or a place to bathe. Hummingbirds appreciate a fine mist of water and will play in it much as children play in a lawn sprinkler. Run a hose to a sunny spot in your yard and up a shepherd's crook; add a misting nozzle and watch the fun on a warm summer day.

If your hose or outdoor faucet is dripping, you'll probably want to fix it to keep your water bill from skyrocketing. But take advantage of the drip, drip, drip until you can make the repair. Put a plastic plant saucer or a birdbath basin under the leak and watch wild things stop in for a bit of refreshment.

If you have a birdbath located beneath a convenient tree limb, you can also rig up a fine little dripper from a plastic milk jug or juice bottle that birds will find delightful. Make a tiny, pin-prick-size hole in the bottom of the jug opposite from the handle, and then hang it over the birdbath. The slow but steady drip of water will invite a steady flow of birds to the bath. If you're not fond of the look of a plastic jug dangling over your birdbath, camouflage it with a large plastic flowerpot. Just run the hanger through the drainage hole and slide the pot down over the jug.

Don't have a birdbath? Make one from a garbage can lid placed upside-down on the ground and held in place with a large stone. Birds are happy to use a surface-level birdbath, provided they are not forced to do so under the watchful eyes of cats or other predators. Four-legged wild things readily make use of any water supply they find at ground level.

ALL ICE IS NOT NICE

Wildlife need water in winter, too, when much of the world is frozen solid. If keeping a birdbath from freezing by using electric surface heaters seems like too much trouble, there is an easier way. Maintain a collection of sturdy, shallow containers such as plastic plant saucers, disposable freezer containers, or plastic take-out dishes, and keep them in a 5-gallon bucket near your door. Each day, at a predictable time (many eyes are watching), simply put out a daily saucer or two of warm water, and gather up the frozen one and toss it in the bucket to thaw.

CHAPTER 7

Solving Pest Problems
in Earth-Safe Ways

*Keep pests of all shapes
and sizes from spoiling your
garden party by using safe,
sensible methods to keep your plants
healthy, productive, and beautiful.*

205

Putting Pest Problems in Perspective

Most of us work hard to make our gardens peaceful places where we can relax and enjoy fresh-picked fruits and vegetables, fragrant flowers, and colorful birds and butterflies. The last thing we want to do in our personal paradise is to battle with pesky creatures, from leaf-eating slugs to destructive deer.

Yet by its very nature, a garden is an interruption of the natural environment, and as a result, nature is constantly trying to take back that ground. Insects and rabbits try to dine on your vegetables; weeds creep into your lawn; birds grow fat on your berry bushes. It's easy to see each of these incidents as outright attacks, but preventing pest problems—and keeping a cool head when they do occur—is much more satisfying than waging war with an ever-changing array of opponents.

The key is to do your best to work *with* nature, instead of against it. By creating a working partnership with nature, you and your plants and all manner of wild creatures can coexist more or less peacefully. The projects in this chapter will help you put down your pesticides and other implements of destruction and share the landscape comfortably with your fellow occupants.

GOOD GARDEN CARE KEEPS PROBLEMS AT BAY

Of all the things you can do to avoid pest problems in your garden, good plant care is the most important. Studies have shown that stressed plants give off chemical signals that attract pests. By keeping your plants healthy and stress-free, you can avoid many problems before they start.

- **Give them what they want.** As much as possible, locate plants where they'll have the right light, soil, and water conditions. A plant that's struggling in too much shade—or too much sun—is much more prone to other problems.
- **Nourish the soil with compost.** Grow your plants in healthy, biologically active soil and skip unnecessary fertilizer applications. Excessive fertilizer often leads to a flush of weak growth that is like a signal flare to pest and disease organisms.
- **Cut down on competition.** Crowding, shading, and reduced air flow also contribute to plant health problems, as does competition for limited nutrients and moisture. Space plants so they have room to reach their full potential, and remove weeds that compete for resources.
- **Mix things up.** Pests have a much easier time finding their targets when those plants are growing all together in a mass. Alternate rows of different vegetables in your garden, and plant a diverse collection of flowers, groundcovers, and shrubs.
- **Water wisely.** Moisture stress (too much or too little) invites numerous other problems. Tending to this basic need will go a long way toward keeping plants healthy.

■ **Rotate garden crops.** Crop rotation isn't just for farmers and market gardeners. Growing the same plants in the same place year after year allows pests and diseases to build up in the soil until their numbers are overwhelming. To thwart these problems, move your veggie plants around from one season to the next.

PREVENTING PEST PROBLEMS

Stopping pests before they reach your garden is much easier than controlling an invasion that's already under way. There's no ridding your apples of maggots that have begun tunneling through the fruits, and picking worms out of broccoli is nobody's idea of fun. Deer that have discovered your tulips are not easily deterred, nor are raccoons that have found your patch of sweet corn.

The projects in this chapter fall into three general categories—deterrents, barriers, and traps. Robust plant health is the first and best deterrent for pests. After that, you may be able to repel pests by confusing their senses. Survival is a strong instinct though, so some pests cannot be deterred. That's when you should move up to barriers—the next level of protection. Traps often are the best way to manage highly mobile pests, such as slippery slugs, or yellow jackets that join you for lunch when you decide to eat outside.

PEST-CONTROL DECISION-MAKING

As you learn more about the pests that are likely to turn up in your garden, as well as their natural enemies, it's important to recognize that plants are not without their defensive talents. When deciding how to handle a pest problem, take your plants' strengths into consideration as you ask yourself the following five questions.

1. **Are there several pests or just a few?** The insects described in the "Eight Challenging Garden Insects" chart on page 213 often invade gardens in large numbers, but many others cause minor damage. And, while wild animals often damage a wide range of plants, it's important to realize that most insects are limited to a very narrow range of host plants.

2. **What kind of damage are they doing?** In some cases, a little leaf eating can be a good thing. Many plants respond to leaf-eating pests by changing their chemistry, and gaseous plumes given off as insects eat leaves attract beneficial insects.

3. **Can you live with the damage?** What are a few blemished leaves that can be easily picked off? When tired old plants develop pest problems, it may be better to send them to the compost heap than to struggle to keep them going.

4. **What's the safest and most effective way to control this pest?** In a home garden, simply collecting insects in a pail of soapy water is infinitely practical. Fencing out animals is always the ultimate cure.

5. **Are there potential side effects or hazards to the chosen method of control?** Never make compromises where your own health is concerned. Solutions that are not good for people usually involve innocent casualties among beneficial insects—your garden's secret security force.

Bring On the Beneficials

The most common pests in gardens are insects, yet a healthy garden is far from insect-free. But instead of huge populations of destructive insects, a healthy landscape includes a dizzying array of helpful insects known as beneficials, which prey upon those that cause trouble for plants. And, in addition to well-known beneficial insects such as ladybeetles and spiders, a diversified landscape provides a good habitat for bug-eating toads, lizards, and birds. If you make beneficials feel at home in your yard (see "Plant a Beneficial Border" on page 210), many potential pest problems will be solved before they start.

One of the most important things you can do to encourage hard-working beneficials in your garden is to avoid using pesticides. Even organic pest control solutions can pose hazards for the insects that are on your side in the garden. Plant-derived rotenone, for example, is deadly to the bees that buzz in to pollinate your vegetables and fruits. Besides, the less tampering you do with insect populations, the faster your yard will evolve into a healthy, balanced ecosystem. Beneficials must have food, too, and denying them access to the life forms they like to eat (or lay their eggs on) can interfere with the good work they can do on your behalf.

GREAT GARDEN DRAMAS

Exactly who are these beneficial insects? A number of species are well known for their pest-control talents, but even experienced organic gardeners often encounter unidentified newcomers that turn out to be tremendous garden allies. When you see an insect on a plant that is not actively eating anything green, keep a close watch to see what it does, especially if there is a pest problem in progress nearby. Keep your hands to yourself, because some predatory creatures, such as assassin bugs and spiders, can cause a nasty bite by injecting you with the same venom they use to disable their prey. To study any type of small insect up close without hurting yourself or the creepy crawler, make a Catch-and-Release Chamber (at right) out of a plastic jar and a couple of straws. Out in the garden, keep your eyes open for these four bug-vs.-bug garden dramas.

High-Action Predators

Be patient and still, and you may be able to catch an assassin bug, spider, praying mantis, or big-eyed bug in the act of nabbing a huge range of insects, from unsuspecting flies to grasshoppers.

Aphid Eaters

Ladybeetle larvae, lacewing larvae, and syrphid fly larvae look like slow-moving, colorful miniature alligators ambling from aphid to aphid, eating them like popcorn. If you're not especially bothered by a small aphid outbreak, wait a few days and you will be treated to a fine show.

Caterpillar Crimes

The juicy bodies of caterpillars are often used as nurseries by tiny braconid wasps and other predatory insects. When you see a caterpillar bearing rice-shaped cocoons, it's in the process of being consumed by its hitchhikers.

Underground Assaults

The soil can be an unsafe place for pests that spend part of their lives as buried eggs or pupae. Firefly larvae, pirate bug larvae, and lumbering ground beetles eagerly devour tasty tidbits they find in the soil.

Make a Catch-and-Release Chamber for Garden Guests

Knowledge is power when it comes to garden insects. Recognizing a friend, such as an aphid-gobbling ladybeetle larvae, or a foe, like a Mexican bean beetle, will help you make smart pest control decisions. This handy homemade device, known in some parts as a pooter, is useful for capturing small insects for study and identification. It's also a fun tool for curious kids who enjoy examining crawly things up close. Remind youthful users that this bug-sucker is not good for capturing stinging insects, since you have to get rather close to your quarry to catch it.

YOU WILL NEED

Tools: Drill with a bit that matches the diameter of your straws or tubing

1 pint-size clear plastic jar (such as a peanut butter or mayonnaise jar)

2 sturdy flexible drinking straws or 8-inch pieces of flexible plastic tubing

Electrical tape

One 2-inch square of nylon stocking or cheesecloth

1. Use the drill to make two holes in the jar lid just large enough to provide a tight fit for each straw (or piece of tubing). Make the holes about 1 inch apart.

2. Push the straws (or tubing) through the holes so each extends to 1 inch from the bottom of the jar. If the straws fit loosely in their holes, use electrical tape to close any gaps around them.

3. Remove the lid, and cover the bottom end of one of the straws with the piece of nylon stocking or cheesecloth. Secure it in place with tape. Put a piece of tape around the other end of the same straw to identify it as the mouthpiece. Screw the lid onto the jar.

4. To collect an insect, put the end of the unmarked straw close to an insect. Suck hard on the mouthpiece straw, and the insect will be pulled into the jar.

Plant a Beneficial Border

Can you use flowers and herbs as a cornerstone of your pest management plan? You'd better believe it! Many of the mightiest predators of garden insects are attracted by flowers that provide plenty of nectar, and bees and other pollinators need an abundant supply of pollen. So, growing beautiful blooms is the best way to roll out the welcome mat for nature's own pest patrol squad.

Some beneficials simply show up when flowers and prey are present, but others—such as ground beetles—need a permanent habitat near where you want them to work. For best results, dedicate a permanent portion of your vegetable garden to a mix of herbs and perennial flowers that will encourage beneficials to make themselves at home season after season. Many gardeners turn fencerows or other underutilized spaces into habitats for beneficials. If limited garden space makes you unwilling to give up even a little ground, squeeze a few friendly flowers in among your veggies—sweet alyssum, marigolds, and nasturtiums are all good choices. In addition, you can install a Toad Palace (see page 200) in a shady spot to provide comfortable accommodations for slug-eating toads. The following project includes a small water source and several perches placed around the garden so bug-eating birds will have a place to watch for tasty tidbits.

YOU WILL NEED

Tools: Garden spade, rake

Seeds or transplants of plants that attract beneficials (see list below)

Shallow container, such as a 10-inch-wide plant saucer

2 cups of clean pebbles

Three 5-foot-long wood or bamboo stakes

2 bushels of organic mulch, such as straw or grass clippings

1. First thing in spring, choose a 2 x 4-foot sunny space as a beneficial border. If the soil has been supporting mostly weeds, dig it deeply and amend it with compost or other organic matter.

2. Plant seeds or transplants of a variety of plants that produce quantities of small flowers over a long season. (See "Good Nectar and Pollen Plants for a Beneficial Border" on next page.) Be sure to include members of the daisy and carrot families. Mix up perennials and annuals, too.

3. Find a spot near both flowers and vegetables, and place the plant saucer there, filled with pebbles. Add water until it's just visible around the edges of the pebbles. Tiny beneficial insects will sun on the pebbles and sip moisture from around them; butterflies will visit this watering hole, too.

4. Push the stakes into the ground among vegetables that are likely to be damaged by caterpillars or grasshoppers—two main food groups in the summer diets of many birds.

5. When the soil is warm and the plants in your beneficial border are actively growing, mulch between them with a 3- to 4-inch-thick blanket of organic mulch.

6. Wait until the following spring to clean up dead foliage and old mulch in your beneficial border. That way, at least some of your beneficials will have a safe place to spend the winter, and you can be assured that they'll be back on pest patrol the following spring.

Plant a Basket for Beneficials

Combine a comfy perch for pest-hunting birds with a haven for beneficial insects. Install a shepherd's crook–type hanger at a corner of your garden and use it to support a hanging basket filled with lantana, nasturtiums, yarrow, or other nectar sources. Beneficial insects will dine at the flowers, while birds will perch on the shepherd's crook as they scan your garden for buggy treats.

Insect-eating birds such as wrens will make a meal out of cabbage loopers, Colorado potato beetles, slugs, and other garden pests. They may also snap up a few beneficials, but they'll mainly go after bigger, more nourishing prey like juicy caterpillars.

Fall-blooming asters (*Aster* spp.)

Baby-blue-eyes (*Nemophila menziesii*)

Baby's breath (*Gypsophila* spp.)

Buckwheat (*Fagopyrum esculentum*)

Caraway (*Carum carvi*)

Clover (*Trifolium* and *Melilotus* spp.)

Coriander (*Coriandrum sativum*)

Cosmos (*Cosmos* spp.)

Daisies (*Leucanthemum* spp.)

Dill (*Anethum graveolens*)

Fennel (*Foeniculum vulgare*)

Feverfew (*Tanacetum parthenium*)

Goldenrod (*Solidago* spp.)

Lantana (*Lantana* spp.)

Lavender (*Lavandula* spp.)

Lemon balm (*Melissa officinalis*)

Marigold (*Tagetes* spp.)

Mints (*Mentha* spp.)

Nasturtiums (*Tropaeolum majus*)

Parsley (*Petroselinum crispum*)

Queen Anne's lace (*Daucus carota*)

Sunflowers (*Helianthus* spp.)

Sweet alyssum (*Lobularia maritima*)

Thyme (*Thymus* spp.)

Yarrow (*Achillea* spp.)

Understanding Insect Appetites

Beneficial insects count on us to provide them with plants that meet their needs, and so do the six-legged creatures we regard as pests. In most gardens, the same insect pests return year after year, and these are the ones you must learn to manage. Eight of the most common pest insects in North American vegetable gardens are described in the "Eight Challenging Garden Insects" chart at right.

With the exception of Japanese beetles, which eat dozens of different plants, most insects have very restricted choices of what they can eat. Colorado potato beetles, for example, can digest only tissues of plants from the Solanaceae family (potatoes, tomatoes, peppers). Similarly, squash bugs may infest squash and other cucurbits, but they pose no threat at all to tomatoes or beans. Even aphids have very specific tastes in plants. The aphids you might find clustered on rose stems in spring are a different species from those that discover your kale in the fall.

It is therefore unlikely that an insect pest of one vegetable family will eat its fill and then move to the next row or bed, assuming the neighboring crop is not closely related to the pest's preferred food plant.

HOMEMADE PEST DETERRENTS

Insects use highly refined sensory receptors to find the host plants they need, and it is sometimes possible to confuse them by dousing plants with confusing smells and flavor compounds. This is the idea behind homemade sprays made from garlic, peppers, citrus peels, or aromatic herbs such as rosemary or mint.

A fragrant or spicy spray often can discourage casual wanderers, but it seldom gives good control of serious insect problems. Once insects begin feeding on their preferred plant, they often give off signals that let their brothers and sisters know that a good food source has been found. These secret signals also put out calls to beneficial insects, so sometimes it is best to let nature take its course. On the other hand, if you know from experience that a certain insect is likely to sabotage a beloved crop, using rowcovers or other barriers can stop the damage before it starts.

WHAT ABOUT INSECTICIDES?

Whether synthetic or organic, insecticides are meant to kill insects, which they do quite well. Many also kill beneficial insects, so even organic pesticides should be used with restraint. If your garden is small and diversified, you may never need to use insecticides, provided you are willing to tolerate minor insect damage. Modern organic insecticides include numerous biological agents that target specific pests, but unless you have a chronic pest problem, using them may not be worth the trouble and expense. For large-scale organic growers, however, becoming familiar with specialized strains of *Bacillus thuringiensis*, spinosad, and horticultural oils is an important part of the job.

Eight Challenging Garden Insects

PEST	DAMAGE	PLANTS AFFECTED	WHAT TO DO
Aphids (*Aphis* spp.)	Suck plant juices, causing curling and distortion; feeding may spread viruses; sticky "honeydew" attracts ants and invites sooty mold growth	Numerous flowers and vegetables, especially roses, peas, petunias, and cabbage family crops	Encourage ladybeetles, lacewings, and other natural predators; pinch off heavily infested stems; spray with insecticidal soap
Colorado potato beetle (*Leptinotarsa decemlineata*)	Yellow and black striped adults and brick red larvae eat the leaves and flowers of potato plants, stunting or killing the plants.	Potatoes, occasionally tomatoes	Encourage spined soldier bugs and other natural predators; use rowcovers; pinch off leaves laden with clusters of orange eggs; handpick adults and larvae
Cutworms (Numerous species)	Soil-dwelling caterpillars feed on stems of seedlings and young transplants, cutting them off at soil level	Numerous vegetables and flowers, especially sunflowers, beans, lettuce, tomatoes, and peppers planted in mid to late spring	Encourage birds and other natural predators; use cutworm collars and other barriers, especially when planting in sites previously occupied by grasses and weeds
Imported cabbageworm (*Pieris rapae*)	Velvety green caterpillars eat large holes in leaves, weakening plants, and further spoil host vegetables with quantities of droppings	Cabbage, broccoli, cauliflower, and other cabbage family crops	Encourage birds and other natural predators; use rowcovers; look for eggs on leaf undersides if you see small white butterflies near cabbage family crops; handpick
Japanese beetle (*Popillia japonica*)	Brightly colored green and copper beetles feed on buds, flowers, and leaves for 6 weeks in summer, weakening plants. Larvae feed on roots of grass.	Numerous flowers, fruits, and shrubs, especially roses, grapes, hollyhocks, and plants of the hibiscus family	Grow resistant plants; use rowcover barriers; handpick
Spotted cucumber beetle (*Diabrotica undecim-punctata*)	Small yellow beetles with 12 black spots feed on blossoms, leaves, and fruits of several vegetables and numerous flowers. Larvae eat plant roots.	Squash, cucumbers, corn, beans, flowers	Use rowcover barriers; handpick, trap
Squash bug (*Anasa tristis*)	Adults and larvae feed on plants, sucking plant juices and often creating ragged holes.	Summer squash, winter squash, pumpkins; sometimes other cucurbit crops	Use rowcovers until plants are in full bloom; destroy shiny dark brown egg clusters; handpick
Tomato Hornworm (*Manduca* spp.)	Fast-growing green and white striped caterpillars hungrily eat leaves, weakening or sometimes killing plants	Tomatoes, peppers, flowering tobacco (*Nicotiana*)	Encourage small wasps and other natural predators; look for excrement trails and handpick

Working with Lightweight Rowcovers

If there are wonder fabrics for gardens, they are lightweight rowcovers—sheets of spunbonded polypropylene that let light and moisture in, but keep insects and most animals out. If you know that it's only a matter of time before a pest shows up to damage a certain crop, installing a rowcover barrier should be your first line of defense. Rowcovers are especially useful for preventing problems with pests such as spinach leafminers (a fly larvae) and squash vine borers (a moth larvae), which often are not spotted until the damage is quite advanced.

Rowcovers create a barrier to pests, but they also exclude pollinating insects. It is therefore best to remove rowcovers when plants begin to bloom heavily. Pest insects will then be able to reach the plants, but the damage they can do will be limited by their late arrival—and the robust health of the plants.

Sold under a number of brand names, a piece of rowcover will last for several seasons when handled properly. The simplest way to anchor the edges of rowcover in place is to bury them, but your rowcover will last longer—and it will be easier to move it to a new planting—if you weight the edges with boards or rocks. Just be sure that insects cannot easily slip under the edges to reach the plants they were born to find.

SUPPORTED OR FLOATING?

Fabric rowcovers are so light that they are often called floating rowcovers, which suggests they can be left to "float" over the tops of plants, with the edges buried in the soil or weighted with stones, boards, or bricks. However, with most crops it is best to support the rowcover to prevent chafing of leaves and growing tips when the rowcover shifts in the wind. The support material must be smooth, so as not to tear holes in the rowcover, so many gardeners use hoops made of wire or half-inch PVC pipe. Or, you can stud the row with upright plants that grow taller than the plant you want to protect, such as corn, wheat, or sunflowers, and let the tall plants work as living supports for your rowcovers.

CONSIDER FROST AND WEEDS

Garden catalogs often proclaim that rowcovers will protect plants from late frosts, but in truth they usually raise the temperature only 3 degrees or so—not enough to be trustworthy as frost protection. Weeds can be an issue, too, because like your garden plants, weeds often thrive in the humid environment beneath rowcovers. If you use a rowcover tunnel like the one in "Grow Undercover Squash" on the next page, open one side of the cover every couple of weeks, pull out weeds, and then promptly replace the cover.

Whenever fabric rowcover is not in use, store it in a dry place away from direct sunlight. Rather than discarding pieces that tear, mend small holes with a needle and thread, or patch them with duct tape.

Grow Undercover Squash

Summer squash is attractive to several serious insects—cucumber beetles, squash bugs, and squash vine borers—all of which can be managed by growing the plants beneath rowcover barriers until they begin to blossom and set fruit. You can use the same procedure described here to exclude insects from potatoes or other low-growing garden crops. More uses for rowcover are discussed on page 217.

YOU WILL NEED

Tools: Measuring tape, handsaw, mallet, pliers, scissors, staple gun

One 5-foot-long piece of 1-inch-diameter PVC pipe

Two 8-foot-long pieces of ½-inch-diameter PVC pipe

1 packet of summer squash seeds

One 10 x 15-foot piece of rowcover

Two 6-foot-long 1 x 2 furring strips

1. Use a saw to cut the 1-inch PVC pipe into six 10-inch pieces. Cut the ½-inch PVC pipe into three 40-inch pieces.

2. Prepare and plant a 2 x 6-foot row of summer squash. At each end corner, pound a piece of 1-inch PVC pipe 8 inches into the ground, pull it back out with pliers, and clear out the plug of soil with one of the ½-inch PVC pipe pieces. Pound them into the ground again to create a hollow sleeve for the hoops. Install another set of sleeves at the middle of the row.

3. Install hoops by placing one end of each ½-inch piece of PVC pipe into a sleeve and slowly bending it over the bed. Insert the other end in the opposite sleeve.

4. Cut the rowcover in half lengthwise, and set aside one half for another use. Place the rowcover over the hoops, and temporarily weight the edges with stones, bricks, or food cans. Roll the long edges of the rowcover around the furring strips twice, and staple it in place.

5. Secure all edges of the rowcover to the ground with stones, bricks, or other weights. Weight the furring strips, too, because they are not heavy enough to stay in place in windy weather.

6. Remove the rowcover 1 week after the plants begin to bloom.

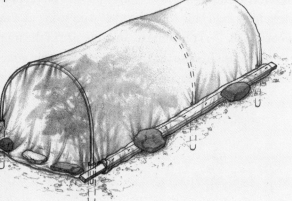

Build an Isolation Box

If you want to protect an individual plant from insect or animal pests, a simple frame that can be covered with row-cover or another lightweight fabric will do the trick. This is a great way to keep Japanese beetles away from a treasured rose during their 6-week feeding period, or to safeguard a tomato from the moths whose larvae become tomato hornworms. An isolation box can serve other purposes as well:

- If you plan to save seeds from a certain plant, you can use your isolation box to exclude pollinating insects (unless the plant is self-fertile, you will need to distribute pollen between different flowers by hand).

- When you decide that you must use an organic pesticide, you can use the box to exclude beneficial insects for a day or two after the plant is sprayed.

- Use the frame to support bird netting if berries or tomatoes need temporary protection.

- Cover the frame with an old sheet to turn the box into a shade cover for seedlings set out in hot weather or for newly seeded beds of slow sprouters such as carrots, parsley, or onions.

This lightweight model goes together in minutes, and because the joints are not glued together, it can be taken apart and stored when not in use. Simply pop the pieces apart, hose them down, and bind them together with string or a large rubber band. Don't hesitate to alter the size of the frame to fit your needs. To raise the frame's height, simply attach additional pieces of PVC pipe to the legs.

YOU WILL NEED

Tools: Measuring tape, handsaw, pruning shears or loppers

Two 10-foot pieces of ½-inch PVC pipe

Four ½-inch-diameter 3-way (90 degree) elbow connectors

Four ½-inch-diameter male connectors

Four 18-inch-long straight sticks or bamboo stakes

One 10-foot-square piece of rowcover

1. Saw the pipe into four 30-inch-long pieces—four for the top of the frame and four for the legs.

2. Arrange four of the cut pieces into a square on a flat surface. Firmly push the ends into the elbow connectors to form a box. With the open ends of the connectors facing up, screw in the male connectors until tight. They may not screw in all the way. Firmly twist the legs into the open end of the connectors.

3. Carry the frame to where you want to use it, and adjust the position of the legs to make the frame square. Mark the places where the legs touch the ground.

4. Use the pruning shears to trim sticks or stakes. Push the sticks or stakes into the ground 10 inches deep at the places marked for the legs, making sure they are perfectly straight. Lift the frame, and slip the legs over the sticks. Push the legs into the soil 3 inches deep.

5. Cover the frame with rowcover, and secure the bottom edges with bricks, stones, or pieces of scrap lumber.

Rowcover Alternatives

Rowcover fabric made for home gardens doesn't have holes in it, so it blocks only a little light, and tiny flea beetles can't get through to damage plants. There are other fabrics that make good stand-ins for purchased rowcover fabric, such as flexible polyester window screening, discarded sheer draperies, or mosquito netting. Another great option is tulle, the polyester net fabric used to decorate ballet tutus, bridal veils, and party tables. Inexpensive and widely available at fabric and craft shops, tulle even comes in festive colors. The openings in the net are less than 1/16-inch wide, so tulle is best used as a barrier for medium to large-size insects, such as various beetles and moths.

Tulle is usually 59 inches wide, which is not wide enough to completely cover a tunnel or box. When using any alternative material that's too narrow to give good coverage, simply sew pieces together with a needle and thread, or use a sewing machine. Rowcover can be cut and sewn, too. If you know how to sew, try creating unique garden fashions from rowcover or alternative fabrics, such as a quick slipcover for the Isolation Box.

Make a Collection of Cutworm Collars

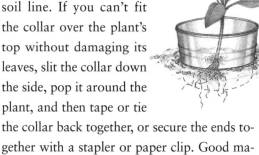

Few sights are more distressing than an entire garden bed of tomatoes or peppers you raised from seed, and then find felled overnight like little trees. The culprits are night-feeding cutworms, which are perhaps the most inefficient of all garden pests. Instead of eating the plants they kill, they simply girdle the stem by curling themselves around it. Seedlings that suddenly disappear without a trace often have been eaten by animals, but when you find the tops of your seedlings shriveling in the sun, you know you have been hit by cutworms. Gray or brown caterpillars that rest in the soil by day and feed at night, cutworms are the larvae of several species of uninteresting-looking gray or brown moths. They are most common in soil that has previously supported grass or weeds, but cutworms can turn up almost anywhere.

The good news is that cutworm catastrophes are extra easy to avoid. Give every transplant in your garden a simple yet effective cutworm collar. There are several styles to choose from, depending on the seedling and its growing situation.

STIFF COLLARS

The most popular and versatile cutworm barriers are round collars, 2 to 3 inches high and about 2 inches in diameter, which can be sunk into the ground around seedlings. The collars should be pushed into the soil 1 inch deep, with about 2 inches showing above the soil line. If you can't fit the collar over the plant's top without damaging its leaves, slit the collar down the side, pop it around the plant, and then tape or tie the collar back together, or secure the ends together with a stapler or paper clip. Good materials for making stiff collars include:

- Small cans, such as tuna or pet food containers, with the tops and bottoms removed
- Plastic drink cups, cut into 3-inch rings
- Plastic soda bottles, cut into 3-inch rings
- Cardboard tubes from paper towels or toilet paper, cut into 3-inch sections
- Strips of poster board or other lightweight cardboard, 2 to 3 inches wide
- Wide plastic or paper drinking straws, cut into 3-inch-long pieces and slit down the side

COWL COLLARS

In fashion lingo, a cowl is a loose collar that drapes around the neckline—a fine style for cutworm barriers, too. The only material cutworms can penetrate is tender young plant tissue, so covering the stems with a tougher sheath keeps them from causing harm. Do be sure that this type of collar extends 1 inch below and 2 inches above the soil line. Avoid making the col-

lar too tight, which can girdle the stem. Good materials for making cowl collars include:

- Aluminum foil, cut into 4-inch squares
- Waxed paper, cut into 4-inch squares
- Scraps of rowcover or cheesecloth, held in place with a dot of glue

STEM SPLINTS

Cutworms sometimes damage direct-seeded crops, too, which may involve so many possible victims that using other types of collars is not practical. If you intervene at the first sign of cutworm trouble, you often can save a planting of beans, cantaloupes, or other veggies by installing hard splints alongside the main stems. When the cutworms try to wrap themselves around the stem, they encircle the splint, too, which makes it much more difficult for them to feed. Good materials for stem splints include:

- Wood or bamboo food skewers, snapped into 4-inch pieces
- Cotton swabs, with the bottom ends snipped off
- Slender 4-inch-long sticks
- 3-inch nails or pieces of wire (be sure to collect them after a week or two)

CURES FOR CLIMBING CUTWORMS

Instead of girdling stems, some types of cutworms climb up plants and eat tender buds and leaves. When you notice unexplained holes in hostas or petunias night after night, or low leaves and buds mysteriously missing from fruit trees, set out a trap beneath the

Use Birds and Barriers

Cutworms have plenty of natural enemies, including hungry birds. Use these techniques to keep cutworms under control with both birds and barriers.

1. Cultivate the soil in fall, if possible, or 3 weeks before planting in spring. Cutworms overwinter as pupae, which are often harvested by birds.

2. Tolerate winter moles. If you see evidence that moles are present in your garden in winter, keep an eye on them but don't immediately run them off. Moles are major cutworm predators.

3. As you set out seedlings in spring, surround each one with an appropriate collar. Keep a few prepared collars on hand for emergencies. Cutworms often return to the scene of their crimes to do more damage night after night.

4. In regions where warm weather lingers long into the fall, a second generation of cutworms may endanger late-planted crops. Use collars on these fall transplants, too.

plants and see what you catch. A cardboard collar laid on the ground beneath the plant and covered with a sticky substance (see page 222) will probably catch the culprit—a climbing cutworm.

Gathering Up Your Bugs

Because insects are small, numerous, and often quite nimble, gathering them up is often more difficult than it sounds. When their peaceful feeding is disturbed, most insects either take to the air or drop to the ground and play dead. And those that are easy to pluck off with a gloved hand, such as imported cabbageworms and tomato hornworms, wear such excellent camouflage colors that they can be difficult to see.

Each species uses different defense strategies, so it's important to tailor your techniques to the specific pest's strengths and weaknesses. If you're new to the world of bug-watching and you have no idea what to expect of a six-legged creature that's damaging your garden, use the time-tested technique known as a beating sheet. Place a sheet of cloth—or a large food tray—beneath the troubled plants, and give the plants a vigorous shake to see what falls out or flies away. This procedure will often help you identify the general type of insect involved—for example, beetle, fly, or hard-backed bug—and you will learn what the critter does when it goes into panic mode.

Should nothing fall into your sheet or tray except a number of small green or black pebbles, you are probably dealing with a caterpillar that can cling to stems and leaves with its numerous sticky feet. Following the trail of "frass" left behind by a leaf-eating caterpillar will lead you to its hiding spot.

USING BOWLS AND BUCKETS

Handpicking pests often means literally reaching into a plant and picking off insects, which is safe and clean if you protect your hand with a thin latex glove (such as a medical exam glove). But when working with a pest that drops to the ground when disturbed—as Japanese beetles, squash bugs, and blister beetles do on cool mornings—you often can capture more bugs by placing broad bowls or cake pans filled with soapy water beneath the plants. The soap makes it impossible for the pests to tread water on the surface for long, so it makes a great low-tech trap.

Many gardeners simply take a pail of soapy water with them when they go on pest patrol and use it as a collection container for unwanted insects. That way, they are never without a place to put pinched-off stem tips heavily laden with aphids, or armyworms found marching up tomato stems.

CREATIVE COLLECTING

You also can use various sticky traps to collect problem insects, including the five described on pages 222 to 223. When faced with large insect outbreaks that defy other collection methods, many gardeners turn to their vacuum cleaners for help. A small handheld rechargeable vacuum is ideal for this task, but any type of vacuum with a hose attachment will do. Be careful to avoid mangling leaves.

Make a Drag Flag for Bad Biters

Among the most worrisome creatures you might encounter outdoors are ticks—spider relatives that require a blood meal in order to reproduce. Some species of ticks carry Lyme disease, and others can transmit Rocky Mountain Spotted Fever. Ticks in search of a warm-blooded host wait patiently on the tips of weeds and tall grasses, where they can be monitored and collected using a simple Drag Flag. Mistaking the flag for a passing animal, they quickly latch on. Once captured, ticks can be killed by soaking the flag in a pail of hot, soapy water for several hours.

YOU WILL NEED

Tools: Scissors, deep bucket

One 14 x 18-inch piece of light-colored corduroy, or a kitchen dish towel

1 old broom or mop handle, or a 5-foot-long bamboo pole

3 large safety pins

Dishwashing detergent

1. If you are using corduroy, cut it to the proper size. There is no need to hem the raw edges.

2. To create a flag, wrap one edge of the cloth around one end of the broom handle and use the safety pins to hold it snuggly in place.

3. Walk slowly along the edge of the place where you think ticks may be present, gently dragging the flag over the tops of weeds and grasses. Repeat for 10 to 15 minutes, because ticks will scramble upward if they sense the presence of a host animal.

4. Inspect the flag for ticks, which often are quite tiny. Detach the flag from the pole and soak it in a bucket of hot, soapy water for several hours. Rinse well and allow it to dry in the sun before reusing it.

Using Icky Stickies

Using sticky traps is another bug-catching option, but it's important that the trap be attractive only to pests, and not to beneficial insects. This can be a problem with yellow sticky traps, which often are intended to trap cucumber beetles or flea beetles, but snare numerous hover flies and beneficial wasps, too. When you use any sticky trap, check it after a day or two to see what you're catching. Stop the campaign if there are too many innocent casualties.

MAKE STOP-'EM-IN-THEIR-TRACKS TRAPS

Sticky traps do have their place in your pest control bag of tricks, and they are easy to make. Certain insects are attracted to specific colors, so the basic idea is to combine an enticing color with an adhesive surface. After choosing a color and shape, make trap maintenance extra easy by covering the trap with plastic wrap or a plastic bag. Then coat the plastic with a sticky substance, such as petroleum jelly, motor oil, or commercial trap adhesives such as Tanglefoot or Stikem. In a pinch, you can even transform purchased sticky ant traps into garden

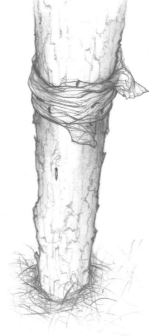

insect traps by decorating them with colorful tape and putting them in specific places. Here are four good sticky trap strategies to try.

Sticky Tree Bands

Stop cankerworms and gypsy moths from munching on the leaves of your favorite tree by taping a 5-inch-wide band of plastic wrap around the trunk about 3 feet above the ground. Then coat it with a sticky substance. Gypsy moth caterpillars and flightless female cankerworm moths will be trapped in the goo and unable to climb into the foliage to gobble leaves or lay eggs. Replace the plastic wrap when it becomes dirty or full of trapped pests. A sticky band will help keep aphid-herding ants out of your trees, too.

Tar-Baby Apples

Meandering tunnels in apples are caused by apple maggots, the larvae of a fast-moving fly. To trap the egg-laying females, place red balls inside plastic bags, coat the bags with sticky stuff, and hang them in your apple trees in the early summer, just as the green fruits are starting to grow. Keep the traps in place throughout the growing season, refreshing their sticky coverings whenever they become dirty or full of trapped flies.

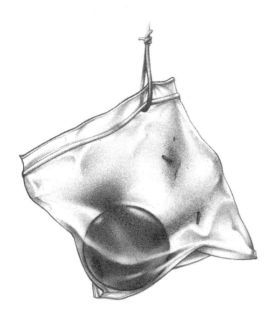

Sticky Whitefly Swatter

Whiteflies sometimes become a nuisance on tomatoes, or they may infest salvias or other summer flowers. You can try placing yellow sticky traps among the plants, but you may capture more bees and other beneficials than whiteflies. To keep the fight fair, tape plastic over the end of a fly swatter, coat it with petroleum jelly or motor oil, and go on a seek-and-destroy mission. Swish one hand through the foliage while waving the swatter through the cloud of whiteflies that rises into the air. Repeat twice daily until you're down to only a few whiteflies.

Houseplant Sitter

Whiteflies or fungus gnats on your indoor plants have no natural predators, so indoors is a great place to use yellow sticky traps made from pieces of yellow poster board or yellow plastic food containers that have been cut into pieces and stapled to a craft stick stake.

Make a Sticky Glove

Instead of discarding old garden gloves when they get holes in their fingers, let them serve a last tour of duty as sticky gloves. Push a spade in the ground, place a dry glove on the end of the handle, and wrap the glove with two or three pieces of packing tape or duct tape, with the sticky sides out. Slip it on your hand, and use it to go after flea beetles, whiteflies, cucumber beetles, and other small pests. It's like wearing a bug magnet on your hand! When you're done, throw it in a pail of soapy water. Remove the tape and dead bugs after an hour or so, then rinse out the glove and let it dry in the sun. Reuse the glove whenever you need to embark on a bug-nabbing mission.

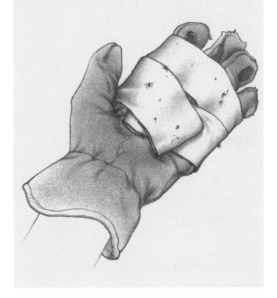

Dealing with Gangs of Grasshoppers

Grasshoppers are a chronic problem in some climates, while in others they pose problems only every few years. In any climate, a bad grasshopper year will find you watching helplessly as the hoppers chew through your leafy greens and beans, and mow down carrot tops in a matter of days. Grasshopper populations grow steadily as the summer wears on, so it's wise to keep a close watch on them and set up barriers and traps if they threaten to get out of hand.

Bran-based baits that infect grasshoppers with a protozoan disease, *Nosema locustae*, are useful for long-term control of these greedy pests, but they're most effective against imma-

ture grasshoppers. The gradual death they inflict is of little use when you have a large-scale invasion in your garden. Protect individual plants or small beds with secure barriers made of window screening. Meanwhile, you may be able to lure grasshoppers away from your garden with a patch of unmowed grass made even more attractive with tempting servings of Hopper Mush. Once you have grasshoppers where you want them, many can be lured to a watery death in a Sweet Hopper Stopper.

MAKE WINDOW-SCREEN BARRIERS

When mature grasshoppers arrive in substantial numbers—a literal "plague of locusts"—

Make Hopper Mush

One way to get grasshoppers to leave your garden is to lure them to another place, such as a grassy ditch or other weedy spot. Entice them to move on by serving up a special dinner of this custom-made mush.

YOU WILL NEED
Tools: Bucket, long-handled spoon or stirring stick, rubber gloves

1 cup molasses

1 cup canola oil

1 quart water

5 pounds whole wheat flour

1. In a bucket, mix together the molasses, canola oil, and water. Add half of the flour, stir for 1 minute, and then stir in the rest of the flour. The mixture will be lumpy.

2. Allow the mush to sit overnight, and then stir it again.

3. Wearing rubber gloves, drop handfuls of the mush in places where you want the hoppers to find it, as far from your garden as possible. Drop coin-size morsels to create a tasty trail from your garden to the site of the grasshopper buffet.

Sweet Hopper Stopper

Plan a sweet reception for grasshoppers to lure these garden-gobbling pests to their doom. Both molasses and canola oil are attractive to grasshoppers, so don't place these traps in parts of your garden where you don't want grasshoppers to go. In addition to attracting grasshoppers, the oil forms a surface film in the trap that prevents problems with mosquitoes.

YOU WILL NEED

One 1-gallon plastic jug

1 cup molasses

½ cup canola oil

9 cups warm water

Several pint-size open-mouthed containers, such as pint jars, plastic drink cups, or plastic soda bottles with their tops cut off

1. In an empty gallon jug, mix together the molasses, canola oil, and warm water.

2. Bury the containers up to their rims in the soil outside the edges of your garden, or in places where you have placed baits or allowed grass and weeds to grow in order to attract grasshoppers.

3. Fill each container halfway full with the molasses solution.

4. Check your traps daily and empty them onto your compost pile as they become full of grasshoppers. Replace the containers and refill with more molasses solution.

late in the summer, barriers that cover whole rows or individual plant covers may be necessary to save your favorite crops from complete destruction. Don't rely on fabric rowcovers to protect your plants—hungry hoppers will chew right through them. Instead, staple aluminum window screening to furring strips and bend it in an arch to fit over the rows in your garden, or surround landscape plants with stakes or bamboo poles and wrap them with aluminum screening. You also can make window-screen cones, which can easily be popped over plants in need of protection. Be sure to evict all hoppers from the plants

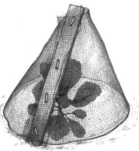

you're covering before you put your screens in place. Otherwise, grasshoppers trapped beneath your screens will have their own private dining area, safe from kestrels and other birds that prey on them.

Simple Ways to Stop Slugs and Snails

Slugs and snails are not insects, but mollusks. Yet the damage they cause—large holes with smooth edges in leaves of lettuce, beans, hostas, and many other plants—looks like it was done by a bug. Slugs and snails usually feed at night and hide in mulch during the day, though you may find them on plants on rainy days, especially early in the morning. Not sure if slugs are your problem? Lightly dust plant leaves with flour in the evening, and check the next morning for meandering trails. Then wash off the flour with a fine spray of water.

Serve After-Dinner Coffee

Gardeners have been trying to spray away their slug problems for centuries, but it has only recently been learned that a substance most of us drink every day—caffeine—is a potent neurotoxin to mollusks. There is enough caffeine in strong coffee to make it an effective slugicide, or you can use two caffeine tablets (over-the-counter "stay awake" pills) dissolved in a pint of water. The challenge is to get the caffeine on the slimers, which means spraying by flashlight. The next morning, remove coffee residue by rinsing plants with a fine spray of water.

Drown Your Sorrows with a Slug Jug

Slugs and snails lay their eggs in soil, so even if you get rid of one batch of slimers with coffee, more will appear within a few weeks. Instead of being taken by surprise, set out slug traps baited with yeasty beer, and slugs and snails will go gladly to their demise. Nearly any container filled with beer and set with its rim flush with the soil surface will attract slugs to a soggy end, but a Slug Jug has three superior features: few flying insects drop in from above, the beer bait does not get diluted by rainfall, and the jug's handle makes it easy to empty, clean, and refill.

YOU WILL NEED

Tools: Utility knife, hand trowel

Plastic milk jug or similar half-gallon or gallon container, with cap

Beer (cheap, yeasty beer is best)

1. Use the utility knife to cut 2-inch-diameter square holes in all four sides of the container, 1 to 1½ inches from the bottom.

2. Choose a spot where slug or snail activity is likely, and use the trowel to dig out a place for the jug. It should be deep enough so that the jug sits down in the ground with the bottom edges of the holes even with the soil surface.

3. Pour beer into the jug, filling the bottom to just below the holes in the sides. Replace the cap on the jug.

4. Check your trap every few days. Pour out the slugs, snails, and aging beer and refill the trap with fresh beer.

More Uses for Your Slug Jug

When you're not using it to trap slugs, a slug jug still makes a handy garden gadget. Here are three ways to keep your slug jug from gathering dust.

■ **Cucumber beetle trap.** One of the substances in cucumbers, squash, and melons that attracts cucumber beetles is cucurbitacin—a bitter compound found just beneath the fruits' skins. Detour cucumber peels or melon rinds on their way to your compost heap by putting them into a slug jug set among any cucurbit crop—cucumbers, squash, pumpkins, or gourds. Take hostages by slipping a produce bag over the jug. Shake the beetles and bait into the bag, and dump it all into a pail of warm, soapy water.

■ **Vinegar sachet.** Cats, squirrels, and many other four-legged critters are disgusted by the smell of vinegar, so a slug jug filled with vinegar makes a great device for deterring digging in newly planted beds. Be careful not to spill the vinegar on plant leaves, because it will leave brown spots.

■ **Flower basket.** If you have no pests to ponder and plenty of short-stemmed flowers you want to gather for bouquets, rinse out a slug jug, place some cool water in the bottom, and use it to collect blossoms. The four holes make it easy to keep different flowers separate, so you can arrange them straight from the jug.

Picnic-Saver Yellow Jacket Traps

Aggressive and able to sting repeatedly, yellow jackets are unwelcome guests at picnics and other outdoor activities. Even though these sturdy little yellow-and-black wasps are beneficials that prey on pests such as caterpillars and flies, their bad manners in (human) social situations make them tough to tolerate in a home landscape. Yellow jackets nest underground, and in the middle of summer, a colony may include hundreds or thousands of wasps. Yellow jacket colonies begin falling apart in late summer, which is when unemployed yellow jackets spend their extra time foraging around picnic tables, garbage cans, and other good sources of food and drink. If your yard falls into a colony's territory, either of the two traps described here can greatly improve outdoor dining—and gardening—when yellow jackets get too bossy to tolerate.

Make a Soda-Bottle Funnel Trap

This trap is cheap and easy to make, but hard to clean. Instead of messing around with funnel traps full of dead yellow jackets, simply dispose of traps that are used up and replace them with new ones.

YOU WILL NEED

Tools: Scissors or utility knife, stapler, hole punch

One 2-liter soda bottle

Wire or string for hanging trap

Soda, fruit juice, sugar water, wine, or cider

1. Cut the top off the bottle just below its shoulders, at the point where the sides become straight.

2. Remove the cap and invert the top so it serves as a funnel going into the bottom part of the bottle. Fasten the funnel in place with a few staples.

3. Punch a hole on either side of the top rim of the trap and attach wire or string for hanging the trap.

4. Pour 2 inches of sweetened liquid—regular (nondiet) soda, fruit juice, sugar water, wine, or cider—in the bottom of the trap. Splash it onto the sides of the funnel as you pour, to increase the trap's attractiveness to wasps.

5. Hang the trap at least 20 feet away from your patio, in an area where you've seen yellow jacket activity. Check traps frequently—they become less effective when they're full of drowned wasps.

6. Take full traps down at night after yellow jackets have returned to their nests. If there are still live wasps in the trap, dunk the entire bottle into a bucket of soapy water before discarding it.

Make a PVC Pipe Trap

This trap uses two kinds of bait—sugary liquid and a bit of meat for protein—to make it twice as attractive to foraging yellow jackets. It's a bit more difficult to make than the soda bottle trap, but it's also easier to clean and reuse.

YOU WILL NEED

Tools: Measuring tape or ruler; handsaw; jigsaw; file or sandpaper; marker; utility knife; electrical tape; drill; long tweezers or slender skewers

One 1- to 2-quart plastic food storage jar with lid

Two 6-inch pieces of ½-inch-diameter PVC pipe

Wire or string for hanging trap

Soda, fruit juice, sugar water, or cider

Meat, such as bologna, tuna, or liver

1. Cut two lengths of PVC pipe so each is ½ inch longer than the diameter of the jar at its maximum width.

2. Use the jigsaw to cut an elongated oval into the middle of each length of pipe. Smooth the cut edges with a file or sandpaper.

3. Trace the diameter of the pipe onto the side of the jar, 2½ inches from the bottom. Cut a hole in the side of the jar and slide the pipe into it. Mark the pipe's diameter where it hits the other side of the jar, and cut a second hole opposite the first.

4. Repeat Step 3 to install the second piece of pipe, placing it about 2 inches above the first pipe and perpendicular to it.

5. Insert the pipes with the oval openings facing upward. If the pipes fit too loosely in

the holes, use electrical tape to keep them from rotating.

6. Drill two holes into the jar lid and run wire or string through them for hanging the trap.

7. Pour 2 inches of sugary liquid, such as regular (nondiet) soda, fruit juice, sugar water, or cider, into the bottom of the jar. Use long tweezers or slender skewers to place a small piece of raw meat in the opening of one or both pipes. Secure the lid and hang the trap.

8. Check the trap daily, and empty it and replenish the baits as necessary. Yellow jackets are not attracted to rotting meat. To kill any live wasps in the trap, submerge it in a bucket of soapy water, preferably at night when new yellow jackets are unlikely to arrive while you're tending the trap.

Preventing Damage from Animals

A hungry raccoon, deer, squirrel, or rabbit can do more damage in an hour than most insects can do in a week, so they can be formidable garden pests. Prevention or early intervention is crucial, because once hungry animals discover good food in your garden, they become much more difficult to manage. Hunger and the availability of other foods are important variables, because starving animals will often eat plants they normally leave alone. If you have a persistent problem with an animal pest, stocking your garden with the non-preferred plants listed on page 233 is a step in the right direction. You may also need to use deterrents and barriers to keep your garden safe from hungry animals.

TRY SCENT FENCES

In landscape situations where an actual fence is not practical, you may have luck deterring animals with various scents. Odor repellents are useful when you have just a few plants in need of protection, and in situations where the pest animals have plenty of other places to go in search of food.

If you choose this "scents-ible" approach to plant protection, be prepared to keep raising a stink as long as animal pests pose a threat. Most repellents need to be refreshed as their aromas fade, especially if they're exposed to the elements. Here are some widely used repellents with reputations for success in keeping plant-munchers at bay.

- **Deodorant soap.** Popular for protecting fruit trees from deer browsing, aromatic bars of soap hung 3 to 4 feet above the ground often are effective. Place a bar in a mesh bag, or drill a hole through the middle and hang on a piece of twine. Each bar will protect an area of about 1 square yard, so large trees and shrubs may need more than one bar. This is a great use for the small bars of soap often provided by hotels.

- **Predator scents.** Rabbits and deer instinctively avoid areas that seem to be frequented by predators. Hang the blanket your dog has been sleeping on over the garden fence, or tuck tufts of dog hair (or human hair) into mesh bags and hang them around your garden or on your favorite shrubs. Put small amounts of used cat litter into the bottoms of coffee cans that have several holes punched in their sides and set them around the outside of your garden (never allow used cat litter inside your garden).

- **Hot stuff.** All mammals can taste the fire in hot peppers, so dousing plants with a spicy spray will often deter casual munchers. Combine 2 cups of water, 2 tablespoons of Tabasco sauce, 1 teaspoon of hot chili powder, and a squirt of dishwashing liquid, and spray or sprinkle it liberally over plants that are being bothered by squirrels, rabbits, deer, or other four-legged creatures. Reapply this spicy cocktail after heavy rains, which usually wash plant leaves clean.

- **Castor oil.** A powerful repellent for moles, castor oil also has proven useful in repelling squirrels, chipmunks, and gophers. If these varmints are rooting around in your flower beds or containers, a castor oil solution is an easy-to-apply deterrent. In a glass jar, combine 1 ounce of castor oil with 1 tablespoon of dishwashing liquid and 1 cup of warm water. Shake the jar to mix the solution. Pour this mixture into a watering can and add 1 gallon of water. Sprinkle onto containers and flower beds where animal damage is occurring, or pour it directly onto mole tunnels. Reapply after heavy rains.

Make an Animal Tracking Box

You know you have an animal pest making secret visits to your garden, but you have yet to catch a glimpse of your wild visitor. Many animals are nocturnal, but you don't have to stay up all night waiting to see who shows up. Instead, make a simple tracking box, and study the footprints the animal leaves behind.

YOU WILL NEED

Tools: Utility knife, scissors, watering can
1 waxed cardboard box
1 roll of duct tape
3 gallons of clean sand

1. Use the utility knife to cut around the sides of the box, removing all but the bottom and 3 inches along all four sides. Use the duct tape to reinforce the box by taping across the bottom in both directions. Also wrap tape around all of the sides and corners of the box.

2. Fill the prepared box almost to the top with clean, dry sand. Place it where animal activity is likely, and sprinkle the sand with water until it is lightly moist. Pat the surface level with your hand. Press your hand lightly to see if it leaves a print. If needed, add more water to the sand and smooth it again.

3. Check the box for prints first thing in the morning. Use the toe-counting method to narrow the field of possibilities.

- Four toes on both the front and back feet, with a fifth central pad, are signs of an animal in the dog, cat, or rabbit family. Dog tracks usually include claw marks, while those of cats do not. Rabbit tracks are elongated, with toe marks barely visible.

- Four toes on the front feet and 5 toes on the back suggest some type of rodent, such as mice, squirrels, chipmunks, or woodchucks.

- Five toes on all four feet are evidence of the raccoon family, which includes weasels, skunks, opossums, and raccoons. The tracks resemble the shape of a small human hand.

- Two elongated toes are proof of a visit by deer, elk, or moose.

Planning an Animal-Resistant Garden

If you are one of the thousands of gardeners who live in an area where deer and rabbit populations are high, you know too well the heartbreak of looking out your window in the morning to find that your garden has been ravaged during the night. You cannot control what wild animals do while you sleep, but you can design a landscape that offers little in the way of attractive foods. As for those plants that rabbits and deer love—such as most fruits and vegetables—the best solution is to fence in the area where you plan to grow your own produce.

Where rabbits are the primary problem, you can install a dependable rabbit fence in a matter of hours (see "Build a Fence That Bugs Bunnies" on page 234). Deer, in comparison, have no trouble leaping over a 6-foot-tall fence, and if they are hungry enough, they will barrel through an electric fence as well. Still, electric fencing is relatively inexpensive and easy to install. Do check your local zoning laws before you start; for safety reasons, some communities restrict electric fence use by homeowners. If you do install an electric fence, post appropriate warning signs and make your neighbors aware of the fence's location.

There is another option—7½-foot-tall black plastic mesh fencing, which is sold by companies that specialize in deer-resistant garden supplies. Plastic mesh fencing's light weight makes it easy to install, and it requires few fence posts to hold it in place. The mesh is nearly invisible at even a relatively short distance, so it doesn't impede landscape views. Deer have a hard time seeing it, too, and are usually so spooked when they run into it that they don't return for a second encounter.

WORKING WITH ANIMAL-RESISTANT PLANTS

You can fence in your food garden, but what about the rest of your landscape? Although rabbit and deer appetites vary with season and region, the plants listed on the next page in "60 Animal-Resistant Plants" are generally unattractive to rabbits, deer, and even squirrels. If you use large numbers of these plants, animals will gradually lose interest in your yard, and you can begin slipping in favorite plants here and there, where their presence will be camouflaged by plenty of neighboring plants animals find distasteful.

For best results, plant nothing but animal-resistant plants around the perimeter of your yard. If you know the direction from which animals tend to enter your property, barriers of thorny blackberries and unpalatable plants may turn them away.

Many of the plants that resist deer and rabbits are also poisonous to people, so take this into consideration if you share your garden with curious kids. Fencing in your edible plants and growing herbs in their own special area make it easy to teach kids the difference between safe and toxic plants.

60 Animal-Resistant Plants

15 PERENNIALS RABBITS AND DEER USUALLY DON'T EAT

Butterfly weed (*Asclepias tuberosa*)

Coral bells (*Heuchera americana*)

Ferns (many species)

Foxgloves (*Digitalis* spp.)

Goat's beard (*Aruncus dioicus*)

Goldenrods (*Solidago* spp.)

Hardy geranium (*Geranium maculatum*)

Hellebores (*Helleborus* spp.)

Irises (*Iris* spp.)

Joe-Pye weeds (*Eupatorium* spp.)

Lamb's ears (*Stachys byzantina*)

Penstemon (*Penstemon digitalis*)

Purple coneflower (*Echinacea purpurea*)

Solomon's seal (*Polygonatum biflorum*)

Spiderwort (*Tradescantia virginica*)

15 ANIMAL-RESISTANT FLOWERS AND HERBS

Ageratum (*Ageratum houstonianum*)

Anise hyssop (*Agastache* spp.)

Bee balm (*Monarda didyma*)

Begonia (*Begonia* spp.)

Catnip (*Nepeta* spp.)

Dusty miller (*Senecio cineraria*)

Lantana (*Lantana* spp.)

Lavender (*Lavandula* spp.)

Mealycup sage (*Salvia farinacea*)

Mint (*Mentha* spp.)

Nicotiana (*Nicotiana alata*)

Oregano (*Origanum* spp.)

Rosemary (*Rosmarinus officinalis*)

Strawflower (*Helichrysum bracteatum*)

Thyme (*Thymus* spp.)

12 ANIMAL-RESISTANT FLOWERING SHRUBS

Abelia (*Abelia grandiflora*)

Blue mist shrub (*Caryopteris clandonensis*)

Bridal wreath spiraea (*Spiraea* spp.)

Butterfly bush (*Buddleia davidii*)

Currants (*Ribes* spp.)

Daphne (*Daphne* spp.)

Forsythia (*Forsythia x intermedia*)

Grape holly (*Mahonia* spp.)

Holly (*Ilex* spp.)

Lilac (*Syringa* spp.)

Rose of Sharon (*Hibiscus syriacus*)

Viburnum (*Viburnum* spp.)

8 DEER-RESISTANT EVERGREEN TREES AND SHRUBS

Chinese holly (*Ilex cornuta*)

Common boxwood (*Buxus sempervirens*)

Fraser fir (*Abies fraseri*)

Junipers (*Juniperus* spp.)

Mountain pine (*Pinus mugo*)

Norway spruce (*Picea abies*)

Scots pine (*Pinus sylvestris*)

White spruce (*Picea glauca*)

10 BULBS SQUIRRELS (USUALLY) WON'T BITE

Autumn crocus (*Colchicum* spp.)

Crown imperial, checker lilies (*Fritillaria* spp.)

Daffodils, narcissus (*Narcissus* spp.)

Glory of the snow (*Chionodoxa* spp.)

Grape hyacinths (*Muscari* spp.)

Grecian windflower (*Anemone blanda*)

Hyacinths (*Hyacinthus* spp.)

Ornamental alliums (*Allium* spp.)

Squills, scillas (*Scilla* spp.)

Surprise lilies (*Lycoris* spp.)

Build a Fence That Bugs Bunnies

Bunnies frolicking in your yard on a summer evening make a charming sight, but it's much harder to romanticize their company when you find your lettuce nibbled down to nubbins, and nothing but stubs where your beans used to be. Scent repellents may have some effect in keeping Peter Cottontail and pals out of your garden, but you have to be rigorous in refreshing them after every rainfall. Even then, they may not do the trick once critters have discovered the goodies in your garden.

It's easy to install a basic fence that will keep rabbits—and groundhogs—from using your garden as their own personal salad bar. The fence doesn't have to be tall—18 to 24 inches is usually enough—but it does need to extend underground. There is also good reason to allow the top of the fence to remain loose and somewhat floppy. Should a raccoon or other climbing animal try to scale the fence, the wire will naturally curl backward toward the animal, making the fence much more difficult to climb. Leaving the top edge unattached also makes it easier to step over when you're carrying tools or harvested vegetables. Although this fence does include a section that can be opened when you need to get inside with a wheelbarrow, you will usually come and go by simply stepping over the fence.

If you want to camouflage the fence, you can do so with handmade wattle panels (see "Weave a Rustic Homegrown Fence" on page 242). Or, you can use a low picket fence, which is easy to install using preassembled panels.

YOU WILL NEED

Tools: Garden spade or trenching spade, mallet, hammer, sturdy gloves, wire cutters

48-inch-tall wood or metal fence posts, 1 for each corner, plus one for every 4 feet of fencing

36-inch-wide chicken wire (also called poultry netting) to enclose the perimeter of your garden

Wire or plastic cable ties for fastening chicken wire to posts, 3 for each post

Two 24-inch-long pieces of 1 x 2 furring strip

Four 1½-inch nails

Two short bungee cords (utility tie-downs)

1. Dig a 6-inch-deep trench around the perimeter of your garden using the garden spade or trenching spade.

2. Use the mallet or hammer to set the posts in the trench, first at the corners of the garden and then at 4-foot intervals in between. Pound them in 8 inches deeper than the bottom of the trench. If necessary, make guide holes for the posts with a rebar stake.

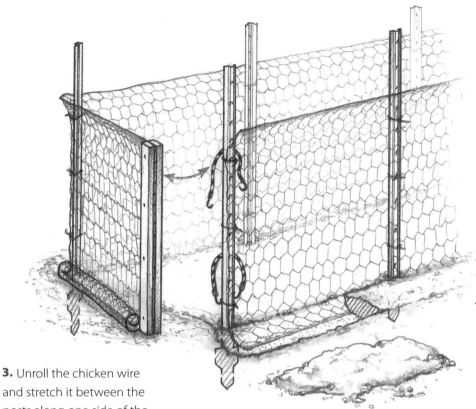

3. Unroll the chicken wire and stretch it between the posts along one side of the garden, aligning the bottom edge of the wire with the bottom of the trench. Use wire or plastic cable ties to fasten the chicken wire to the posts in three places—1 inch, 13 inches, and 25 inches above the soil. Do not attach the top edge of the chicken wire to the posts.

4. Repeat Step 3 with the remaining sides of the garden. When you reach the section between the last post and corner, cut the chicken wire to the proper length, and rein- force the cut edge with the furring strips. Lay the cut edge on the ground, and sandwich the edge of the chicken wire between the two furring strips, with the tops of the furring strips 6 inches from the top edge of the chicken wire. Nail them together.

5. To make a convenient opening in the fence, make an 8-inch-long vertical cut in the chicken wire 4 feet from the last corner post. Roll up the lowest 6 inches of chicken wire between the cut and the furring strips so it will not be buried. Fasten the reinforced end of the fence to the last corner posts with bungee cords.

6. Before refilling the trench, angle the bottom edge of the chicken wire outward, so that any animal trying to dig under the fence will be almost stand- ing on top of the wire as it digs. Refill the trench with soil, and pack it down firmly.

Make a No-Dig Barrier

Whether you want to foil cats intent on digging up newly planted carrots or squirrels after your tulip bulbs, a wire barrier will do the trick. As long as these and other animals can't get their paws into soft, freshly dug soil, your work won't be ruined. You can leave the barriers in place as long as you like. If digging mice and squirrels are a problem all winter, it's best to provide protection for bulbs until spring, when other foods become available. You can hide the wire barriers from view by covering them with a thin layer of chopped leaves or other organic mulch.

YOU WILL NEED

Tools: Sturdy gloves, wire cutters or tin snips, scissors

Chicken wire (also called poultry netting)

1 wire clothes hanger

1 yard of colorful ribbon or yarn

1. Wearing gloves to protect your hands, use the wire cutters or tin snips to cut a piece of chicken wire large enough to cover the area where your seeds or bulbs are planted. Lay it on top of the soil, and bend the edges down so they stick into the soil.

2. To make staples to secure the chicken wire in place, use the wire cutters or tin snips to cut off the two corners of the clothes hanger, 5 inches from the corners. Bend the ends in until the sides are parallel.

3. Bend the two wires attached to the hanger's hook downward until the ends are parallel. Bend the remaining straight piece of wire into a U-shape.

4. Pin down the four corners of the chicken wire with the wire staples. Tie a 9-inch piece of ribbon or yarn to each staple to make them easy to find.

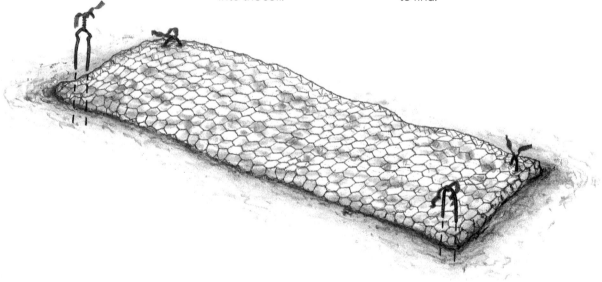

Block Bark Biters, Too

Save your fruit trees from fatal gnawing by installing protective cylinders around the trunks each winter. Mice, voles, and rabbits are notorious for nesting under mulch and snow around the base of fruit trees and nibbling away at the tender bark. By spring, the tree is often completely girdled and dead or dying from the damage. A basic barrier is all that is needed to prevent this distressing result.

Two materials are easy to fashion into cylinders to protect tender tree trunks. Chicken wire is best if the trunks are large. Simply cut a piece of chicken wire four times as long as the diameter of the tree, and make four evenly spaced 2-inch slits along the bottom edge. Bend the sections of wire between the slits outward to create a flared base, and encircle the trunk with the wire barrier. Secure the cut edges together with string or short pieces of flexible wire.

To protect smaller trees, make barriers from 4-inch-diameter plastic drainpipe, which is sold in 10-foot lengths in hardware stores and home centers. Use a utility knife to cut the plastic pipe into 18-inch segments, then slit each piece down its length. Carefully snap a section around the base of a fruit tree, taking care not to gouge the bark with the pipe as you put it in place. Install either type of rodent barrier in late fall and remove them when spring arrives to avoid creating places where insect pests can hide. Both types of barriers can be reused several times.

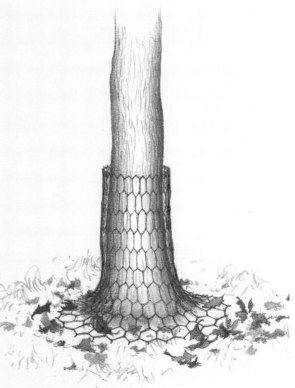

Bird-Deterrent Basics

Most gardeners regard birds as friends rather than foes, but large numbers of crows, blackbirds, jays, and even mockingbirds can become a nuisance when they discover your seeds, seedlings, or almost-ripe berries. Birds are quick to grow accustomed to the devices gardeners use to try to scare them away, so success at protecting your garden from bird damage requires a multifaceted approach.

Use motion. Whirligigs, wind socks, compact discs dangling on strings, or other devices that wiggle or wave will help keep birds wondering if the objects are alive and, therefore, if they should avoid them. Relocate these devices regularly, before birds figure out that they are actually harmless. Reflective foil tape moves in the wind, so it makes a good deterrent for tomatoes, berry bushes, and other plants that need protection for several weeks.

Use color. Put brightly colored pinwheels and flags around your garden to take advantage of birds' color vision. Some gardeners use colorful stuffed animals, purchased at yard sales, to populate their gardens with curious, colorful "predators."

Use sound. Things that make noise help to keep birds away, too. Just be careful to avoid noisemakers that drive you and your neighbors bonkers in the process. Try wind chimes or similar unobtrusive and unpredictable sound sources. One old-fashioned method that works well in windy areas is to bury empty soda bottles around the garden, with their open mouths 2 inches above the soil line. As wind blows over the bottles, it creates an eerie song that spooks birds. You can also try playing a battery-operated radio in the part of your garden you want to protect. Change the station each day so birds don't become too accustomed to the sound.

Use danger. Scarecrows such as the Flashy Scarecrow on page 240 and other things that look like threats—including rubber snakes, plastic owls, or reflective balloons —will make birds think twice about dining in your garden. The Solar Snake (see page 162) also can be used to discourage birds. Be sure to change the location of your scare devices often enough to convince birds they are real.

Use netting. Birds that are too smart or persistent for other methods can be kept from raiding the garden with plastic bird netting. Some birds will reach through netting that is draped over plants, so it's best to attach the netting to posts to create a few inches of space between the netting and the plants. Use clothespins to gather the edges of the netting together, and to secure it to strings tied between the posts.

"Go Fish" for Seed and Seedling Protection

Stop birds from dropping in to devour newly planted seeds and tender seedlings with a few strands of fishing line strung between stakes. Thin and strong, nylon fishing line is hard to see when it's stretched taut above plants or cultivated soil. You won't notice it, and neither will birds intent on getting their beaks on young corn or peas. One surprise encounter with the "invisible" line is enough to discourage most birds from going after your garden.

Installing the fishing line close to the ground also can put a stop to pets' parading through young flower beds. Dogs and cats will quickly learn to stop running through your beds when they find themselves tripped up on the hard-to-see lines. Take care not to string the fishing line where it will be likely to trip you or get in your way as you pull weeds or attend to other maintenance. The plants will hide the fishing line and stakes from view as they grow, so you can leave them in place as long as you like.

YOU WILL NEED

Tools: Hammer, scissors

6 or more wood stakes

1 spool of nylon fishing line

1. Drive a stake into the soil at the end of each row in your garden, especially rows to be planted with corn, beans, or other seeds birds like to harvest.

2. Tie fishing line to one stake about 3 inches from the top. Stretch the line tightly along the row and tie it to the stake at the other end.

3. If you're planting in blocks or wide rows, place a stake at each corner and stretch two lengths of fishing line in an "X" over the block. Then tie lines along the outside edges of the bed, too.

4. Leave the lines in place until your plants grow to the height of the lines. Snip the lines, roll them around a spool, and save them to reuse for your next planting.

Fashion a Flashy Scarecrow

Most gardeners enjoy the sight and sound of birds in the landscape—until those feathered friends take a liking to newly planted seeds, tender seedlings, and just-ripened berries. Songbirds are most likely to visit the garden in search of caterpillars and other tasty bugs, but crows, mockingbirds, jays, and a few other species sometimes become "beaks gone bad." Before these clever creatures learn that your garden is a great place for lunch, put a scarecrow or two on patrol.

Anyone who's ever done battle with crows or jays knows that the term "bird-brained" is less of an insult than most people think. These birds are bold and intelligent, and they quickly recognize the difference between genuine threats and our feeble attempts to chase them off. You can make a traditional scarecrow stuffed with straw, but this flashier version is more likely to do a good job of spooking birds. Birds quickly become accustomed to stationary stuffed scarecrows and will eventually use them as perches. They are much less likely to cozy up to a scarecrow that flashes in the sun, flaps in the wind, and has brightly colored dangling hands. A successful scarecrow may not win a prize in the fall porch-decorating contest, but its features will make it scarier to birds than any benign straw-stuffed dummy.

YOU WILL NEED

Tools: Wood saw, scissors or wire cutters, pliers, stepladder, rubber mallet

1 sturdy bamboo pole or tall fence post

3 yards of string or thin, pliable wire

1 metallic compact disc (or aluminum pie pan)

1 wire clothes hanger

Two 18-inch-long wood stakes

8 wood or plastic clothespins

1 suit of old clothes, including a long-sleeved shirt and pair of baggy pants or billowy skirt

1 pair of brightly colored rubber gloves

1. Use the saw to cut a shallow 1-inch-deep V-shaped notch in the top of the bamboo pole or fence post. Use string or thin wire to hang a shiny compact disc or a pie pan from the top of the pole, running the string through the notch to keep it from slipping. This forms the scarecrow's "head." If desired, use a waterproof marker to draw eyes on the scarecrow's face.

2. Attach a second piece of string or wire to the top of the pole, and pull a loop through the center hole of the disk (or through a hole punched near the lowest rim of the pie pan). Hook the clothes hanger through the loop. Use pliers to close the hanger's hook to help keep it on the loop.

3. Use the rubber mallet to drive the prepared pole in place in your garden. Pound 2 stakes into the ground on either side of the pole, and secure it with guy wires tied or wired to the stakes.

4. Use clothespins to fasten the pants or skirt to the hanger's cross bar. Slip the shirt over the hanger. Don't worry about stuffing the clothes—it's better if the scarecrow's "body" flaps in the slightest breeze.

5. Fasten the rubber gloves to the ends of the sleeves with clothespins. If the weight of the gloves makes the sleeves too heavy to move freely, slip a long branch, a straight piece of wire, or a yardstick into the sleeves to hold them out from the scarecrow's "body."

6. Let your scarecrow blow in the breezes. If necessary for stability, use string or fine wire to loosely attach the clothing to the pole. Keep birds guessing by moving your scarecrow around in the garden. The best time to change its location is in the evening. The next morning's early birds will be surprised to find it in a different spot.

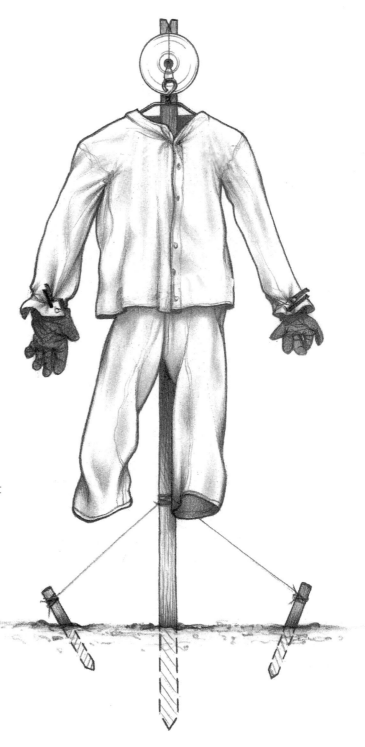

Weave a Rustic Homegrown Fence

Kids and dogs rarely mean to trample the dahlias or break off the begonias, but the damage they cause while chasing errant balls or neighborhood cats can be severe.

Here's a pretty yet practical handmade fence that can save your garden from destruction and save your family from stressful discord.

This version is 12 feet long and 3 feet high, but you can make a smaller version if you want to create a low edging around flower beds. If you live near woods, you can gather your materials as you thin out unwanted undergrowth. Or, grow your own wood for weaving (see "Grow Great Wood for Weaving" on page 252). If your own property lacks a supply of wattle-worthy wood, check with a local tree-trimming business or your local parks department to see if you can acquire what you need from them. The misguided pruning practice of "topping" trees causes them to produce a gold mine of growth that's perfect for wattle fence construction—loads of long, straight, whippy branches. If your neighbor is inclined to this type of arboreal abuse, offer to prune the afflicted tree of its resulting suckers (those long, straight stems) and put them to good use in your fence.

YOU WILL NEED

Tools: Pruning saw, loppers, pruning shears, hatchet, measuring tape, hammer, scissors

One 18-inch-long rebar stake

Small piece of scrap lumber

Five 4-foot-long, 2-inch-diameter posts

Thirty-two 4-foot-long flexible branches

Jute or twine

1. Use the pruning saw and loppers to gather your materials. Trim off stubs and leaves with pruning shears. Shape one end of each post to a point with a sharp hatchet.

2. Mark places for posts 3 feet apart. Use the rebar stake, topped with a piece of scrap lumber, to make guide holes for the posts. Pound the posts into the guide holes 12 inches deep. They may be slightly wobbly.

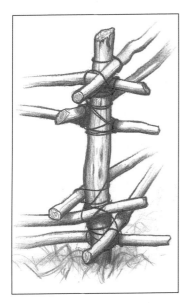

3. Starting at each end, weave flexible branches between the posts, alternating the position of each branch on either side of the posts. Use at least four horizontal rows of branches to make the fence sturdy enough to work as a barrier. As you weave, adjust the posts as needed to keep them upright. The fence will become sturdier as each row of horizontal branches is added.

More Woven Wood Barriers

If you have a supply of thin, flexible suckers but don't want to weave them between posts, you can still make a pretty rustic barrier to protect garden beds from tumbling children or pets. Bend long, flexible branches into arches, and stick the ends in the ground. Overlap the end of each arch by about 3 inches. Then use string to tie the arches together at each place where the branches overlap. If you like, you can then weave thin branches in and out through the upright parts of the arches, or do the same with long pieces of grapevine or string.

To protect individual plants or small newly seeded areas from unwanted foot traffic, surround them with a wreath woven from grapevines or thin, flexible saplings (see "Make a Grapevine Wreath" on page 258). Place a few upright sticks around the wreath to hold it in place and serve as a visual marker. When the plants gain size and no longer need protection, move the wreath to a new section of your garden.

4. When you are satisfied with the woven pattern of the branches, use jute or twine to tie the ends of protruding branches to adjacent horizontal branches to hold them in place. Trim off any awkward ends.

5. Weave jute or twine through the ends of the horizontal branches on both outside edges of the fence, lashing them to the outermost posts to keep them from sliding up and down. Trim the ends of the branches on the outside of the fence to make them even.

Five Fine Pest Barriers

Faced with unexpected pest problems, creative gardeners have come up with a long list of easy-to-make barriers. The more you garden, the more you will probably invent solutions to pest challenges. Like the ones described here, they may surprise you with their simplicity—and with how well they work.

MILK JUG MELON CRADLES

Protect developing melons from mice and mold. Cut a 1-gallon plastic milk jug in half vertically, and then use an ice pick to punch three or four drainage holes in each half. Slip a prepared cradle beneath a growing melon or winter squash. The plastic cradle will create enough of a barrier to protect the fruit from nibbling mice and other determined varmints, and it will also reduce the risk of rot due to soil-dwelling fungi and bacteria.

BAG UP YOUR CORN

If you think that raccoons or crows are watching your sweet corn for signs of ripening, beat them to the punch by covering almost-ripe ears with small paper bags (such as lunch bags) fastened in place with clothespins or rubber bands.

MAKE FLEA BEETLE TEEPEES

If you grow eggplant, you've seen the tiny jumping flea beetles that chew hundreds of holes in eggplant leaves. Flea beetles often move to eggplant from early potatoes, or from horse nettle, a common host weed. To keep them off your eggplant, make a teepee around the plants with several sticks fastened together at the top with string, and cover the structure with scraps of rowcover or a piece of cheesecloth. Either can be held in place with clothespins.

BUBBLE WRAP BARRIER

Broccoli, cauliflower, and other cabbage family cousins often thrive in the fall garden—if you can keep them safe from cabbage root maggots, the larvae of a fast-moving fly. To frustrate these flies, surround each seedling with a mat that covers the root zone and fits snugly around the stem. Tar paper is a popular choice, or you can use bubble wrap. Cut either material into a 10-inch-wide circle, cut a slit from one edge to the center, and place it around seedlings right after transplanting.

STICK SQUIRREL BARRIER

In a good acorn year, squirrels are eager to hide their treasures everywhere, including in large containers left outdoors through the winter. Keep hardy plants safe from squirrel digging by covering your pots with a simple barrier woven from sticks. Collect a dozen or so sticks a few inches longer than the diameter of your pot, and weave them together, waffle-style, on a flat surface. Then go back and tie the joints together with string. Place the barrier over the soil in your containers.

CHAPTER 8

Special Crops for Handy Gardeners

Your garden can become a great source of craft, project, and building materials if you grow these multitalented plants.

245

Creating a Super-Resourceful Garden

Few experiences in a gardener's life are more satisfying than growing a robust vegetable garden that's nicely trimmed with beautiful flowers, but why not let your garden work a little harder by growing your own plant stakes and trellis-building supplies? Or how about growing some nutty grains for popping, fragrant herbs to brew into tea, or gourds to craft into birdhouses, dippers, or unique works of art? Growing multipurpose plants is great fun, and they will make you a more self-sufficient gardener, too.

This is not a new idea. Only a century ago, resourceful gardeners made room for a plot of broomcorn every few years so they would have the perfect materials for making new whisk brooms to replace old ones that had been singed in the fireplace. In Europe, many gardeners maintained coppice plots of willow, from which they could cut wonderfully pliable stems for weaving into fences and trellises. To this day, Asian gardens often include clumps of bamboo that are as beautiful as they are practical, providing a steady supply of canes for use as stakes, panels, or even water pipes. Whether you are creating a tea garden or growing wheat to use in food or crafts, the plants and projects in this chapter will help you celebrate the true bounty of Nature's global garden.

LANDSCAPING WITH USEFUL PLANTS

You do not need a huge garden to make use of many of these resourceful plants. Instead, simply look for ways to work them into your existing landscape.

- Clump-forming bamboos make wonderful screening plants for property boundaries, and you can carve secret passageways through mature stands.
- Use grapes to cover a pergola or overhead trellis such as the Found-Wood Rustic Arbor on page 110.
- A few willows grown for coppice can be tucked into a woodland edge or slipped into a shrub border.
- Many grains are perfectly at home planted anchoring the edge of your vegetable garden. Tall-growing grains such as millet and amaranth can even be used as a Single-Season Windbreak (see page 167). Or, let small clumps of ornamental wheat support your spring peas.
- Grow kitchen herbs near your back door, where sprigs can be quickly gathered when you need them for cooking.
- Include flowers that dry well in any flower bed, or let them provide color and diversity when woven into your vegetable garden.

GROWING POSSIBILITIES

Many of us are quite happy when our gardens keep us well supplied with fresh food and flowers, but there is nothing wrong with expecting a little bit more. Why should you have to buy plant stakes when you can grow or gather your own? If you enjoy the companionship of flowers, you will surely be delighted by everlasting flowers that keep their good looks for months when displayed indoors.

This is the kind of resourceful thinking that has made the plants in this chapter such valuable garden assets. All are easy to grow, but because they are so different from more familiar garden plants, you should expect them to take you into new and exciting gardening frontiers. Perhaps you will discover a deep fascination with amaranth or other ancient grains that have been serving mankind for thousands of years, or find yourself so delighted with the wreaths you can make with grapevines that the fruits (or lack of them) are of little importance.

DIGGING DEEPER

Use this chapter as an introduction to these interesting plants that have been serving gardeners for centuries. Should the easy projects here, such as making a Bamboo Rainstick (see page 250) or weaving a Good Luck Charm (see page 264), whet your appetite for more, do take the time to find more in-depth information on the plants that have captured your interest. You can begin with the specialty nurseries suggested on page 296. Also take your curiosity to your local library, which may have excellent sourcebooks to help you explore primitive yet practical garden-grown crafts.

Putting these plants to work in your garden is a simple and interesting way to let your landscape work harder. For example, a garden stocked with culinary herbs can help fill its keeper's spice cabinet (see "Plant a Potted Kitchen Herb Garden" on page 270); gourds will produce garden-grown bird housing (see "Grow Gorgeous Gourds" on page 280); and including bamboo or willow in your garden will reduce the number of trips you must make to the garden center for supplies, and increase your ability to rely on your garden for more of your basic needs.

Ready to get started? This chapter begins with bamboo and ends with gourds—Nature's most versatile containers. In between, you will get to know grapes, grains, and dozens more hardworking plants.

Using Multipurpose Plants

When you welcome super-resourceful plants into your garden, you are taking a major step toward developing a more sustainable landscape. This practice has a name, *permaculture*, which was coined by Bill Mollison, an Australian ecologist, in 1978. Since then, people around the world have sought and found ways to enrich their land with easily grown plants that have multiple uses. When you thoughtfully observe what you need from your garden (such as food, beauty, building materials, or habitat for wildlife) and employ plants that can be added without destroying what Nature has already put in place, you are practicing a form of permaculture. This can be a tremendously satisfying journey, in which you help Nature to make a place more productive while enhancing its environmental integrity.

The Best Bamboo for You

Despite its treelike appearance and the woody texture of its canes, bamboo is actually a giant grass. Like many grasses, it spreads by a network of underground stems, or rhizomes. New canes (culms) sprout from the rhizomes in spring and summer, and usually grow to their maximum size within a few months. A bamboo cane does not become entirely woody until its third or fourth year; as a general rule, the canes are best harvested when they are 2 years old. Left uncut, canes usually begin to decline after they are 4 to 5 years old.

Cane size varies with species, and ranges from 70 feet tall and 6 inches in diameter to only 2 feet tall and ¼ inch in diameter. The canes produced by young clumps often are small compared to those that spring from established mature plants. Even small canes, less than ½ inch in diameter, make wonderful plant stakes, while larger ones can be used to make trellises, fences, or dozens of other garden projects (see "Great Things to Do with Bamboo" on page 251). Once you have a clump of bamboo nicely situated in your yard, you may wonder how you ever gardened without it.

TYPES OF BAMBOO

Bamboo falls into two groups: clumping species and running types. Within each group, species vary in their tolerance of cold weather, as well as their mature size. See the "Eight Great Bamboos" chart to get acquainted with species suitable for your garden.

Clumping Bamboos

In small yards, clumping types are a wise choice because they stay put and never threaten to take over a garden. The canes of clumping types are shorter than those of most running species, but they are large enough to use as plant stakes and in small projects. Heat-craving clumping bamboos often wait until midsummer to produce their new growth, and the new canes continue to grow until late fall. New culms often do not develop branches or leaves until their second summer. Below ground, clumping bamboos develop short rhizomes in late summer in preparation for new growth the following year. Clumping bamboos do spread, but they do so modestly and are much easier to control compared to running types.

Running Bamboos

Running species develop much longer rhizomes than clump-forming types, so they are naturally invasive plants. Established clumps may send out rhizomes more than 20 feet from the parent clump. Do not plant running bamboo unless you are willing to commit to its control, which is not difficult as long as you stay on top of the task (see "Prevent the Spread of Running Bamboo" on page 251). The rewards for your dedication can be great, because many running bamboos reliably produce huge crops of strong canes, and you can harvest and eat the unwanted shoots.

GROWING BAMBOO

Bamboo is typically sold in containers, or you can take divisions from established clumps. Bamboo has shallow roots, so it is easy to dig and transplant short shoots that appear at the edge of a colony. Make new plantings from spring to early summer, when all types of bamboo make vigorous new growth. Set plants at the same depth they grew in their pots or parent clumps, and be sure to water

Eight Great Bamboos

THREE CLUMPING BAMBOOS

NAME	HARDINESS	SIZE	CHARACTERISTICS
Dragon head bamboo (*Fargesia dracocephala*)	Zones 5 to 10	10- to 15-foot arching canes, 1 inch in diameter	Tall, arching canes form a beautiful clump; lower sections of canes make good plant stakes. Evergreen in Zones 7 to 10.
Hedge bamboo (*Bambusa multiplex*)	Zones 8 to 10	10-foot upright canes, 1 to 2 inches in diameter	Best clump-forming bamboo for making stakes, fences, and other craft projects. Mature clumps spread slightly.
Umbrella bamboo (*Fargesia murieiae*)	Zones 5 to 10	10- to 15-foot arching canes, ½ to 1 inch in diameter	Umbrella-like canes arch overhead; lower sections make good plant stakes, or longer ones can be tied together to form trellises or arbors. Evergreen in Zones 7 to 10.

FIVE RUNNING BAMBOOS

NAME	HARDINESS	SIZE	CHARACTERISTICS
Dwarf goldenstripe bamboo (*Pleioblastus viridistriatus*)	Zones 7 to 10	2- to 4-foot-tall canes, ½ inch in diameter	New growth emerges striped with yellow and ripens to green; tolerates shade and grows into a dense groundcover. Good for containers.
Dwarf timber bamboo (*Phyllostachys bissetii*)	Zones 6 to 10	15- to 20-feet tall, canes 1 to 2 inches in diameter	Good bamboo for a hardy hedge; yields edible shoots and versatile canes for use as stakes or trellises. Invasive unless controlled.
Kumazasa bamboo (*Sasa veitchii*)	Zones 7 to 10	4- to 5-feet tall, canes less than ½ inch in diameter	Small canes make good plant stakes, and dried leaves can be used in flower arrangements. Easier to control than larger running types.
Timber bamboo (*Phyllostachys bambusoides*)	Zones 7 to 10	20- to 35-feet tall, canes 2 to 4 inches in diameter	This big, running bamboo produces large, strong canes for construction projects, plus tasty edible shoots. Invasive unless controlled.
Yellow groove bamboo (*Phyllostachys aureosulcata*)	Zones 6 to 10	15- to 30-feet tall, canes 1 to 2 inches in diameter	Canes ripen from yellow to green as they mature, and shoots are edible. Invasive unless controlled.

them thoroughly. When planting a running type of bamboo, install a root barrier before setting out the plants (see "Prevent the Spread of Running Bamboo" on the next page).

Established bamboo requires minimal care. Being a grass, it needs plenty of nitrogen for healthy growth, especially during the first two seasons after planting. Any balanced organic fertilizer recommended for lawns will work well for bamboo when applied in early summer. Established bamboo colonies often thrive with no supplemental fertilizer.

Make a Bamboo Rainstick

Each time a bamboo rainstick is turned upside down, it gives off the sound of gently falling rain. If desired, you can paint your rainstick or decorate it with beads and woven string.

YOU WILL NEED

Tools: Handsaw, drill, hammer, pruning shears

One 2-foot-long piece of bamboo at least 2 inches in diameter

One 18-inch-long metal or wood stick

20 to 30 round wooden toothpicks

All-purpose glue

4 tablespoons of raw rice or plastic craft pellets

One cork or round of wood, cut to fit inside the bamboo

1. Cut the bamboo to length, with one end just beyond a node. This end will remain closed.

2. Stand the cane on its end, and use a drill to make several holes in the membrane within the nearest node. Use the hammer and stick to knock the insides of the nodes open. Shake out the broken pieces.

3. Drill 20 to 30 holes in the cane the same diameter as the toothpicks. Snip the ends from the toothpicks before poking them through the holes as far as they will go. Pull them back out ¼ inch, trim with pruning shears, and then push them back into the cane. Seal the toothpicks in place with a drop of glue.

4. Place the rice or craft pellets in the rainstick. Close the open end by gluing a round of cork or wood into the open end.

PREVENT THE SPREAD OF RUNNING BAMBOO

Bringing any invasive plant into your garden requires careful planning, and bamboo is no exception. Decide ahead of time how much space you want to allow for your colony, and install a barrier before setting out your first plants. To bring a neglected colony of spreading bamboo under control, you will need to dig out all unwanted plants before implementing one of these control strategies.

- Isolate the colony within a broad, 15-foot-wide mowing strip. Mow the perimeter often, especially in the spring, when new growth is tender. Use a sharp knife to sever shoots that appear in unwanted places. (The shoots of most big running bamboos are edible. Boil them for a few minutes to make them tender and to remove any bitterness.)
- Use a buried barrier to slow the spread of the roots. A 2-foot-wide piece of aluminum flashing, buried vertically in the soil around the entire clump, makes a good preventive control.
- Surround the planting with a 12-inch-deep trench filled with mulch. Every few weeks from spring to fall, chop through the trench with a sharp spade to sever rhizomes that have spread into the trench. In the fall when chopped leaves become available, replenish the trench with a fresh supply.
- Grow small spreading species in large containers that have had their bottoms removed.
- Place your planting near water. Running bamboos will not grow into a pond or stream.

Great Things to Do with Bamboo

- Use bamboo canes as plant stakes. Use an ordinary handsaw to cut stakes to length, rotating the canes as you saw to help prevent splintering.
- Tie three or more long canes together at the top to form a Teepee Trellis (see page 94). Shorter canes can be used to make smaller teepees for cucumbers or flowering vines.
- Combine bamboo with wood to make a Tie-Together Trellis (see page 98).
- Make a *shishi odoshi*, a traditional Japanese-style bamboo fountain, by linking a small submersible pump to hollow pieces of bamboo (see "Make a Terra-Cotta Fountain" on page 144 for easy basic instructions on making a fountain). To prevent water loss, push the plastic tubing attached to the pump all the way through the length of the bamboo pieces.
- Build a bamboo fence by tying together canes in either a horizontal or vertical pattern. Bamboo decomposes quickly when buried, so it's best to attach a fence to wood or metal posts.
- Tie together small canes to create a bamboo mat that can be used as a shade cover over young seedlings. Roll it up and store it in a dry place when it is not in use.

Grow Great Wood for Weaving

When you cut a vigorous young tree back to a stump, it often tries to regrow by producing several long, slender whips. Many gardeners regard these as a nuisance, but they can be such a rich source of materials for garden projects that you may want to grow them on purpose. This practice is called coppicing, and it is the oldest form of forestry, employed in England and France since Neolithic times. From the early Middle Ages through the late 19th century, many types of trees and shrubs in lowland England were coppiced in order to supply sufficient material for firewood, posts, stakes, props, poles, hoop-wood, laths, fencing, charcoal, baskets, and even brooms. When managed properly, coppiced willows—and several other species—will produce whips for many years. Meanwhile, a small coppice plot provides food and shelter for birds and other wildlife.

WORKING WITH FOUND WOOD

Any wood that is cut when it is young and pliable can be used as hoops (which are placed over plants to support rowcover or winter blankets, or to simply stabilize stems), or you can use them to weave fences, edgings, or trellises. The new wood of willows is quite pliable, so willows are the first choice among gardeners who want to grow their own weaving woods (see "Seven Great Woods for Weaving" on the next page). But if you have a small woodlot, you often can gather plenty of pliable whips from other trees, including maples, oaks, dogwoods, and Pawlonia (empress tree). Trees that regrow rapidly after being cut back often produce huge crops of coppice. Once you develop a good eye for weaving wood, you may be able to find treasures in piles of prunings left on the curb by your neighbors or professional tree-trimming crews.

The best times to gather wood for weaving are late winter and late fall, when new stems are bare of leaves. Then use loppers or pruning shears to trim the branches to the length you want. Freshly cut green sticks are quite pliable, but quickly stiffen as they dry. If you cannot use found wood right away, push the trimmed sticks into a bucket filled with damp sand to keep them from drying out.

GETTING STARTED WITH WILLOWS

Willows are easy to grow, require little space, and will produce plenty of weavable wood when cut back every other year. Many also produce pretty catkins in spring. In addition, willow stems contain soluble compounds similar to those present in commercial rooting powders, so you can use willow twigs to make your own rooting solution to speed root development in plants being propagated by rooting stem tip cuttings (see "Wows for Willow Water" on page 67). These compounds serve willows as well. When stuck into the ground in spring—at about the same time you plant tomatoes—8-inch-long willow stem tip cuttings root readily. Specialty nurseries that sell willows for weaving ship cuttings in spring.

Once you have a plant growing in your garden, you can increase the size of your coppice plot by simply poking cuttings into the ground just before the branches leaf out in spring.

Seven Great Woods for Weaving

FOUR WONDERFUL WILLOWS

NAME	HARDINESS	DESCRIPTION	USES
Almond-leafed willow (*Salix triandra*, 'Black Maul')	Zone 4	Large shrub, up to 35 feet tall when left uncut. New growth is maroon-black; best when rods are cut every other year, when less than 6 feet long.	Fences, trellises, hoops, basketry; catkins make good cut flowers.
Corkscrew willow (*Salix matsudana*)	Zone 5	Large shrub or 40-foot tree when left uncut, with unusual twisted branches. New growth turns yellow or red in spring, depending on variety. Rods can be cut annually.	Trellises, arbors. Makes good specimen plant; branches produce excellent cut flowers.
Golden twig willow (*Salix alba*, 'Vitellina')	Zone 3	Large shrub or 60-foot tree when left uncut. New growth is bright golden yellow. Best when half of rods are cut annually when they are 6 feet long.	Trellises, fences, hoops, basketry; makes a good hedge.
Purple willow (*Salix purpurea*)	Zone 3	Medium-size shrub grows 16 feet tall when left uncut. Deep purple rods best cut in spring, when less than 3 feet long. Can be cut every 1 to 2 years.	Plant supports, small trellises, basketry. Catkins make good cut flowers.

THREE MORE WEAVABLE WOODS

NAME	HARDINESS	DESCRIPTION	USES
Catalpa (*Catalpa bignonioides*)	Zone 5	Medium-size tree grows up to 45 feet tall when left uncut. Best tree for coppice in warm climates. Rods can be cut yearly from established stumps.	Fences, trellises, plant stakes, hoops.
European hazel (*Corylus avellana*)	Zone 4	Large shrub grows up to 15 feet tall when left uncut. When grown as coppice, 6-foot-long pliable rods can be cut every other year.	Fences, trellises, plant stakes, hoops.
Red osier dogwood (*Cornus sericea*)	Zone 3	Small to medium-size shrub grows 3 to 5 feet tall when left uncut. Rods cut in spring may be red or yellow, depending on variety. Cut one-third of most supple rods each year.	Small trellises, basketry, other crafts.

Grow a
Living Fedge

hat do you get when you cross a fence with a hedge? The answer is a fedge, which you can make by weaving fresh willow branches together, with their bases nestled into moist soil so they take root and grow. You can start a fedge with willow or other woody cuttings gathered from woods or roadsides, or use one of the species described in the "Seven Great Woods for Weaving" chart on page 253. Or, use whatever green branches you have on hand, including those pruned from fruit trees, grapes, or forsythia or other flowering shrubs. As long as you make the fedge in spring, when deciduous plants are just emerging from dormancy, many of them will take root and leaf out.

In traditional fedges, branches are arranged diagonally, so they cross each other within the structure. However, you also have the option of setting branches into the ground vertically, so they grow straight up. A fedge can be temporary—lasting only a few years—or you can make it a permanent part of your landscape. If your goal is to establish a permanent coppice plot, you can plant your first cuttings in a fedge, and then cut all of the plants back to the ground after 2 years. In subsequent seasons, the plants will regrow into a hedge that will produce a steady supply of young branches to use in garden projects made of weavable woods.

YOU WILL NEED

Tools: Spade, handsaw, wire snips, staple gun

Three 5-foot-long wood posts

30 feet of 10-gauge wire

Twelve 8-inch-long willow stem tip cuttings (or cuttings from other deciduous plants)

Mulch for a 12-foot-long row

1. Prepare the soil in a 12-foot-long row by digging in organic matter and removing weeds, roots, and rocks. Set the posts in the ground, 12 inches deep and 4 feet apart.

2. Install 2 tiers of wire between the posts, with the bottom tier 12 inches from the ground and the top tier 36 inches from the ground. Wrap the ends of the wire around the end posts before snipping off the ends. Staple the wire to all three posts.

3. Push half of the cuttings into the ground 2 feet apart and 3 inches deep, setting them at a diagonal angle. Push the remaining cuttings into the soil 6 inches from the first set, crossing the cuttings so they form right angles. Water well.

4. As the cuttings begin to leaf out, remove any weeds and then mulch over the soil. Train the new growth to twine in and out between the wires.

Great Things to Do with Weavable Woods

- Make a Twig Tower in a Pot (see page 112).
- Build a Found-Wood Rustic Arbor (see page 110).
- Use 6-foot-long green, pliable branches as support hoops for rowcover or plastic over an Easy-Does-It Raised Bed (see page 12). Replace the branches yearly, as they become brittle.
- Weave a Rustic Homegrown Fence (see page 242).
- Bend pliable branches into hoops, and place them over bushy perennials such as peonies or asters as grow-through plant supports. For the best support, place two arches over a plant side by side and 3 to 4 inches apart. Then cross these with a second pair of arches.
- Make a Waffle-Weave Squirrel Barrier (see page 244).
- Use the trimmings from your other projects to tie together a twig mat, which makes a great shade cover for newly seeded beds. Tie 30 or so 2-foot-long sticks together with two long pieces of hemp or jute string. Roll up the mat and keep it in a dry place when it is not in use.
- Turn a plain glass jar into an attractive vase by covering it with small sticks placed side by side. Place two rubber bands over the jar, and slip twigs under the bands until the jar is completely covered. Cover the rubber bands with raffia or decorative ribbons.

Good Things from Grapes

Most gardeners who grow grapes begin with visions of sun-ripened clusters, but long-lived grapevines have much more to offer. Large grape leaves do a great job of providing summer shade when the vines are trained to grow over a sturdy arbor. Beginning 2 years after planting, grape flower clusters will perfume the air with their fruity fragrance in late spring, and even tart, seedy grapes make delicious juice or jelly.

Grape leaves are handy in the kitchen, too. All summer long, you can pick young leaves, blanch them in boiling water for a minute, and then use them as wrappers for spicy rice-and-meat fillings, as Greek and Middle Eastern cooks have been doing for thousands of years. When you want to dress up a summer platter of any cold salad, use blanched grape leaves like lettuce for lining the plate. The gnarled woody trunks make grapes an attractive plant in winter, too, and pruned branches will provide you with a good supply of vines to weave into wreaths and other crafts. See "Great Things to Do with Grapevines" on page 259 for clever ways to use grapevines in other garden projects.

SELECTING GOOD GRAPES

Many of the most flavorful table grapes and wine grapes are descended from European varieties. These are worth a try if you are lucky enough to live in a good grape-growing climate, where summer days are warm yet nights are cool, and there is only a little late summer rain. Humid conditions set the stage for numerous disease problems, which commercial growers manage by spraying plants often with fungicides. This is neither practical nor pleasant in a home garden, so it's better to choose grapes known for their tough constitutions. Time-tested varieties descended from native species, such as those described in the "Six Great North American Grapes" chart, are the best candidates for a low-maintenance edible landscape.

You will need a sunny, well-drained site and a sturdy trellis. Consider building a Found-Wood Rustic Arbor (see page 110) or a T-Trellis (see page 108) for grapes. When grown in soil that has been enriched with organic matter, grapes do not need much fertilizer—a late winter topdressing with good compost is usually sufficient.

Grapes are notorious for varying in flavor depending on where they are grown and the season's weather. Fruit flavor is often weak or sour in cool, damp summers, or you may lose the crop altogether to disease. This is no great loss when you consider the other things you can get from grapes—eye-pleasing greenery, cooling shade, edible leaves, and craft-worthy vines. If you simply do not like the flavor of the grapes your vines produce, wild birds will be delighted to have them.

Six Great North American Grapes

North America is home to dozens of wild grape species, and varieties descended from native grapes are the easiest grapes to grow. Some are true heirlooms dating back to the early 1800s, when fruit growers developed varieties that tasted better than wild strains, yet did not succumb to cold or disease as the European strains tended to do. If you want to try more modern seedless varieties, ask your local Extension Service for suggestions, because grapes vary in their tolerance of cold and heat, as well as their ability to stand up to insects and diseases.

VARIETY	ZONES	DESCRIPTION	USES
Beta (*Vitis riparia* hybrid)	3 to 7	Extremely cold-hardy cross between 'Concord' and the wild "riverbank" grape found growing along streams from Canada to Colorado.	Jelly
Concord (*Vitis labrusca*)	5 to 8	Purple-fruited seedling selected in Concord, Massachusetts, in 1849. Easy to grow in a wide range of climates and soils.	Jelly, juice
Delaware (*Vitis labrusca*)	5 to 8	Red-fruited selection made in Ohio in the early 1800s, valued for its sweet, fruity flavor	Jelly, juice, wine
Muscadine (*Vitis rotundifolia*)	6 to 9	Numerous varieties are available of this Southeastern native species. Plant two varieties for good pollination.	Table, jelly, juice
Niagara (*Vitis labrusca*)	5 to 8	White-fruited descendant of 'Concord,' selected in Lockport, New York, in 1867. Bears fragrant, full-flavored berries.	Jelly, juice
Sunbelt (*Vitis labrusca*)	5 to 9	Modern 'Concord' type better adapted to climates with warm, humid summers. Developed in Arkansas in 1993.	Jelly, juice

HOW TO GROW GRAPES

The best time to plant a new grapevine is spring, when the plants are just emerging from winter dormancy. Nurseries sell 1- or 2-year-old vines, which should be planted at the same depth they grew in their containers. Trim back long roots as you set the plants in fertile, well-drained planting holes, because roots pruned to less than 10 inches long quickly develop a strong network of good feeder roots. After planting, water the plants thoroughly and cover the area over the root zone with a 2-inch deep blanket of compost, chopped leaves, or other organic mulch.

Fertilize grapes in early summer by scratching a balanced, organic fertilizer into the soil beneath the mulch. In autumn, rake up and compost fallen grape leaves to interrupt the life cycles of pests and diseases. If your soil is extremely acidic, sprinkle on a small amount of lime as you give your grapes a fresh helping of mulch in early winter. Grapes thrive in slightly acidic soil with a pH between 5.0 and 6.0.

PRUNING GRAPES

Commercial grape growers follow strict pruning regimens, but you can be much more casual when growing a vine as an edible ornamental. The second spring, prune off long branches until only the trunk and two strong lateral branches (which sprout from the main vine) remain. Fruit production usually begins in the third year. Consult a fruit-growing manual if you want to follow pruning practices intended to maximize fruit production. However, if you want to grow a lush vine that cascades over

Make a Grapevine Wreath

When gathering vines from wild or cultivated grapes for making wreaths, use pruning shears to nip off the leaves (save pretty young leaves for cooking). Leave the curled tendrils intact. If you will not be using the vines right away, wind them into a coil in a large washtub or laundry basket, and cover them with a wet towel.

You can make grapevine wreaths freehand, but it's easier to use a form made from a piece of scrap plywood. Decorate your wreath after it has dried.

YOU WILL NEED

Tools: Measuring tape, pencil, hammer, pruning shears

One 2-foot-square piece of scrap plywood

Four 4-inch nails

4 or more pieces of grapevine at least 4 feet long

Several 8-inch-long pieces of string

1. Draw an 18-inch-wide circle on the plywood, and hammer four 4-inch nails at equal intervals around the circle. Hammer them only as deep as needed to hold them secure.

2. Holding the thickest end of a cut piece of vine, wind it loosely around the nails, and then tuck in both of the ends. Repeat with as many vines as you like.

3. To help hold the wreath tight, tie it together with pieces of string before slipping it off of the form.

4. Lay the wreath on a flat surface to dry, and expect it to shrink a little. Should a wreath begin to warp as it dries, weight it with a board held in place with a brick.

an arbor and provides plenty of edible leaves and supple vines, limit late winter pruning to relieving crowded conditions in the canopy. In summer and fall, you can freely gather vines that are not holding fruit as you need them for craft projects. Vines taken in winter are craftable, too, but they break more easily than green ones.

TROUBLE-SHOOTING GRAPES

Mature grapevines that refuse to develop blossoms and fruit may be overfertilized, which is not a problem if you are growing grapes for shade, leaves, and craft-worthy vines. If fruit clusters develop but are then ruined by a fuzzy mold, the problem is gray rot, a fungal disease that overwinters in soil and mulch and is encouraged by damp weather. Fruits that dry into hard mummies are infected with another fungal disease called black rot. Remove and dispose of infected fruits to reduce black rot problems in future seasons.

In many areas, leaf-eating Japanese beetles are the most serious insect pest of grapes. Collect them in a pail of soapy water during their 6-week summer feeding season.

TRY AN ORNAMENTAL GRAPE

The ornamental claret vine (*Vitis vinifera purpurea*) produces small, sour fruits, but its burgundy leaves—and vigorous vines—make it a great plant for arbors. Adapted in Zones 6 to 9, this European grapte often resists disease since it expends so little energy producing fruit. Claret vine is increasingly available in nurseries.

Great Things to Do with Grapevines

- Weave pieces of grapevine into any type of trellis. Grapevines are perfect for the horizontal rings in the Twig Tower in a Pot (see page 112), or you can use them to add shapely curves to the Found-Wood Rustic Arbor (see page 110).
- Use short pieces of vine as decorative trim for birdhouses, bird feeders, or an outdoor mirror, hung on a fence or wall.
- Make three small wreaths that can be stacked up and used to encircle a pot of flowers kept on your deck or patio.
- Make a grapevine ball to use as a decorative finial atop a fence post or trellis. If you have a lot of vines, you can make a large grapevine ball by winding green vines around a beach ball. Deflate and remove the beach ball after you have enough vines woven together to form a sturdy sphere. Then add more vines!
- Place a grapevine wreath on the ground to protect newly seeded beds, or to mark the location of a dormant perennial.
- Use thick pieces of grapevine to add texture to woven stick fences such as the Rustic Homegrown Fence (see page 242).

Grow Gifted Grains

If you're looking for a really different garden project this year, why not try your hand at growing grains? Many gardeners grow corn, but there are many other garden-worthy grains to try in your garden. And, although grains are often regarded as "field" crops, you don't need 40 acres or heavy-duty farm machinery to grow grains—a sunny, well-drained spot and a few basic garden tools will get you started.

In the following pages, you will get to know eight easy-to-grow grains that have been serving mankind for many centuries. From amaranth to the special strain of sorghum known as broomcorn, these plants can diversify the food supply produced by your garden and serve as the basis for interesting and useful garden projects.

GOOD COOKING GRAINS

With a world of grains to choose from, it can be tough to decide which ones to try first. It helps if you think about what you'd like to do with the grains. Do you want to grow grains as food or crafts, or do you want to use them both ways? You can narrow down your choices from there.

- If you want to grind your own flour for baking—and have some decorative dried material for flower arrangements—wheat, rye, or triticale (a wheat-rye cross) are all excellent choices.
- Amaranth, barley, buckwheat, or millet can be ground into a coarse meal using an ordinary coffee mill. When mixed with wheat flour, they add fantastic flavor and texture to breads or muffins, or you can cook them into nutrition-packed hot cereals.
- Enjoy cooked amaranth, barley, or quinoa grains whole as an alternative to rice or potatoes. Add them to soups and stews.
- Expand your snack options by popping amaranth or sorghum seeds over medium heat in a dry nonstick skillet. Enjoy the popped grains hot from the pan, or allow them to cool and mix them with dried fruits and nuts.
- The tender young leaves of amaranth and quinoa make a fine addition to salads, and the steamed older leaves can stand in as a hot-weather spinach substitute.

BEYOND THE KITCHEN

Pretty and productive, grains also provide a wealth of inspiration for clever crafters, and grains with colorful foliage or seeds can do double duty as garden ornamentals. The seed heads of amaranth, millet, sorghum, and wheat all look great in wreaths and arrangements, either alone or mixed with dried flowers (see "Grow Flowers That Last Forever" on page 274). And, if you'd like to try making your own brooms, then broomcorn (a type of sorghum) belongs on your list of grains to try. Just want to grow grains for the fun of it? Don't bother harvesting at all, and instead enjoy watching wild birds feasting in your garden until the last morsel is gone!

HOW TO GROW GRAINS

Grains don't require much special soil prep-aration, but it's critical to get weeds under control before planting, because it's hard to weed while the plants are growing. The soil doesn't need to be very rich, but most grains will grow even better if you've worked some compost into the soil. Rake the seedbed well to remove stones, large lumps, and other de-bris. Use a seeder, or broadcast the seed by hand as evenly as possible, then rake to cover the seed. The "Eight Gifted Grains" chart on page 262 suggests sowing rates for 100 square feet, which should provide plenty of material for crafting or experimenting with grains in the kitchen. If you're serious about baking or cooking with homegrown grains, you can increase the amount of space you plant with your favorite grains. To insure pollination by both insects and wind, plant grains in blocks rather than in long, narrow rows.

Keep the seedbed evenly moist until sprouts appear. After that, most grains don't need supplemental water during the growing season. You can harvest small patches with pruning shears or a garden knife. When har-vesting larger patches, a sickle, machete, or string trimmer makes the job go faster.

TROUBLE-SHOOTING GRAINS

Pests and diseases usually aren't a major prob-lem in home-garden plantings. One serious exception on rye is ergot, a fungal disease that is poisonous when ingested; if you see black kernel-like growths among the usual light-colored grains, destroy the affected heads. Do not eat them.

Great Things to Do with Gifted Grains

- If you garden in a windy area, include grains in a Single-Season Windbreak (see page 167).
- Fill a fabric pouch with cleaned grain, and put it in your freezer. It makes a great reusable ice pack for minor injuries!
- After harvest, use the leftover stems (straw) and leaves (hay) as animal bedding or garden mulch.
- To make your own straw bales, allow the grain foliage to dry, and then drape three long pieces of string inside a large cardboard box. Stuff the box with your homegrown hay, and tie the bundles tightly.
- Use tall millet or sorghum as living trellises for pole beans or flowers. Use wheat or rye as living trellises for gar-den peas. See "Working with Living Trellises" on page 92.
- Decorate wreaths, baskets, and other crafts with wheat, millet, or other grain seed heads. Use whiskered wheat to add a beautiful accent to hand-wrapped gifts.
- Store an assortment of grains in a rodent-proof container, and feed it to birds.

THRESHING AND CLEANING GRAINS

These methods sound primitive, but if you need to thresh and winnow only a small amount of grain, they are incredibly practical.

■ Holding the cut ends of the stems in one hand, whack the heads against a log or post so the seeds fall into a clean sheet spread over the ground.

■ Spread the stalks on a clean sheet spread over a hard surface, and beat the seed-bearing heads with a broomstick or plastic baseball bat.

Eight Gifted Grains

NAME	PLANTING	HARVESTING	USES AND VARIETIES
Amaranth (*Amaranthus hypochondriacus*)	Sow in late spring, planting seeds ¼-inch deep and 4 to 6 inches apart in rows 18 to 24 inches apart. Thin plants to 12 inches apart. Sow 1 ounce of seed per 100 square feet.	Gather seed heads when seeds begin to break free when tapped or shaken, usually about 100 days after planting. Rub the clusters to dislodge seeds.	Pop whole seeds, add them to breads, grind them into flour, or cook them as a hot cereal. Eat young leaves as cooking greens. 'Manna' and 'Golden Giant' have yellow-orange seed heads; 'Burgundy' and 'Hopi Red Dye' have deep red stems, leaves, and seed heads.
Barley (*Hordeum vulgare*)	Sow in fall or early spring. Broadcast over the soil and rake to cover the seed. Sow 4 ounces of seed per 100 square feet.	Cut in early summer, after the seed heads turn golden brown.	Hull-less varieties are best for eating popped, sprouted, or cooked in salted water until soft and chewy. Grow regular barley for crafts or birdseed. Try hull-less 'Jet' for grain. For crafts, 'Black Heart' produces deep black grains with black whiskers.
Millet (*Panicum, Pennisetum,* and *Setaria* spp.)	Sow from late spring to late summer; broadcast over the soil and rake to cover the seed. Sow 1 ounce of seed per 100 square feet.	Cut when the heads are heavy and full of visible seeds, usually about 50 days after planting.	Grind seeds of proso millet into flour; simmer pearl millet with 4 parts water to 1 part grain for about 30 minutes. Use seed heads in wreaths and other crafts, or feed to winter birds. Colorful ornamental varieties include 'Purple Majesty', with dark purple foliage and seeds, and bronze-seeded 'Highlander'.
Oats (*Avena sativa*)	Sow in fall or early spring. Broadcast the seed evenly and rake to cover with soil. Plant 4 ounces of seed per 100 square feet.	Cut stalks when plants begin to dry and seeds are hard. Hang bundled stalks to dry for several weeks before threshing. For crafts, cut when seed heads are formed but still green.	Grind grains into flour, or cook cracked oats in water for hot cereal. Use unthreshed seed heads in crafts. Try 'A.C. Baton' for spring planting; 'Kynon' can be planted in fall or spring. 'Forest Bouquet' is planted in spring and picked green for crafts.

- Winnow the threshed grain by pouring it from one pan to another in front of a fan powerful enough to blow away the chaff.
- Use a framed screen, such as the Handy Sink Screen (see page 63) to sift the grain from side to side. Grains are heavier than chaff, so they naturally roll to the low end of the tilted screen.
- Use a coffee mill or grain mill to process small amounts of grain into meal or flour. Store milled grain in an airtight container in your freezer.

NAME	PLANTING	HARVESTING	USES AND VARIETIES
Quinoa (*Chenopodium quinoa*)	Sow in spring, planting seeds ¼-inch deep and 4 inches apart in rows spaced 18 inches apart. Thin plants to 8 inches apart. Sow 1 ounce per 100 square feet.	Cut heads when the first seeds start to drop, about 100 days from sowing, or wait until they turn brown. Gather heads into a large tub, and shake to remove seeds.	Eat tender young leaves fresh in salads; steam older leaves. Rinse whole quinoa seeds in several changes of water to remove bitter compounds before cooking for 10 minutes. 'Cherry Vanilla' bears pink seed heads; 'Red Faro' bears red ones. Several shades are present in 'Temuco'.
Rye and Triticale (*Secale cereale, Secale x Triticosecale*)	Sow in fall or early spring. Broadcast over the soil and rake to cover the seeds. Sow 8 ounces of seed per 100 square feet.	Gather when the stalks and seed heads turn golden brown. Thresh them, and then winnow or screen to remove the chaff. For crafts, cut when seed heads are formed but still have not yet dried.	Grind into flour for baking, or simmer whole grains in water for about 1 hour. Use dried seed heads in crafts. 'Silver Tip' has heavy tan seed heads with long awns, or whiskers.
Sorghum and Broomcorn (*Sorghum bicolor*)	Sow outdoors in late spring or early summer, planting seeds 1 to 2 inches deep and 6 inches apart, in rows 18 to 24 inches apart. Sow 2 ounces of seed per 100 square feet.	Gather broomcorn when the brushy tops turn from yellow to green. Harvest grain sorghum when the seed heads turn brown, about 110 days after planting.	Pop whole seeds in a hot pan, add them to soups and stews, or simmer in water for about 45 minutes. Use broomcorn for crafts or decorating. Grow 'Black Amber', 'Mennonite', or 'White-Seeded Popping' for grain. Try 'Multicolor' or 'Texas Black' broomcorn.
Wheat (*Triticum aestivum*)	Sow spring wheat in early spring; sow winter wheat in early fall. Broadcast over the soil and rake to cover seeds. Sow 1 pound per 100 square feet.	Gather when the seed heads and stalks turn golden brown. Thresh them, and then winnow or screen to remove the chaff. For crafts, cut when seed heads are formed but still have not yet dried.	Grind grain into flour, or simmer whole berries in water for 1 hour. Use dried seed heads in crafts. For grain, plant 'Polk' in spring or 'Hard Red Winter' in fall. For crafts, 'Utrecht Blue' and 'Black Tip' have long awns, or whiskers.

Make a Woven Wheat Good Luck Charm

For thousands of years, people in different parts of the world have captured and preserved the fertility of summer by making woven wheat charms, which were hung in the kitchen through winter as a blessing for the house. The following spring, many rituals involved burying the woven wheat in the garden as a good luck charm for a bountiful season.

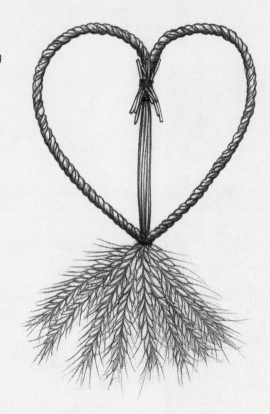

YOU WILL NEED

Tools: Scissors

9 stems of wheat, with the seed heads intact

Three 10-inch-long pieces of waxed dental floss

2 heavy books

1. Gather almost-mature wheat stems, with the whiskered heads attached, and hang them upside down in a bundle to dry. If you don't grow your own wheat, ask permission to gather some stems from a farm field, or look for dried wheat stems in craft stores.

2. When you're ready to weave, soak 9 dried wheat stems in warm water for 15 to 30 minutes to make the stems pliable.

3. Working on a flat surface, tie the wheat stems together with dental floss just below the seed heads. Separate the stems into three sections. Tie the middle three stems together three inches below the cluster of tops.

4. Braid the 3 stems on one side of the cluster, and then braid the other 3 stems. Curve the ends of the braids together to form a heart shape, and tie them tightly to the center bunch of stems. Trim off the ends.

5. Arrange the seed heads the way you want them, and place the weaving between two books to dry for at least 3 days. Hang your finished weaving on a wall or over your kitchen door.

Make a Broomcorn Whisk Broom

Making a perfect broom requires practice, but anyone can make a pretty yet primitive whisk broom. The secret is to bind the stems together as tightly as you can, which is best done with the help of a handy doorknob. You can use a straight stick or dowel for the handle, or turn your broom into an art piece by using a curved branch of rhododendron or other gnarled wood.

YOU WILL NEED

Tools: Ruler, drill, hammer, wire snips, scissors

About ½ bushel of cleaned broomcorn tops

One 18-inch-long stick, 1 inch in diameter, or an old wooden broom handle

One 2-inch-long finishing nail

One 36-inch-long piece of flexible wire

One 24-inch-long piece of cotton string

1. Harvest the seed-bearing tops from mature broomcorn, and hang them in small bundles to dry for several days. To remove the seeds, lay several stems on a flat surface and pull a ruler over them until the seeds break free.

2. Drill a small hole through the handle, one inch from the end. Tap the finishing nail through the hole, so that ½ inch (or more) of the nail extends on either side of the handle. Attach one end of the wire around one end of the nail, leaving 3 inches of wire extend-ing outward from the nail. Attach the other end of the wire to a post, doorknob, or other stationary fixture.

3. Arrange a handful of broomcorn stems around the nail, with the tops of the stems one inch above the nail. Pull the wire taut, and rotate the broom to wrap the wire around the stems.

4. Repeat Step 3 twice, until the broom is full and tight and the nail is completely covered. Wind the two wire ends together tightly, and trim the ends.

5. Tie the string around the bundle, just above the nail. Wind it around the bundle tightly several times, and tie off the ends. Use scissors to trim the tops and bottoms of the broomcorn stems.

Grow a Kitchen Herb Garden

Anyone who likes to cook needs a kitchen herb garden—a small collection of culinary herbs located close enough to the kitchen door to allow you to quickly gather sprigs in only a few seconds. It doesn't need to be a big space. A single Easy-Does-It Raised Bed (see page 12) can support a robust collection of herbs, or you can grow them in containers on your deck or patio. The important thing is that the plants be close at hand, so you can easily dash out and harvest what you need while you are cooking. Don't worry if your cooking skills are limited, because your cooking will naturally get better as you learn to enhance the flavors of foods with garden-grown herbs. All of the herbs described in the "12 Terrific Kitchen Herbs" chart on page 268 are easy to grow, and only a few plants are needed to provide plenty of sprigs for salads, sandwiches, and dozens of savory cooked dishes.

PICKING THE PERFECT SPOT

Herbs develop their best flavors when they get plenty of warm sun, so choose a location that gets at least 6 hours of sun each day. If you have only a small puddle of sun, you can make good use of it by planting your herbs in pots and rotating them in and out of the sun-drenched spot every 2 weeks. Do plan ahead for easy access when growing kitchen herbs in your garden. Install stepping-stones if needed to make sure you can pop out to the herb bed without putting on your shoes. It doesn't mat-

ter what shape or length you make the herb beds or rows as long as you can easily reach all of the plants without stepping on the soil. Since you'll be seeing your kitchen garden often, feel free to liven it up with decorative edgings, and maybe a few edible flowers such as pansies or nasturtiums.

GETTING STARTED WITH KITCHEN HERBS

Prepare the planting site for kitchen herbs the same way you would before planting vegetables or flowers. Remove any existing grass and weeds, spread 2 or more inches of compost or other organic matter over the site, and then dig or till to loosen the top 6 to 8 inches of soil (see "Do a Lawn-to-Garden Turnover" on page 10). If your soil tends to be on the wet side, or if it's so rocky that it's difficult to dig that deeply, an Easy-Does-It Raised Bed (see page 12) can solve these problems. Most herbs thrive when grown in soil that drains quickly after heavy rains, so be sure to amend heavy clay soil with a generous helping of organic matter. When growing herbs in containers, keep in mind that large containers retain water longer than small ones. See "Plant a Potted Kitchen Herb Garden" on page 270 for more tips on growing herbs in containers.

Now comes the fun part—deciding what to plant! Most herb gardeners regard the classic quartet of parsley, sage, rosemary, and thyme as essentials because they complement a wide range of cuisines. Also include herbs that taste best when picked fresh, such as basil, chives, cilantro, dill, fennel, and tarragon. One or two plants of each herb is usually enough. Plant more of herbs you know you will use often.

Whether you begin with seeds or plants depends on the herbs themselves. Fast-growing annual herbs including basil, cilantro, and dill are easy to grow from seeds, and the same is true of parsley, sage, and some types of thyme. Yet some of the best strains of perennial herbs are best grown from rooted stem cuttings, so it is often wise to start with purchased plants when growing rosemary, oregano, and special mints. The "12 Terrific Kitchen Herbs" chart on page 268 suggests the best options for starting new plantings of a dozen fine culinary herbs.

CARING FOR KITCHEN HERBS

Once all of your herbs are planted, spread a 1- to 2-inch-deep layer of chopped leaves or other organic mulch over the soil. Besides suppressing weeds, moderating soil temperature, and reducing watering chores, mulch will prevent the soil from splashing up onto the plants. Cleaner plants mean less washing before your herbs are ready to use. If you live in a humid climate, consider mulching your herbs with ½ inch of pea gravel spread over a fabric weed barrier. Most herbs love the extra warmth provided by a gravel mulch, and it reduces the chances of them rotting from excessive moisture.

When you harvest, it's usually best to snip off the parts you need with sharp scissors.

Pulling off leaves or shoot tips can lead to broken stems. Snipping herbs often helps to make them produce more leaves and branches, and it often delays flowering as well. Snipping off the tops of basil, sage, and most types of thyme every few weeks makes the plants much more productive by encouraging them to produce more leaf-bearing branches.

Warm-natured basil turns black when lightly touched by frost, but most herbs will continue growing well into the fall. Leave the tops of perennial herbs intact through winter, which helps to insulate shallow roots from damage caused by cold weather. If you live from Zone 5 northward, protect perennial herbs with a mulch of loose straw or evergreen branches laid over the plants. There will still be some casualties, so you will need to replace plants that fail to leaf out by mid-spring.

Preventing Runaway Herbs

A few herbs can be invasive if given free rein in the garden. Among kitchen herbs, mints often spread out of bounds by sending out wandering underground rhizomes. The simplest way to prevent this problem is to grow mint in containers. Chives are quite well behaved in most gardens, but in cold climates some strains reseed so prolifically that they become a weedy nuisance. Gathering the flowers to use in arrangements—or to shred into salads—will keep chives from producing unwanted seeds.

12 Terrific Kitchen Herbs

NAME	DESCRIPTION	GROWING TIPS	USES
Basil (*Ocimum basilicum*)	Bushy, upright plants from 1 to 3 feet tall bear flavorful, aromatic leaves and spikes of small flowers; a summer annual that requires warm weather.	Sow seed indoors in spring or outdoors after the soil has warmed in early summer. Harvest shoot tips often to delay flowering and promote new growth.	Add fresh leaves and flowering tips to salads, sandwiches, pesto, or stir-fry. Chopped basil is a classic complement to fresh tomatoes.
Chives (*Allium schoenoprasum*)	Slender green chive leaves and pink, early summer flowers have a mild onion flavor. Leaves grow to 1 foot tall, with flowers slightly taller. Perennial, adapted in Zones 3–9.	Sow seeds indoors in late winter, or outdoors in spring or fall. Or, start with a purchased plant. Pinch off flowers as they fade to prevent reseeding. Divide in fall or early spring.	Snip the leaves into small pieces and use to season potatoes, egg dishes, or steamed vegetables. The blooms add welcome color and flavor to green salads and potato salads.
Cilantro (*Coriandrum sativum*)	Seedlings develop rosettes of parsleylike leaves, and quickly develop umbels of white flowers on upright central stems. The ground seeds are the spice known as coriander. Cool-natured annual.	Sow seeds in the garden or containers in mid-spring, followed by a second sowing in early fall. Purchased plants often are so mature that they quickly develop seeds, so it's best to grow from seeds.	Young leaves add flavor to salsas and many Mexican and Thai dishes. Add to cooked dishes at the last minute. Ground seeds can be used to flavor rice, casseroles, and breads.
Dill (*Anethum graveolens*)	Thin, threadlike leaves form feathery fronds. Plants mature quickly and bear flattened clusters of yellow flowers followed by flavorful seeds. Fast-growing annual.	Sow seeds in the garden or containers in mid-spring. A second sowing may be made in late summer. When buying plants, look for small, young seedlings. Easiest to grow from seed.	Chopped, fresh leaves are used to flavor vegetables, salads, sandwich spreads, cheese dishes, and breads. Seeds impart flavor to pickles, marinades, and breads.
Fennel (*Foeniculum vulgare*)	Beautiful clumps of feathery, bright green, licorice-flavored leaves send up 3- to 5-foot-tall stems topped with clusters of tiny yellow blooms in midsummer. A hardy perennial, Zones 5–9.	Buy a plant to start with, or grow your own by sowing seeds outdoors in mid- to late spring. Harvest or pick off the flower heads often to prevent self-sowing, unless you plan to harvest the seeds.	Fennel foliage is great cooked with fish or used fresh in salads (you can use the flowers this way, too). The seeds are also flavorful; enjoy them whole or ground in baked goods or beverages.
Mint (*Mentha* spp.)	Mints come in numerous shapes, sizes, and flavors. Versatile spearmint (*M. spicata*) has deeply veined, bright green leaves. Peppermint (*M. x piperita*) has smooth leaves with a stronger flavor. Perennial adapted in Zones 5–9.	Buy a starter plant or root a stem tip cutting. Mints spread quickly, so it's usually best to grow them in containers. Mints are easy to grow in either full sun or partial shade.	Mints are marvelous for flavoring desserts, beverages, and cold fruit- or grain-based salads. Mint is also a classic complement for roasted lamb, steamed peas and carrots, and yogurt with cucumbers.

NAME	DESCRIPTION	GROWING TIPS	USES
Greek oregano (*Origanum heracleoticum*)	Greek oregano forms mounded plants about 12 to 18 inches tall, with aromatic, deep green leaves topped by clusters of tiny white flowers in summer. Perennial, Zones 5–9.	Start with a purchased plant or rooted cutting. Rub and sniff a leaf before buying, to make sure you're getting the rich-flavored Greek oregano and not the bland common oregano (*O. vulgare*), which is the type grown from seed.	A key ingredient in tomato sauces and pizza, Greek oregano is also great in soups, stews, and omelets. Sprinkle chopped fresh leaves over bread loaves before baking to add extra flavor.
Parsley (*Petroselinum crispum*)	First-year plants grow 12 inches tall; in the second year, they bear clusters of yellow flowers. Italian parsley has flat, glossy leaves; curly parsley has crinkled foliage. Biennial, Zones 6–9, usually grown as an annual.	Set out new plants each spring, or sow seeds in spring or fall. Germination is often slow, and can be hastened by soaking seeds for 2 days in several changes of water. Young seedlings transplant better than larger ones.	The flavor of flat-leafed parsley holds up better to long cooking, but any type of parsley adds color and flavor to numerous dishes. Particularly good with potatoes and steamed vegetables.
Rosemary (*Rosmarinus officinalis*)	Upright, bushy plants bear pungent, deep green, needlelike leaves, plus small blue flowers. Perennial, Zones 8–9. Keep indoors in winter in colder climates.	Begin with a purchased plant, or root a stem tip cutting offered by a friend. To keep a plant from year to year, grow it in a pot sunk into the ground in summer. Keep the plant in a sunny, cool windowsill through winter.	This strong-flavored herb complements a variety of roasted meats as well as cheese dishes, breads, and potatoes. Tender new leaves and flowers are also wonderful in fresh salads.
Sage (*Salvia officinalis*)	Shrubby, 12- to 30-inch-tall plants produce an abundance of flavorful, gray-green leaves, as well as spikes of purple-blue blooms in summer. Perennial, Zones 4–9.	Start with a purchased plant, or grow from seed sown indoors in early spring. Prune plants back by two-thirds each spring to promote vigorous new growth. Propagate by rooting stem cuttings.	Culinary sage is a traditional partner for poultry and a classic ingredient in stuffing; try it in cream sauces and egg-based dishes, too. Toss flowers into salads for extra color and flavor.
French tarragon (*Artemisia dracunculus*)	These bushy, 2- to 3-foot-tall plants have slender stems clad in narrow, medium green leaves. Perennial, Zones 4–8.	Start with a purchased plant, and be sure it is labeled as French tarragon; seed-grown plants are Russian tarragon, which tends to have a bitter flavor. Propagate by division, or rooting stem tip cuttings.	A traditional flavoring for hollandaise sauce, tarragon's delicate licorice flavor is also wonderful in herb vinegars. Try it with eggs, cheese, chicken, and tomato sauce, too.
Thymes (*Thymus* spp.)	English thyme (*T. vulgaris*) is the classic cooking thyme, while lemon thyme (*T. x citriodorus*) has bright green, lemon-flavored foliage. Both bear tiny white flowers in summer, grow 6 to 12 inches tall. Perennials, Zones 4–9.	Start with purchased plants to make sure you're getting the flavors you want. Good drainage is critical to prevent root rot, especially in winter. To keep plants bushy, shear them back by half in midsummer.	English thyme's warm flavor complements a variety of savory dishes, from meats and eggs to cheese and vegetables. Add lemon thyme to salads, chicken, and stir-fry as well as to drinks and desserts.

Plant a Potted Kitchen Herb Garden

Think you don't have room for a kitchen garden? Think again! Planting culinary herbs in pots lets you dress up your deck, porch, or patio with plants that are pretty as well as productive. Plus, it's easy to move them around or replace plants that are past their prime, so they'll always look their best.

Herbs can grow equally well in individual pots or grouped into larger planters. Even for gardeners who have plenty of garden space, single pots are ideal for herbs that spread rampantly by creeping roots or stems, such as mints. Containers also make it easy to bring herbs indoors in fall and extend your harvest into winter. On the down side, individual pots have limited space for roots, so they tend to need frequent watering and fertilizing. Larger planters provide more rooting room, but they also tend to be heavy and difficult to move. Consider using a mix of container sizes to enjoy the advantages of each.

There's no one best type of container for kitchen herbs—anything that can hold potting soil will do the job, as long as it has holes in the bottom for drainage. If your potted garden is in a highly visible spot, set the herbs directly into decorative planters, or grow the herbs in plastic nursery pots and slip them into prettier planters. Fill your chosen containers with an all-purpose potting soil, but not regular garden soil, which can compact tightly with regular watering.

During the growing season, water regularly to keep the soil evenly moist; small pots may need to be watered as often as once a day during dry, windy weather. Also, fertilize once every 2 to 3 weeks with diluted fish emulsion or a commercial organic liquid fertilizer to keep the plants healthy and vigorous. Herbs normally aren't bothered much by pests or diseases, but if you notice any problems, pinching off the affected parts is an easy way to stop them from spreading.

The possible combinations of plants and pots is limited only by your imagination, but to get you started, here's a simple plan for a basic container herb garden comprised of three containers. Once you get the hang of growing herbs, personalize the planting plan for your particular needs!

YOU WILL NEED

Tools: Watering can, hand
trowel

1 round container, 14 inches
in diameter

1 rectangular window box
container

1 hanging basket container

One 40-pound bag of
potting soil (more for larger
containers)

Container-grown herb plants

For the large round planter:

1 clump of chives

1 fennel plant

1 sage plant

1 French tarragon plant

For the window box:

1 basil plant

2 parsley plants

1 spearmint plant

For the hanging basket:

1 Greek oregano plant

1 creeping rosemary plant

1 English thyme plant

1. Thoroughly water the purchased herbs, and trim away
any yellowed leaves or damaged stems.

2. Fill all three containers to
within 2 inches of the top
with purchased potting
soil. Push the herbs
from their pots by
squeezing on the
bottoms and jiggling the
plants free. Set the plants
in place as shown, begin-
ning with the largest
plant in each group.

3. Add potting soil to fill in
spaces between the herbs. Tap
or gently shake the containers to help settle the soil in
place. Add additional soil until
the tops of the root balls are
barely covered.

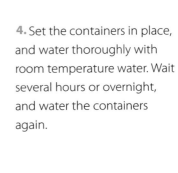

4. Set the containers in place,
and water thoroughly with
room temperature water. Wait
several hours or overnight,
and water the containers
again.

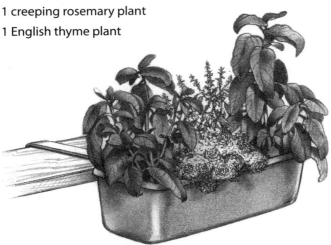

Grow a Tea Garden

After a long day, there's nothing like the luxury of a hot cup of tea from your very own garden to help you unwind. Picking the herbs just before brewing gives your beverage a burst of flavor that you just can't get from dried leaves, and the simple pleasure of touching the herbs and releasing their scents as you gather them is a sensory treat in itself.

If the occasional cup of tea is all you need, a few suitable herbs tucked into your kitchen herb garden can serve the purpose. But if you're serious about tea, why not set aside a special place for a garden just for tea herbs? This simple plan includes a variety of minty, lemony, and spicy perennial herbs to please any taste. Suited for sun or partial shade, this little garden is ideal for tucking into a sheltered corner, where you can sit and sip your tea amid the leafy and flowering herbs. It even includes a few alpine strawberry plants, which provide leaves for tea along with tiny, intensely flavorful berries.

YOU WILL NEED

Tools: Measuring tape, garden spade, rake

3 rectangular stepping-stones

Two 8-inch plastic pots

Tea herb plants:

6 alpine strawberries (*Fragaria vesca*)

1 anise hyssop (*Agastache foeniculum*)

1 bee balm (*Monarda didyma*)

6 Roman chamomile (*Chamaemelum nobile*)

1 lemon balm (*Melissa officinalis*)

1 peppermint (*Mentha x piperita*)

1 sage (*Salvia officinalis*)

1 spearmint (*Mentha spicata*)

1 English thyme (*Thymus vulgaris*)

1 lemon thyme (*Thymus x citriodorus*)

1 chair or small bench

1. Measure a triangular space for your tea garden. Install stepping-stones so their tops are 1 inch above the level of surrounding soil. Cultivate the surrounding spaces where you will plant your herbs, mixing in at least 2 inches of

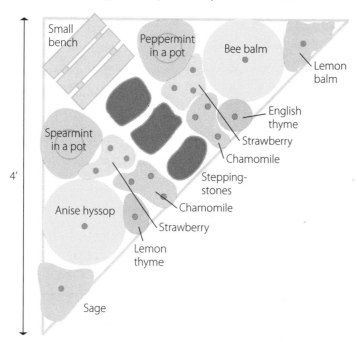

good compost or other rich organic matter.

2. Water the plants well before removing them from their containers. Transplant the peppermint and spearmint to plastic pots. Set the plants in place, and bury the potted mints up to their rims. Water again after transplanting.

3. When the plants begin to show new growth, weed the tea garden thoroughly, and spread a thin mulch of dry grass clippings, shredded leaves, or weed-free straw between the plants. Also mulch over the sitting spot, and add a chair or bench.

4. Snip off leaves and flowers as you need them for tea. Bring a kettle of fresh water to a rolling boil, and pour it into a non-metal teapot with 1 heaping tablespoon of lightly crushed fresh herbs per cup of water. Cover, and let steep for about 5 minutes. When the strength of the brew suits your taste, strain out the herbs and enjoy your tea.

Great Things to Do with Kitchen Herbs

■ Most kitchen herbs are as nice to look at as they are tasty to eat, so dress up your dinner table with a bouquet of fragrant, fresh-picked leaves and flowers. Then use the arrangement to season your breakfast omelets the next morning.

■ If you're a true pasta aficionado, create a special "spaghetti garden" to have all of your favorite fixings right at your fingertips. Include plenty of basil for zesty pesto, plus Greek oregano, rosemary, thyme, garlic— and tomatoes, too, of course!

■ Keep your harvest coming by potting up a few of your favorite herbs in late summer, then bringing them indoors to a sunny windowsill. They'll keep growing for weeks or months, so you can enjoy fresh-picked herbs even when your outdoor garden is frozen solid.

■ Dry some of your herbs to use in winter, especially thyme, rosemary, and mint, which hold their flavor well when dried. Gather stems on a dry day and hang them upside down or spread them on screens to dry for a week or two. Store dried herbs in airtight containers.

■ You can also preserve herbs in ice. Fill an ice-cube tray halfway with water, clear juice, or broth, and let it freeze. Add a leaf or flower of your favorite herb and cover it with liquid. Put the tray back into the freezer. Transfer the cubes to freezer bags when they are frozen hard.

■ Enjoy the fresh aromas of basil, mints, or rosemary indoors by crushing a few leaves in your hands. Then set them in a shallow dish. Outdoors, simply swish your hand through the foliage of any herb to release its invigorating fragrance.

Grow Flowers That Last Forever

Who says you have to put up with faded dried flowers in your house—or substitute a dusty artificial version? It's easy to grow and dry flowers straight from your garden, which you can enjoy for months in a vase, or use to make colorful wreaths, swags, and bookmarks, or to add a special touch to a hand-wrapped gift. Best of all, dried flowers from your own garden serve as reminders of the glory of summer when winter has you in its chilly grip.

Even a small yard can provide an abundance of beautiful blooms for use in wreaths, arrangements, and other fun projects. And, by growing your own flowers, you can choose the perfect colors to complement your indoor décor. You may be familiar with several excellent flowers for drying—perhaps they are already blooming in your garden—but exploring everlasting flowers may take you into new flower gardening frontiers. You may decide to grow your favorites in a special cutting garden.

THE BEAUTY OF BRACTS

While it's possible to dry nearly any bloom one way or another, the easiest flowers to dry are those that naturally tend to hold their shape and color as they age. The most well-known candidates are so-called everlastings, which have flowers that are composed mostly of colorful, papery bracts that are easily mistaken for petals. For example, the tiny true flowers hidden between the bracts of a rounded gomphrena blossom are hardly noticeable. Instead, what we call a flower is actually a cluster of bracts. Bracts contain much less water than true petals, so they hold their form and color for weeks in the garden—and even years when properly dried indoors.

Not all of the good flowers for drying have blossoms comprised of bracts. Some that have small, thin petals also dry well, such as baby's breath and larkspur. The "Six Easy Everlastings" chart on the next page describes a half-dozen good flowers for drying, and you can experiment with many other species, including flowers that produce showy seed capsules, such as poppies and lunaria. Grasses, grains, and even weeds often dry into beautiful specimens, which can greatly expand your crafting options. Gather these and other filler materials when they catch your eye, and combine them with more colorful dried flowers. Their unusual textures will help to showcase the dried flowers you grow in your garden.

TAKE CARE WITH COLOR

Overall, blue, orange, and pink blooms tend to hold their colors best during the drying process. Red and purple flowers usually darken noticeably, while bright yellows often turn light yellow and whites typically turn cream-colored or even brown. Growing a variety of different flowering annuals and perennials will give you a wide range of colors and flower shapes for all kinds of craft projects.

Six Easy Everlastings

NAME	DESCRIPTION	GROWING TIPS	DRYING TIPS
Celosias, cockscombs (*Celosia* spp.)	From midsummer to frost, 1- to 4-foot-tall stems are topped with plumes, spikes, or crinkled heads in shades of pink, red, orange, or yellow. Annual.	Start seeds indoors in spring, or sow outdoors in late spring, after the soil has warmed.	Cut when the blooms are bright and appear fully open, but before the outer edges start to fade. Hang bundles upside down to dry, or stand them upright in a dry container.
Globe amaranth (*Gomphrena* spp.)	Slender stems topped with small, rounded to oblong heads of papery bracts in white, red, orange, pink, or purple. Annual.	Start seeds indoors 6 weeks before your last frost date; set outdoors after danger of frost is past.	Harvest blooms at any stage—from just-formed to fully opened. Dried stems are fragile, so reinforce them with floral wire before drying upside down or on a drying rack.
Love-in-a-mist (*Nigella damascena*)	Bushy plants produce numerous blue, pink, or white summer flowers followed by inflated, deep green seedpods striped with deep purple. Annual.	Sow seeds directly in the garden in early to mid-spring. Love-in-a-mist grows best in full sun and fertile, well-drained soil.	Gather stems laden with seedpods as soon as they swell; hang upside down in small bunches to dry. Or, pull up the entire plant when it becomes heavy with seedpods and hang it upside down to dry.
Statice, annual (*Limonium sinuatum*)	Sturdy, 1- to 2-foot-tall stems produce one-sided sprays of tiny white flowers surrounded by papery calyces in soft pastel colors. Annual.	Start seeds indoors in late winter or early spring; set outdoors after danger of frost is past. Annual statice can tolerate heat and drought.	Harvest statice when about three-quarters of the florets in the cluster are open; the rest will open during the drying process. To dry, hang upside down in bundles.
Strawflower (*Bracteantha bracteata*)	Daisylike blooms in shades of pink, yellow, orange, red, or white. Blooms close in wet weather and reopen when dried by the sun. Annual.	Start seed indoors in early spring; set out after danger of frost is past. Or sow directly in the garden in late spring.	Cut flowers from bud stage to half-open; they will continue to open as they dry. To dry, hang upside down in bundles, or dry the heads alone on a drying rack.
Yarrows (*Achillea* spp.)	This tough perennial bears flat-topped to slightly domed flower clusters atop sturdy stems in summer; colors include white, red, pink, rust, or yellow. Perennial, Zones 3–8.	Sow seeds indoors or out in spring (they will bloom starting in their second year). Or, start with purchased plants.	Harvest at full-bloom stage, when the individual flowers in the cluster are open but before they start to fade. Hang upside down in bundles to dry.

Few flower gardeners are happy to restrict their color choices to those that dry well, and many dried flower crafts require an abundant supply of blossoms. One solution to this dilemma is to sprinkle repetitious plantings of a flower you intend to dry throughout your garden. Repetition has a unifying effect in the landscape, and it's and easy way to grow all the celosia, globe amaranth or strawflowers you need for a variety of craft projects. Light pastel colors such as yellow plume celosia, or pale pink globe amaranth blend well with brighter bloomers, and their unusual forms contrast nicely with flowers that produce daisy-shaped blossoms.

If you plan to do lots of crafting, consider creating a separate cutting garden, where you can harvest flowers and foliage to your heart's content without thinking about how the plants look. It could be as simple as a partial row in your vegetable garden, or as elaborate as a special craft garden bursting with everlasting flowers and ornamental grains. Remember to include plenty of paths so you can easily reach the blooms for picking. Need just a few flowers for drying? Include everlasting flowers in your regular flowerbeds, and gather blooms from the least visible sides of the plants.

Flowers on a Wire

If you harvest blooms with very short stems, or if their natural stems tend to be brittle, reinforce them with floral wire (available at craft stores) before you dry the flowers. Take a straight piece of wire and bend one end into a small, U-shaped hook. Insert the straight end of the wire into the center of a bloom from the top, and carefully pull it down until the hook nestles into the top of the petals. Before using the flowers, you can wrap the wire and stem together with green or brown floral tape to create a more natural look.

GROWING EVERLASTING FLOWERS

Like most other heavy-blooming flowers, the best everlastings require full sun and fertile soil. You may need to provide supplemental water while the plants are young, but flowers that produce bracts rather than petals tend to require less water after they develop extensive root systems. Do include some type of mulch between plants, which will reduce weed problems and keep mud from splashing onto your flowers during heavy rains.

PINCHING YOUR PLANTS

Unlike many of the flowers you may have grown as bedding plants, most everlasting flowers do not develop numerous branches without a little help. The natural tendency of celosias, strawflowers and other annuals is to quickly produce a flower at the tip of a single upright stem. If you interrupt this process by pinching off the primary growing tips when the plants are 5 to 6 inches tall, the plants will respond by producing several new bushier branches. Plants that are pinched back often produce three or four times as many blossoms as those left unpinched.

HARVESTING EVERLASTING FLOWERS

When you are ready to gather flowers for drying, choose a dry day, and wait until mid-morning, after the dew has dried. Choose only perfect blooms, because any imperfections will still be noticeable when the flowers are dry. Feel free to experiment with picking flowers at different stages—from buds to fully open—and keep notes of when and what you harvested, so you'll remember the results. Try to get as much stem as possible—long stems give you the most crafting options—but even stemless flowers can be handy for making potpourri or gluing onto wreaths.

Air-drying is the easiest route for preserving most homegrown flowers, foliage, and seed heads. The secret is to choose the right site: a warm, dry, dark place with good air circulation, such as a garden shed or garage. The faster your flowers dry, the brighter their colors will stay! Prepare them for drying by pulling or cutting the leaves off of the bottom half of the stems. Most flowers are fully dry within 1 to 3 weeks. The blooms will look dry, and the stems will snap when you bend them. Store your dried flowers in boxes or plastic snap-lid containers in a cool, dry area until you are ready to use them.

DRYING IN BUNDLES

The most space-efficient drying technique is to hang bundles of blooms upside down, so they're out of the way. Small bunches—usually 5 to 10 stems each—are best. Wrap a rubber band a few times around the base of each bunch to hold the stems together, and then hang the bundles cut-ends-up from over-head ropes, rafters, or hooks. If you're short on space, attach the bundles to wire clothes hangers with clothespins. Space them out so they don't touch each other, because crowded bundles tend to develop mold.

RACKING THEM UP

A drying rack—basically, a piece of ¼-inch wire mesh propped up on bricks or draped between two chair backs—takes up more space, but it gives you several options. To dry long-stemmed blooms, slip the stems into the holes and let the flowers slide down until they are resting on the wire. If the stems are very short or lacking altogether, simply spread the blooms, buds, or pods in a single layer right on the surface of the rack. Either way, they'll get plenty of air on all sides for quick drying.

STANDING ROOM ONLY

Some plants dry so easily that you can simply stand the cut stems in a coffee can or wide-mouth jar and let them dry right there. For extra support, punch holes in a plastic lid, and insert the stems through the holes. This works great for materials that are already almost dry (such as grasses or seedpods), and it's a particularly good way to handle wheat, barley, and other grains, because the heads can develop a graceful arch as they dry. If you want them to stay straight, hang them upside down instead.

Make a Batch of Potpourri

Why spend money on artificial air fresheners when you can create your own right at home? Making potpourri is a great way to use up odds and ends of dried herbs and flowers, and you can add little pinecones, seeds, or even dried bits of fruit if you like. There's no one set recipe for potpourri, so it's easy to tailor the look and fragrance of each batch to make one-of-a-kind creations.

To pump up the fragrance of potpourri, you will need one or more small bottles of pure, organic essential oil—highly concentrated extracts made from fragrant plants, which are available at health food stores. Most retail displays include tester bottles,

so you can sniff before you buy. If you can't decide, choose essential oils based on where you plan to use your potpourri. Lavender oil is quite popular for closet sachets and active living areas; some people like rose oil for potpourri kept on bedside tables; and various citrus scents are always welcome in the kitchen.

Your potpourri will hold its scent longer if you use a fragrance fixative such as orris root, which is made from a type of iris. Craft stores sell other fixatives, too, such as calamus (which has a mild fruity scent) and spicy-smelling benzoin. However, orris root is widely available and works well in any type of potpourri.

YOU WILL NEED

Tools: Measuring spoon, wooden spoon, scissors

1 package of orris root crystals or other fixative

1 small bottle of pure, organic essential oil

1 pint-size glass jar with lid

6 cups of dried flowers, herbs, and seedpods

One 2-quart airtight glass or plastic container

1. Place 3 tablespoons of fixative and 15 to 20 drops of essential oil in a glass jar. Mix lightly with a wooden spoon and screw on the lid. Set aside for 2 days.

2. Select materials for your potpourri that include colors and scents to complement the room where you'll display your potpourri. Use scissors to cut them into small pieces. Place the materials in an airtight glass or plastic container.

3. Add the infused fixative to your dried materials, and toss everything together lightly with the wooden spoon. Put on the lid, and place the container in a dry, dark place for 2 weeks.

Great Things to Do with Dried Flowers

■ Press individual blossoms within the pages of a heavy book. Enclose the dried blossoms in plastic laminating sheets to create beautiful bookmarks, or glue them inside homemade greeting cards.

■ Decorate a Grapevine Wreath (see page 258) with dried flowers and foliage; change the dried materials every few months to fit the seasons.

■ Make a seasonal table display by combining dried flowers, seed heads from grains and grasses, and ornamental gourds in a large oval platter.

■ If dried blossoms break off from their stems, use a hot glue gun to attach them to gift-wrapped boxes, baskets, wreaths, and other decorative objects.

■ Turn a perfect dried blossom into a unique accessory by tucking it into your hair barrette or ponytail holder.

■ Use short-stemmed dried flowers to make a tiny arrangement in a pretty teacup. Place an inch of dry sand in the teacup to help hold the stems in place.

4. Place your finished potpourri in an open bowl to use as an air freshener, or tuck it into cloth pouches to use it as drawer or closet sachets.

Grow Gorgeous Gourds

Gourds grow in summer, and then you have the rest of the year to enjoy crafting them into birdhouses, planters, water dippers, musical instruments, and dozens of other useful items. Or, you can carve, paint, or etch them with a wood-burning tool to create original works of art. Whether you grow your own gourds or buy them from someone who does, don't be surprised if crafting gourds becomes habit-forming.

The most useful gourds for crafting are hard-shell gourds (*Lagenaria siceraria*), or you can grow luffas or fast-maturing ornamental gourds. All gourds are easy to grow, even for beginning gardeners, and the galloping vines will quickly cover a trellis or arbor. After the blossoms give way to green fruits, you will enjoy a mesmerizing show while the fruits swell daily before your eyes. Among hard-shell gourds, there are numerous shapes and sizes, from little egg gourds to birdhouse gourds to bulbous gourds the size of a bushel basket. Smaller varieties mature faster than very large ones. Several of the most common shapes are described in the "Seven Great Gourds to Grow" chart on the next page.

LUFFAS AND ORNAMENTAL GOURDS

Luffas, also called vegetable sponge, are edible when young, or you can let them mature into garden-grown sponges. The inside of the fruit grows into a stringy, spongy mass that, when dried and cleaned, makes a wonderful kitchen or bath scrubber. Like hard-shelled gourds, luffas require a long, warm growing season, and you will need to trellis the vines if you want long, blemish-free fruits.

If you live in a cool climate where hard-shelled gourds and luffas aren't likely to produce well, you can grow ornamental gourds instead. Ornamental gourds are vining squash cousins grown for their dramatic shapes and colors. Maturing in less than 90 days, ornamental gourds are usually small enough to hold in your hand. They have intriguing names defined by their shapes, such as turk's turban, egg, or spoon gourd, and seed packets are widely available that include a range of varying shapes and colors. When allowed to mature until their rinds are hard, ornamental gourds make great display pieces for autumn decorating. They are an easy crop for children to grow, too.

GROWING HARD-SHELL GOURDS

Hard-shell gourds are a warm-season crop that should not be planted outdoors until 2 to 3 weeks after the last spring frost has passed. If you live in a cool climate, start the seeds indoors 3 weeks before you hope to transplant them, and keep the seeded containers in a warm place, such as atop your refrigerator or hot water heater. Gourds germinate best at temperatures above 80°F.

Plant gourds in a sunny place, in soil that has been generously enriched with organic

Seven Great Gourds to Grow

NAME	DAYS TO MATURITY	DESCRIPTION	USES
Birdhouse (*Lagenaria siceraria*)	110 to 120	Bulbous base with a short neck, 12 to 14 inches tall and 6 to 8 inches wide	Birdhouses, hanging planters, bowls, painted or decorated art
Bottle (*Lagenaria siceraria*)	100 to 120	Hourglass with larger bulge on bottom than on top; range of sizes, from 3 to 5 inches tall (small) to 12 to 14 inches tall (large)	Vases, decorative bowls, candle holders, painted or decorated art
Corsican (*Lagenaria siceraria*)	100 to 120	Round and flattened, like a wheel of cheese; range of sizes from 10 to 15 inches wide	Bowls, planters, containers with hinged lids, painted or decorated art
Dipper (*Lagenaria siceraria*)	110 to 120	Small bulbous bottom with long necks that can be straight or curved; 12 to 30 inches tall	Water dippers, animal feed scoops, painted or decorated art
Egg (*Lagenaria siceraria*)	80 to 90	Thin-shelled and about the size of a goose egg	Painted or decorated art, table displays
Luffa (*Luffa* spp.)	95 to 100	Elongated spheres 3 inches wide and up to 15 inches long	Bath or dish sponges, scrubbers, dried flower arrangements
Ornamental (*Cucurbita pepo* var. *ovifera*)	75 to 80	Huge range of shapes and colors, most less than 6 inches tall and wide	Seasonal decorations

matter. Or, grow them in an old compost heap (see "Make a Cucurbit Compost Pile" on page 28), which is how gourds have been grown for thousands of years. Large-fruited gourds become so heavy that they are best grown on the ground. Placing growing bottle or other large gourds upright on a piece of cardboard has the additional advantage of helping them to develop flat bases. Small-fruited egg or skinny snake gourds are easy to grow on a sturdy trellis. Many gardeners have watched in amazement as gourd vines took off and covered their chain-link fence—and nearby utility poles—in a matter of weeks.

Once gourd vines are off and running, there is little to do except sit back and watch—unless you want to intervene and fine-tune the shape of your gourds. While they are growing, young, green gourds are soft and pliable. If you tie a string around the middle of a bottle gourd, it will develop a tinier waist. Or, you might use stretchy cloth or old panty hose to train the neck of a dipper gourd into an acute curve. Should your goal be gourds with solid bottoms that sit up straight when set on a tabletop, set small boards beneath gourds grown on the ground, and go out every few days and position the gourds upright. To help a gourd with a rounded bottom sit flat, you also can make a little wreath of woven grapevine, wheat stems, or corn husks to help hold it upright. Keep in mind that trellis-grown gourds usually develop rounded bottoms, which is fine if you plan to use them to make birdhouses such as the Gourd Birdhouse on page 192.

TROUBLE-SHOOTING GOURDS

Hard-shell gourds usually have few insect and disease problems, though cucumber beetles can weaken plants when the larvae feed on the roots. Floating rowcovers are the easiest way to keep them off of your plants. If powdery mildew appears, control it by spraying plants weekly with a solution of ½ teaspoon baking soda to 1 quart of water, with a few drops of dishwashing liquid added to help the mixture stick to the leaves.

HARVESTING AND CURING GOURDS

Hard-shell gourds are mature when the vine turns dry where it connects to the gourd. Cut (do not twist off) the gourd from the vine, leaving as much stem attached as possible. You don't need to rush to harvest your gourds before a light frost, but do move them to a dry place before they are exposed to temperatures below about 26°F.

Depending on their size, gourds are cured in 6 weeks to 6 months. Small gourds dry much faster than large ones. Be patient, because the inner walls become much harder as gourds dry. Many gourds develop patches of black mold on their skins as they dry. Curing gourds in a warm, dry place reduces the amount of mold that forms, but a bit of mold on drying gourds is completely normal. You can easily scrub it off later, just before you make a gourd project.

CLEANING CURED GOURDS

When you can hear seeds rattling inside the gourd, it's ready to clean and craft. Wrap it in a towel soaked with hot water, and after 10 minutes or so see if it will scrub clean with a copper dish scrubber. If not, wrap it in the towel again, and give it a second scrub. Use soap and water if you like, because the cleaning process also removes the thin outer layer from the gourd's skin. With most gourds, natural mottled patterns remain after the gourd is thoroughly cleaned. After cleaning, let the gourd dry for several hours. Cleaned gourds can be combined with dried flowers (see "Grow Flowers That Last Forever" on page 274) in decorative garlands or table arrangements, and then later used for crafts.

CRAFTING HARD-SHELL GOURDS

Dried, cleaned gourds can be treated much like wood. They can be sawed, engraved, drilled, painted, stained, dyed, or embellished with wood-burning tools. Whenever you saw, sand, or drill into a gourd, wear a dust mask to avoid breathing the fine particles, which can easily irritate your respiratory system.

Most crafts begin by making an opening in the gourd, which is most easily done by drilling several small, closely spaced holes. Then you can use a craft saw, keyhole saw, or sharp serrated knife to enlarge the hole, or to cut the gourd in half. If a gourd cracks during cutting, fill the crack with household glue, wipe away the excess with a damp cloth, and sand the repaired area lightly with fine-grit sandpaper while the glue is still wet. That way, gourd particles will help fill the crack.

Make a Bottle Gourd Candle Holder

You can make a candle holder from any size of bottle gourd, but it's a great use for very small ones. Remember that gourds are flammable, so do not leave your candle holder unattended or allow the candle to burn very low.

This is a good starter project to introduce you to gourd crafting. Be as creative as you like with the outside finish. Plain shoe polish or furniture wax are all you need to give your gourd a natural finish, or you can use paints, leather dye, or a coat of clear polyurethane.

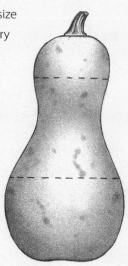

YOU WILL NEED

Tools: Pencil, dust mask, craft saw, knife, sandpaper, paint and paintbrushes, brown shoe polish

1 small bottle gourd, cured and cleaned

1 broad candle

12-inch piece of velvet ribbon that matches the candle

1. Place the gourd on a soft surface, such as a foam pad or old pillow, and use the pencil to mark 2 parallel cutting lines on either side of the gourd's waist. One will be the bottom of the candle holder, and the other will be the top.

2. While wearing the dust mask, use the craft saw to remove the top and bottom from the gourd. Scrape away loose material from inside the gourd with the tip of the knife. Sand the cut edges and inside surfaces until they are smooth.

3. Paint the interior surfaces of the gourd, allow them to dry, and then apply a second coat.

4. If desired, paint the outside of the gourd. If you prefer a natural look, finish the gourd with two coats of brown shoe polish.

5. Set the candle holder on a level surface and insert a candle. If needed, use the knife to shape the bottom of the candle so that it sits firmly in place. Tie the velvet ribbon into a bow around the middle of the candle holder.

More Great Things to Do with Gourds

- Make a Gourd Birdhouse for small wrens or titmice (see page 192).
- Make a planter by cutting the top off of a bulbous gourd. After painting or finishing the gourd, screw small brass knobs or other upholstery hardware onto the bottom to help the planter sit flat. Fill the planter with a plant grown in a small plastic pot.
- Make a garland by stringing together gourds of different shapes and sizes, and hang it under the eaves of your garage or potting shed.
- Cut the side from a bulbous gourd and use it as a dipper for water, animal feed, or soil amendments.
- Create lidded storage containers for potpourri, jewelry, or even seeds. Small metal hinges can be screwed into a gourd the same way they are installed in wood.
- Use acrylic paint to make imaginative holiday ornaments from gourds, from Thanksgiving turkeys and Santas to permanent Easter eggs and pumpkins.
- Use a small bottle gourd as the basis for a homemade doll. If you already have doll clothes, look for a gourd they will fit. Paint on a face, and make hair from soft yarn.
- Paint or burn a design on the surface of a cleaned gourd to create a one-of-a-kind art piece. Or, use gourds as the beginning of decoupage projects. For example, glue autumn leaves all over a gourd and then seal them in place with polyurethane spray.
- With a gourd as your canvas, use paint to help transform it into a penguin, whale, goose, bird, or anything else the shape suggests to you.
- Cut rings from a gourd, sand them smooth, and make them into napkin rings or bracelets.
- Make a percussion instrument from a gourd by making a hole through which you can remove the seeds and replace them with beads. Or, cover a gourd with a loosely tied and beaded macramé net.

Glossary of Tools

Most of the projects in this book can easily be completed with tools you already have in your garden shed or garage. If you find that you need to buy new tools, this quick review of tools will help you make the best choices. All of the tools described here are readily available at any hardware or home supply store, often in several versions. For example, look under Saws for various types of saws, and read through Wrenches to learn the difference between an adjustable wrench and a ratchet wrench. You may want to rent or borrow tools you will use only once, but having a basic collection of good tools on hand makes many gardening tasks much easier and will increase the satisfaction derived from both large and small gardening projects.

Digging fork. In addition to a garden spade, every gardener needs a digging fork, which is the best tool for cultivating compacted soil, turning compost, or mixing soil amendments into beds and planting holes. Digging forks have shorter handles than garden spades, and most have a D-shaped grip at the end to help increase leverage—a great advantage when you are prying up rocks and roots.

Drill. If you own only one power tool, it should be a drill. Choose a drill with rechargeable batteries so you won't have to deal with cumbersome extension cords and plugs. Most drills also come with screwdriver heads, which make short work of screwing (or unscrewing) large numbers of screws. The manual option to a power drill is called a *brace and bit*. A brace and bit is fine for making holes in wood, but it can't help with screws and lacks sufficient power to drill into metal or masonry.

Drill bits (the drilling points) can be purchased individually or in sets. A set of a half-dozen or so regular bits, in various diameters, is all you will need for drilling guide holes for screws into wood. When drilling guide holes, choose a bit slightly smaller than the shaft of the screw, and drill the hole no deeper than three-quarters of the length of the screw. That way, the screw's frets and tip will firmly bite into the wood. Be careful when using very narrow drill bits, which break easily (but are easily replaced at a reasonable price). Special bits with super-hard carbide tips are needed for drilling into metal or masonry. These special bits cost more and usually can be purchased individually.

To drill holes more than 2 inches deep, you will need a longer bit, called an *extension bit*. Extension bits can be purchased individually or in small sets. When using an extension bit, it is important to hold the drill perfectly straight. For best results, center yourself behind the drill, and hold it firmly with both hands. It also can help to begin by drilling a shallow hole with a regular bit before switching to an extension bit.

To drill holes more than ½ inch in diameter, you will need an *expansion bit*. Expansion bits have short pointed tips, with broader wing-shaped blades behind the tips that rasp out a wide hole. It is often helpful to drill a guide hole with your largest diameter regular bit, and then switch to an expansion bit to widen the hole.

Dust mask. Never subject your respiratory system to the particles released when wood, gourds, or other materials are sawn or sanded, which can lead to nasty and persistent infections. Disposable dust masks are inexpensive and are usually sold alongside paint and sanding supplies.

Gloves. There are many types and styles to choose from among gardening gloves, so simply use your taste and comfort as your guide. When cutting wire fencing, you will need a pair of heavy-duty cloth or leather gloves to protect your hands from painful pricks. Also wear heavy-duty gloves when handling stone, and protect your hands from chemical damage by wearing waterproof gloves when working with concrete.

Hammer. A regular hammer, called a claw hammer, is an essential tool in any household. Use the head to drive nails, and the claw end to pull them out. A heavier type of hammer, called a *sledgehammer,* is useful for driving stakes into the ground. If you are a small person who has trouble handling a sledgehammer, a *rubber mallet* is lighter and easier to control than a sledgehammer.

Hoe. While far from fancy, there is no better tool than a hoe for breaking up clods of soil or for lopping off the heads of weeds. Try on different hoes before you buy, and choose a hoe with a handle length and head weight that feels comfortable to you. Sharpen your hoe often with a *steel file,* sometimes called a bastard mill file.

Level. You will never have to guess whether or not a horizontal line is level or whether a vertical one is perfectly straight if you use a level, sometimes called a carpenter's level. The most versatile version is 18 inches long and includes three oil-filled tubes with bubbles in them—one for horizontal, one for vertical, and one that measures 45-degree angles. When the bubble in the tube is perfectly centered, you know that the place you are measuring is perfectly straight.

Measuring tape. Rulers and yardsticks are fine for measuring short distances, but you will need a measuring tape to measure lengths longer than 3 feet. Metal measuring tapes that retract into a case that clips onto your belt are inexpensive and well worth their cost.

Pliers. Objects that you could never grasp firmly with your fingers can be manipulated easily with pliers. A small- to medium-size pair of pliers is most useful because they can fit into tight places. For bending small wire or fitting into little nooks and crannies, sharp-tipped *needle-nose pliers* are invaluable. Look for needle-nose pliers that include a pair of cutting blades just behind the tips; they will double as lightweight *wire cutters*.

Posthole digger. Sometimes called a clam-shell digger, a posthole digger features two blades that are thrust into the ground to help loosen and remove soil. The digger makes a narrow hole (usually the size of a fence post) when you pull the handles apart and pick up the soil that has been loosened by the blades. When setting posts, a narrow hole is great be-cause the sides of the hole remain firm, which helps support the post. Using a posthole dig-ger effectively takes a bit of practice as well as upper-body strength. For best results, thrust the digger down into the hole as hard as you can. Turn a quarter turn between strikes to help keep the hole symmetrical and straight.

Pruning shears. Plants deserve clean pruning cuts, which require the use of pruning shears. You can use scissors—or even a knife—to cut tender green growth, but pruning shears are better for cutting fibrous or woody stems. Anvil-type shears press a blade through the stem and cut it against a solid counter-blade. Bypass-type pruners fit into tight spaces better, but require regular sharpening to keep them working well. Pruning shears are usually suf-ficient for cutting stems up to ½ inch in diam-eter. To cut larger stems or branches, you will need *pruning loppers*.

Rake. Most gardeners need two types of rake—a stiff, steel-toothed garden rake for working in soil, and a leaf rake, with flexible tines, for gathering up leaves, pine needles, and mulch materials.

Sandpaper. The splinters that often result when wood is sawn—by you or by the saw-mill—can be smoothed out by going over the surface with sandpaper. Always sand with the grain of the wood. Use coarse sandpaper to begin smoothing very rough surfaces, and then switch to medium sandpaper. Finish the job with fine sandpaper. You can buy packets of sandpaper that include a selection of grades. Before painting or staining sanded surfaces, wipe them with a clean, damp cloth to remove loose particles.

Saws. Many of the projects in this book re-quire the use of a *handsaw*. A general-purpose handsaw with a blade at least 12 inches long will do a good job of sawing soft wood, such as pine, that is less than 2 inches in diameter and no more than 6 inches wide. You also can cut PVC pipe with a basic handsaw. To cut small pieces of metal by hand, invest in a small *hacksaw*.

You will need a *power saw*, often called a circular saw, to cut fence posts or very thick or wide pieces of wood. Most circular saws have safety features built in, such as a blade sheath, but they should still be handled with care. A circular saw is great for cutting straight lines, but you will need a different type of saw, called a *jigsaw* or *saber saw,* to cut curves. Wear eye protection when using any type of power saw to avoid getting sharp particles in your eyes.

Two types of small specialty saws are used for a few of the projects in this book. A *keyhole saw* is a small manual saw used to shape the interior of holes. A *craft saw* is even smaller—not much larger than a pencil—and it is used to shape holes in gourds or in thin pieces of wood.

Scissors. Along with desk scissors and kitchen scissors, a household with a gardener in residence also needs at least one pair of garden scissors. Any large scissors will do for big jobs, and a small pair you can slip into your pocket is perfect for cutting string. Scissors with brightly colored handles are less likely to get lost when used outdoors.

Screwdrivers. Unless you stumble into electrical projects, a simple set of household screwdrivers that includes a large and small flat-blade screwdriver and another pair of Phillips-head screwdrivers (those with an X pattern on the end) will do quite nicely. If you do not have strong hands or wrists, look for screwdrivers with good grips on the handles. A rechargeable electric screwdriver is also an excellent option.

Spade. Whether you call it a spade or shovel, this is the most essential gardening tool of all. Before buying, try on various models, and choose a spade that fits your size and strength.

Also buy a small metal file, and use it regularly to refresh the sharp edge on your spade. A sharp spade works much better than a dull one. If you (or your kids) tend to leave your tools in odd places, place a piece of brightly colored tape on the handle of your spade to keep it from getting lost. If you need to dig a narrow trench, you will love the work done by the long, narrow blade of a *trenching spade,* also called a plumber's spade.

Staple gun. Inexpensive and versatile, a staple gun makes fast work of attaching wire, cloth, or plastic to wood. A standard model, with half-inch staples, is sufficient for most garden projects. When not in use, store your staple gun indoors out of the reach of children. When stapling paper, cardboard, or lightweight plastic, a regular *office stapler* is all you will need.

Tin snips. Like giant scissors with powerful, short blades, tin snips are used for cutting metal or semirigid plastic. They come in various sizes. A pair of tin snips that is rated to cut 1.2 mm cold rolled steel or 0.7 mm stainless steel is adequate for most tasks.

Utility knife. This versatile yet dangerous tool is basically a razor blade within a handle-type housing. Invaluable for cutting through cardboard and thin sheet vinyl, a utility knife should always be handled with care and stored out of the reach of children. Buy a box of blades along with the knife, and replace them when they become rusted or dull. Use pliers to pull out the old blade, and leave the new blade sheathed until it is installed. Instead of pushing in a new blade with your fingers, get it started in the correct position, and then shove it into place by pushing the tool against a hard surface.

Wheelbarrow. Most gardeners cannot go a day without using a wheelbarrow to transport soil, mulch, plants, or tools. A small cart can be used in place of a wheelbarrow, but in both cases it's important to choose one that fits you well. Small models carry lighter loads, but they are easier to control than large, heavy ones. Wheelbarrows with tubs made of plastic also tend to be lightweight. Tubeless tires are less likely to go flat than tires with inner tubes.

Wire snips. Needle-nose pliers with small blades can be used to cut small-diameter wire, but true wire snips do a better job when you are cutting chicken wire or landscape fencing. To easily cut galvanized steel cable or concrete reinforcing wire, consider upgrading to what are called *bolt cutters*. The 14-inch size is usually sufficient.

Wrenches. The most common purpose of a wrench is to hold a nut or pipe while the other end is screwed or rotated, but the wrench itself also can be the tool that does the turning. Mechanics often keep huge collections of wrenches in a range of sizes, and having the exact size you need is important when bolts must be very tight. However, an adjustable wrench, in which the bottom lip can be moved up and down, is quite adequate for most garden projects. Exceptions are projects that involve lag screws, which have boltlike heads. Lag screws (and bolts) must be installed with a *ratchet wrench,* which gives you much more leverage than a regular wrench. A ratchet wrench comes with various size heads that fit over the tops of lag screws and other smooth-topped screws with square edges.

Picking Projects for Your Garden

As you enrich your garden with the projects in this book, use these lists to make sure you don't miss out on ideas that are especially well suited to your type of garden. In addition to matching projects to your garden's size and style, choose projects based on your mood and motivation. When you feel like making or building something, simply pick out a promising project. Do the same when you want to get something new and wonderful growing in your garden.

PROJECTS FOR STARTING A NEW GARDEN

PROJECTS THAT MAKE THE MOST OF A SMALL GARDEN

PROJECTS FOR LARGE GARDENS

Sources for Seeds, Plants, and Supplies

CHAPTER 1: DIGGING IN

Eight Great Green Manures, page 15

Seeds of green manure plants often are available at farm supply stores. They can be ordered by mail from:

Johnny's Selected Seeds
955 Benton Avenue
Winslow, ME 04901
800-854-2580
www.johnnyseeds.com

Peaceful Valley Farm Supply
PO Box 2209
Grass Valley, CA 95945
888-784-1722
www.groworganic.com

Make an Indoor Worm Farm, page 30

Red worms often can be purchased at bait shops. They can be ordered by mail from:

Green Culture, Inc.
32 Rancho Circle
Lake Forest, CA 92630
800-233-8438
www.composters.com

Magic Wiggler Worm Ranch
1130 Bush Road
Raymond, MS 39154
601-885-6096
www.magicwiggler.com

CHAPTER 3: TEEPEES, TRELLISES, AND OTHER SMART PLANT SUPPORTS

Try Restrained Runners, page 95

Check retail seed racks for the bean varieties described, or order them by mail from these companies:

Park Seed
1 Parkton Avenue
Greenwood, SC 29647
800-213-0076
www.parkseed.com

Southern Exposure Seed Exchange
PO Box 460
Mineral, VA 23117
540-894-9480
www.southernexposure.com

Grow a Patio Climbing Rose, page 114

Look for the miniature climbing roses at local nurseries, or order them by mail first thing in spring from these mail-order companies:

Bridges Roses
2734 Toney Road
Lawndale, NC 28090
704-538-9412
www.bridgesroses.com

John's Miniature Roses
24062 NE Riverside Drive
St. Paul, OR 97137
503-538-1576
www.johnsminiatureroses.com

Nor'East Miniature Roses
PO Box 440
Arroyo Grande, CA 93421
800-426-6485
www.noreast-miniroses.com

CHAPTER 4: INGENIOUS WAYS TO WATER

Make a Bucket Drip System, page 134

Polyethylene drip irrigation tape may be available at local farm supply stores, or you can order it by mail from these and other mail-order companies:

Drip Works, Inc.
190 Sanhedrin Circle
Willits, CA 95490
800-522-3747
www.dripworksusa.com

Peaceful Valley Farm Supply
PO Box 2209
Grass Valley, CA 95945
888-784-1722
www.groworganic.com

Grow a Potted Lotus, page 142

Hardy water lotus and other aquatic plants often are sold at garden centers that sell pond supplies. They also can be ordered by mail from these and other mail-order companies:

Slocum Water Gardens
1101 Cypress Gardens Boulevard
Winter Haven, FL 33884
863-293-7151
www.slocumwatergardens.com

Spring Time Nursery
23902 County Road H
Sugar City, CO 81076
719-267-4166
www.ewaterlily.com

Van Ness Water Gardens
2460 North Euclid Avenue
Upland, CA 91784
800-205-2425
www.vnwg.com

CHAPTER 5: STRETCHING EVERY SEASON

Grow an Asian Stir-Fry Garden, page 173

Numerous seed companies, including the ones listed below, offer seeds of Asian vegetables.

Johnny's Selected Seeds
955 Benton Avenue
Winslow, ME 04901
800-854-2580
www.johnnyseeds.com

Nichols Garden Nursery
1190 Old Salem Road NE
Albany, OR 97321
800-422-3985
www.nicholsgardennursery.com

CHAPTER 6: ATTRACTING WILDLIFE TO YOUR GARDEN

Make a Gourd Birdhouse, page 192

If you don't grow your own gourds and can't find them locally, good selections of cured gourds for crafting into birdhouses are available from these mail-order companies:

Northern Dipper Farm
RR 1
Wilsonville, ON N0E 1Z0
Canada
519-443-5638
www.northerndipper.com

Sandlady's Gourd Farm
10295 N 700 W
Tangier, IN 47952
765-498-5428
www.sandlady.com

Welburn Gourd Farm
31252 Pepper Tree Street
Winchester, CA 92596
888-873-3622
www.welburngourds.com

CHAPTER 7: SOLVING PEST PROBLEMS IN EARTH-SAFE WAYS

Grow Undercover Squash, page 215; Using Icky Stickies, page 222

Many garden centers and seed companies sell floating row-cover. The companies below offer multiple choices so you can choose a type of row-cover that suits your needs. They are also good sources for Stickem or Tangletrap for making sticky traps.

Gardens Alive!
5100 Schenley Place
Lawrenceburg, IN 47025
513-354-1483
www.gardensalive.com

Peaceful Valley Farm Supply
PO Box 2209
Grass Valley, CA 95945
888-784-1722
www.groworganic.com

CHAPTER 8: SPECIAL CROPS FOR HANDY GARDENERS

The Best Bamboo for You, page 248

Shop regionally for bamboo for your garden. Here are five bamboo nurseries located in a range of climates that ship plants in spring.

Bamboo Sourcery
666 Wagnon Road
Sebastopol, CA 95472
707-823-5866
www.bamboosourcery.com

Lewis Bamboo
Oakman, AL 35579
205-686-5728
www.lewisbamboo.com

MidAtlantic Bamboo
1458 Dusty Road
Crewe, VA 23930
434-645-7662
www.midatlanticbamboo.com

New England Bamboo Company
5 Granite Street
Rockport, MA 01966
978-546-3581
www.newengbamboo.com

Tradewinds Bamboo Nursery
28446 Hunter Creek Loop
Gold Beach, OR 97444
541-247-0835
www.bamboodirect.com

Grow Great Wood for Weaving, page 252

If you cannot find willows at local nurseries, special varieties of willow and other woods to grow for weaving into fences and other projects are available from these mail-order sources:

Bluestem Nursery
1946 Fife Road
Christina Lake, BC V0H 1E3
Canada
250-447-6363
www.bluestem.ca

Forest Farm
990 Tetherow Road
Williams, OR 97455
541-846-7269
www.forestfarm.com

Willow Dreams Farm
1979 Casey Fork Cook Road
Edmonton, KY 42129
270-432-4486
www.willowdreamsfarm.com

Good Things from Grapes, page 256

Many nurseries sell grapevines in spring, but the selection of varieties may be limited. Excellent selections of varieties are available from these and other mail-order nurseries:

Concord Nurseries
10175 Mile Block Road
North Collins, NY 14111
800-223-2211
www.concordnursery.com

Ison's Nursery and Vineyard
PO Box 190
Brooks, GA 30205
800-733-0324
www.isons.com

Lon Rombough
PO Box 365
Aurora, OR 97002
503-678-1410
www.bunchgrapes.com

Grow Gifted Grains, page 260

You often can find several types of grain seeds at local farm supply stores. Or, order special varieties from these mail-order companies:

Johnny's Selected Seeds
955 Benton Avenue
Winslow, ME 04901
800-854-2580
www.johnnyseeds.com

Peaceful Valley Farm Supply
PO Box 2209
Grass Valley, CA 95945
888-784-1722
www.groworganic.com

Seeds of Change
PO Box 15700
Santa Fe, NM 87592
888-762-7333
www.seedsofchange.com

Grow a Kitchen Herb Garden, page 266

Try to find a local herb grower who can provide you with locally adapted plants. Or, order either seeds or plants from these and other mail-order sources:

Garden Medicinals and Culinaries
PO Box 320
Earlysville, VA 22936
434-964-9113
www.gardenmedicinals.com

Goodwin Creek Gardens
PO Box 83
Williams, OR 97544
800-846-7359
www.goodwincreekgardens.com

Richters Herbs
357 Highway 47
Goodwood, ON L0C 1A0
Canada
905-640-6677
www.richters.com

Grow Flowers That Last Forever, page 274

You will find plenty of planting possibilities among the seeds and plants offered by these companies:

Goodwin Creek Gardens
PO Box 83
Williams, OR 97544
800-846-7359
www.goodwincreekgardens.com

Johnny's Selected Seeds
955 Benton Avenue
Winslow, ME 04901
800-854-2580
www.johnnyseeds.com

Park Seed
1 Parkton Avenue
Greenwood, SC 29647
800-213-0076
www.parkseed.com

The Thyme Garden
20546 Alsea Highway
Alsea, OR 97324
541-487-8671
www.thymegarden.com

Grow Gorgeous Gourds, page 280

Seeds of the most popular types of gourds are widely available from mail-order seed companies. These and several other small family companies specialize in unusual gourd seeds:

Carolina Gourd Seeds
259 Fletcher Avenue
Fuquay Varina, NC 27526
919-557-5946
www.carolinagourdsandseeds.com

Wuv'n Acres Gourden
14280 North Sunset Valley
   Road
Hulbert, OK 74441
918-772-2800
www.wuvie.net

More Great Things to Do with Gourds, page 284

If you get bitten by the gourd-crafting bug, special crafting supplies are available from:

The Caning Shop
926 Gilman Street
Berkeley, CA 94710
800-544-3376
www.caning.com

Turtle Feathers
PO Box 1227
Waynesville, NC 28786
828-926-4716
www.turtlefeathers.com

Index

Underscored page references indicate boxed text. **Boldface** references indicate illustrations.

snap connectors, 127
splitters (Y-connectors),
126–27
timers, 127
coiling, <u>127</u>
as faucet extenders, 126,
128–29, **128**, **129**
guides for, <u>129</u>
outdoor shower using,
140–41, **140**
recycling old, <u>131</u>
soaker hoses, 138
homemade, 138, <u>139</u>, **139**
sprinkler, 138
Houseplants, insect pests on,
223
Hummingbirds
create a haven for, 194–95
feeders for, 194–95, <u>195</u>,
195
flowers attractive to, 194,
<u>196</u>
nectar for, 195
providing water for, 204
western, <u>195</u>, **195**
Humus, 6

I

Impatiens (*Impatiens
walleriana*), <u>196</u>
Insect pests
aphids, 208, <u>213</u>
appetite of, 212
apple maggots, 222, **223**
barriers for
bubble wrap, 244
cutworm collars, 218–
19, **218**, <u>219</u>, **219**
isolation boxes, 216–17,
217
milk jugs, 244
paper bags, 244
rowcovers, 214, <u>215</u>,
215, <u>217</u>, 225
rowcover teepees, 244
tar paper, 244

cabbage root maggots, 244
cabbageworms, imported,
<u>213</u>
cankerworms, 222
Colorado potato beetles,
<u>213</u>
cucumber beetles, <u>213</u>
rowcovers and, <u>215</u>, **215**
trap for, <u>227</u>
cutworms, <u>213</u>
birds and, <u>219</u>
climbing, 219
deterrents for, 218–19,
218, <u>219</u>, **219**
eight major, <u>213</u>
evaluating damage by, 207
flea beetles, 244
fungus gnats, 223
grasshoppers, 224–25, <u>224</u>,
<u>225</u>, **225**
gypsy moths, 222
handpicking, 220
homemade deterrents and,
212
identifying, 220
with catch-and-release
chamber, <u>209</u>, **209**
on indoor plants, 223
insecticides and, 208, 212
Japanese beetles, <u>213</u>
protecting roses from,
216–17, **217**
plant health and, 206
slugs, 226–27, **226**
snails, 226–27, **226**
soil solarization and, 36
sources for traps and
deterrents, 295–96
squash bugs, <u>213</u>
rowcovers and, <u>215</u>, **215**
squash vine borers
rowcovers and, <u>215</u>, **215**
sticky traps for, 222–23,
222, <u>223</u>, **223**
gloves, <u>223</u>, **223**
sticky apples, 222, **223**

tree bands, 222, **222**
whitefly swatter, 223
ticks, <u>221</u>, **221**
tomato hornworms, <u>213</u>
whiteflies
sticky glove for, <u>223</u>, **223**
swatter for, 223
yellow jackets
traps for, 228–29, **228**,
229
Insects. *See also* Beneficial
insects; Insect pests
identifying, <u>209</u>, **209**, 220
Intercropping, 206
Invasive plants
bamboo
running, 248, <u>249</u>, 251
chives, <u>267</u>
mints, <u>267</u>
vines, 85
Ipomoea species and hybrids,
<u>83</u>
Ivy, English, 85

J

Japanese beetles, <u>213</u>
protecting roses from,
216–17, **217**
Joe-Pye weed, <u>197</u>

K

Kale, season-stretching with,
<u>153</u>
Kiwi, hardy, <u>84</u>

L

Labels, <u>61</u>
Lacewing larvae, 208
Ladybeetle larvae, 208
Lagenaria species, <u>83</u>, 280, <u>281</u>
Landscaping
trellises in, 76
useful plants in, 246–47
wildlife and, 178–79
Lantana (*Lantana* species and
hybrids), <u>197</u>

sour (acid), 3–5
sweet (alkaline, basic), 4–5
testing, 2, _4_
texture, 2–3, _3_, **3**
   watering and, 138
warming in spring
   with painted rocks, _163_,
      163
   with solar snake, _162_,
      162
Soil conditioner, 6
Solarizing, 36–37, **36**, _37_, 37
Solidago cultivars, _197_
Sorghum (broomcorn)
      (Sorghum), _263_
   as living windbreak, _167_
   whisk broom from, _265_,
      265
Sources, 294–97
Spanish flag, _83_
Spiderflower, _196_
Spiders, handling, 208
Spigots, extending, 126,
      128–29, **128**, **129**
Spinach
   growing from seed, _45_
   Malabar, _82_
   season-stretching with, _153_
Squash
   growing from seed, _45_
   rowcover for, _215_, **215**
   in three sisters circle garden,
      90–91, **90**
   when to water, _125_
   winter, _153_
Squash bugs, _213_
   rowcovers and, _215_, **215**
Squash vine borers, _215_, **215**
Squirrels
   deterring, 230
      from container plants,
         244
      with hot pepper, 230
      with no-dig wire mesh
         barrier, 236, **236**
      vinegar and, _227_

feeder for, 190–91, **190**, **191**
flying, _185_
plants resistant to, _233_
Stakes. _See also_ Wickets
   bamboo, _251_
Statice, annual, _275_
Sticky traps, 222–23, **222**,
      _223_, **223**
   for apple maggots, 222, **223**
   sources for, 295–96
   sticky gloves, 223, **223**
   for trees, 222, **222**
   for whiteflies, 223, _223_,
      223
Straw
   as mulch, _33_
   raised bed of, 54–55, _54_, 55
Strawflower, _275_
Stropharia, winecap (king)
      _(Stropharia rugoso-
      annulata)_, _35_
Succession planting, 152
Sunflower, Mexican _(Tithonia)_,
      _196_
Sunflowers, annual
      (Helianthus)
   growing from seed, _45_
   growing in compost, _29_
   as living windbreak, _167_
   as teepee playhouse, _91_
Swales, controlling water with,
      120–21, _121_, **121**
Sweet potatoes, 58, 61,
      164–65
Sweet William, 172
Swiss chard, _153_
Syrphid fly larvae, 208

T
Tarragon, French, _269_
Teepees
   creative twists to, _94_
   sunflower, _91_
   tied, 94–95, _94_, 95
Terraces, building, 38–39, _39_,
      39

Thunbergia alata, _83_
Thyme, _269_
Thymus species, _269_
Ticks, capturing, _221_, **221**
Tithonia rotundifolia, _196_
Toads
   attracting, _201_
   house for, 200–201, **200**
Tobacco, flowering, _196_
Tomatoes
   caging, _175_
   green manure mulch and,
      18–19, **19**
   growing in winter, 74
   propagating
      from cuttings, 74
      from seed, _45_, 74
   trellising, 76
   volunteer, 74
   when to water, _125_
Tomato hornworms, _213_
Tools and equipment
   glossary of, 285–89
   light box, 50–51, **51**
   lights, _50_
   planting bar, _59_, **59**
   potting table, building, **41**,
      64–65, _64_, **65**
   sink screen, _63_, **63**
   soil sifters, 40, **40**
Transplanting, of crowded
      seedlings, 62
Transplants, shading, _69_
Trees
   animal resistant, _233_
   living fence of, 254–55,
      254
   protecting bark from
      rodents, _237_, **237**
   sticky bands for, 222, **222**
Trellises. _See also_ Plant
      supports
   anchoring, 78–79, _79_, 79,
      _80_, **80**
   colorful pyramid pole,
      100–101, _101_, **101**

USDA Plant Hardiness Zone Map

		Average annual minimum temperature (°F)
Zone 1		Below -50°
Zone 2		-40° to -50°
Zone 3		-30° to -40°
Zone 4		-20° to -30°
Zone 5		-10° to -20°
Zone 6		0° to -10°
Zone 7		10° to 0°
Zone 8		20° to 10°
Zone 9		30° to 20°
Zone 10		40° to 30°
Zone 11		Above 40°

This map was revised in 1990 and is recognized as the best indicator of minimum temperatures available. Look at the map to find your area, then match its pattern to the key above. When you've found your pattern, the key will tell you what hardiness zone you live in. Remember that the map is a general guide; your particular conditions may vary. *Map courtesy of Agriculture Research Service, USDA.*